GRACE
PITTSBU   SO-CUJ-406

THE CONSCIENCE OF THE AUTOBIOGRAPHER

STUDIES IN LITERATURE AND RELIGION

General Editor: David Jasper, Director of the Centre for the Study of Literature and Theology, University of Glasgow

Studies in Literature and Religion is a series of interdisciplinary titles, both monographs and essays, concerned with matters of literature, art and textuality within religious traditions founded upon texts and textual study. In a variety of ways they are concerned with the fundamental issues of the imagination, literary perceptions and theory, and an understanding of poetics for theology and religious studies.

Further titles in preparation

The Conscience of the Autobiographer

Ethical and Religious Dimensions of Autobiography

Associate Professor of Religion
St. Olaf College
Northfield, Minnesota

M
MACMILLAN

CT
25
B28
1992

CATALOGUED

© John D. Barbour 1992

All rights reserved. No reproduction, copy or transmission of
this publication may be made without written permission.

No paragraph of this publication may be reproduced, copied or
transmitted save with written permission or in accordance with
the provisions of the Copyright, Designs and Patents Act 1988,
or under the terms of any licence permitting limited copying
issued by the Copyright Licensing Agency, 33–4 Alfred Place,
London WC1E 7DP.

Any person who does any unauthorised act in relation to this
publication may be liable to criminal prosecution and civil
claims for damages.

First published 1992 by
MACMILLAN ACADEMIC AND PROFESSIONAL LTD
Houndmills, Basingstoke, Hampshire RG21 2XS
and London

Companies and representatives
throughout the world

Edited and typeset by Grahame & Grahame Editorial, Brighton

ISBN 0–333–55492–2

A catalogue record for this book is available
from the British Library

Printed in Great Britain by
Billing and Sons Ltd, Worcester

GRACE LIBRARY CARLOW COLLEGE
PITTSBURGH, PA 15213

For Ian Graeme Barbour
and
Deane Kern Barbour

IIIW 4-13-93 $59.95 engl

Contents

General Editor's Preface

Since the *Confessions* of St. Augustine, autobiography has been a crucial literary form in the Western tradition. Augustine, centered on God, and Rousseau, centered on the self, are touchstones of this book, which is concerned with autobiography as the struggle for self-knowledge. With its central involvement with ethics and the conscience, the autobiography seeks to uphold the values of integrity, coherence and truthfulness, against the grain of the disintegrative tendencies of contemporary deconstructive and post-modern criticism.

John Barbour's range of reference is wide, yet he never loses sight of specific texts, leading always from the particular to the general, from the individual to the public. The practice of autobiography as an 'exercise in the still-developing conscience' looks both to the past and the future and within the conventions and formulas of literature in the pursuit of truthfulness (as opposed to any narrow definition of truth), character and narrative coherence.

The underlying moral and theological themes of the study are traced through questions of religious conversion, public and political life, racial sensitivities and the intense personal quest of Mary McCarthy. What we are continually reminded of is the significance of specific literary narratives working against the theological tendencies towards generalization. As Barbour reminds us, 'while the theologians are most interested in continuity of character, and in the achievement of wholeness and order, literary critics usually focus on the dramatization of change, and on the fragmentation, alienation, and disorder of the self'. Self-scrutiny, or in Rousseau's case self-deception, are deeply embedded in the religious, cultural and political life of our society. The themes of this book are, therefore, central to the most pressing questions concerned with the relationship between theology and literature. From Augustine, to the 'essays' of Montaigne and Johnson, to *The Autobiography of Malcolm X* and the two autobiographical works of Mary McCarthy, a close critical analysis maintains a focus on the themes of conscience, moral and theological reflection in the pursuit of self-knowledge and integrity.

DAVID JASPER

Acknowledgements

The generosity of individuals and support of institutions have been as indispensable to me as the works of other scholars acknowledged in the notes to this book. Several colleagues at St. Olaf College have commented helpfully on drafts of one or more of these chapters: Mark Allister, David Booth, Rick Fairbanks, Carol Holly, Edmund Santurri, Doug Schuurman, Frederick Stoutland, and Charles Wilson. I am grateful as well to David Barbour, Heather Barbour, Paul John Eakin, Karl Weintraub, and Eric Ziolkowski for each responding to a chapter in manuscript. Mary McCarthy graciously corrected some details of my interpretation of her autobiographies. Jody Greenslade's typing and computing skills made the editing process much easier.

A National Endowment for the Humanities Summer Seminar on 'The Forms of Autobiography', directed by James Olney in 1983, led to an early version of Chapter 4. Chapter 7 was written when I received a St. Olaf faculty development grant during summer 1987. Chapter 5 grows out of my participation in a Mellon Faculty Seminar during 1988 on 'Individualism and Community' directed by Frederick Stoutland.

Chapter 6 is a considerably rewritten version of some of the material in 'Religious *Ressentiment* and Public Virtues', *The Journal of Religious Ethics* 11 (1983) 264–79. Chapter 3 is a revision of 'Character and Characterization in Religious Autobiography', *The Journal of the American Academy of Religion* 55 (1987) 307–27.

Another form of gratitude is due to my family. Meg Ojala, Graham, and Reed have given me their love and their presences. My parents, Ian and Deane Barbour, read and commented on the entire manuscript and shaped my conception of its ideal reader. In addition to gifts of love beyond recall, their insights into conscience over the years have contributed substantially to the writing of this book, which is dedicated to them.

JOHN D. BARBOUR

1
Introduction

Conscience refers to a person's moral judgment of his or her own actions and character. In this book I define it simply as moral self-assessment. Appeals to conscience are autobiographical claims, first-person assertions about how one measures up to standards that may or may not apply to others. Conscience testifies about how moral principles, ideals, and aspirations pertain to one's own character, and it encompasses the states of consciousness which result from applying these standards to oneself. Conscience is better interpreted as an act or function of the entire self than as a faculty or a separate part of the mind. As the act and process of self-assessment, conscience is inextricably bound up with many other moral concepts, such as ideals of character or virtue, feelings of guilt and shame, and the religious loyalties or ultimate concerns which shape a person's identity.

The central thesis of this book is that autobiography is not simply a description or report on how the author's conscience operated in the past, but itself represents an act or exercise of conscience. In addition to exploring the past workings of conscience, the writing of autobiography raises many issues for conscience, including such problems as the nature of truthfulness, the dangers of self-deception, the validity of certain fictions and figures of self-representation, and other ambiguities involved in knowing, depicting, and assessing the self. Conscience is a dimension of self-knowledge and of moral agency which is constantly activated by autobiography's inherent structural tension between the author as protagonist (his past self) and as narrator (his present self). The work of conscience creates in autobiography various dramas of the moral imagination, as a writer faces sources of shame in the past, analyzes his dependence on literary and moral conventions, strives to overcome self-deception in understanding experience, or traces the development of present religious convictions. Since writing an autobiography is itself a major event in a person's life and a matter for moral reflection,

1

autobiography offers an opportunity for continuing evolution of a writer's conscience, and sometimes for religious transcendence.

This study reflects a theoretical model of conscience which focuses on the narrative structure of moral reflection. The construction of a narrative is essential to the operation of conscience, as a person selects events as relevant for inclusion in one's story, characterizes oneself and other agents, locates the self in a community and culture, and construes how intentions, circumstances, and consequences of human action are linked and should be assessed. The act of imagining and fashioning a coherent narrative is a central function of conscience, both in its ordinary workings and in that unusually extended and articulate form of self-examination and expression we call autobiography.

The role of conscience in autobiography is varied and complex, and it deserves much closer scrutiny than it has received. This subject is of deep interest to several scholarly fields, including religious studies, theology, philosophy, and literary criticism. Autobiography's exploration of ethical and religious issues is a primary reason why this form of writing engages most readers, including the students to whom I teach many of the books examined here. Surprisingly, however, the topic of conscience in autobiography has not been given extended or detailed treatment.

In theology and the fields of religious studies, scholars agree that autobiography provides a valuable source of theological insights and a crucial kind of evidence of the role of religion in the moral life. While numerous thinkers have asserted the promise or value of narrative for ethical reflection, such theoretical proposals and affirmations rarely lead to encounter with particular texts. Theologians' reflections on autobiography tend to be general or abstract, and only rarely explore specific narratives. Furthermore, the discussion in religious studies remains largely uninformed by the important work in autobiographical theory that has appeared within the last two decades. Theologians tend to treat autobiography as simply one more illustration of the general characteristics of 'narrative' and consequently neglect its distinctive qualities. They forget that as do other genres such as creation myths, wisdom literature, or scriptural parables, autobiography has distinctive functions in the moral life of an individual and of a community.

What is needed is an integration of theoretical reflection with analysis of particular narrative texts, focusing on what such analysis contributes substantively to ethical and religious reflection.

Autobiographies such as Augustine's *Confessions*, Bunyan's *Grace Abounding*, and Dorothy Day's *The Long Loneliness* have an essential place in the Christian literary tradition, the life of the church, the self-understanding of individual believers, and the agenda for theological thinking. Such 'secular' works as Montaigne's *Essays*, Rousseau's *Confessions*, or Mary McCarthy's *Memories of a Catholic Girlhood* may also play a determinative role as moral paradigms, and should serve as a resource for philosophical and theological ethics. Ethical reflection may be renewed, challenged, and enriched by closer attention to the diverse ways in which autobiographies present issues for conscience.

Although recent literary theory and criticism of autobiography raise crucial moral issues, no study has focused specifically on ethical dimensions of autobiography. While a number of recent books discuss the ethical dimensions and the ethical criticism of fiction, both the writing and the evaluating of autobiography raise equally significant, if somewhat different, moral issues. Assumptions about how conscience functions in autobiography are necessary, though usually unexamined, both for the person who sets out to write the story of his or her life and for the critic or scholar who analyses and evaluates such a work. The critic assesses the ways in which an autobiographer assesses his own past; both forms of assessment reflect basic assumptions and beliefs about conscience. Critics inevitably rely on moral categories, even when their work centers on formalist analysis, aesthetic values, or the deconstruction of traditional concepts of the self or the text. Evaluations of autobiography depend not only on aesthetic and historically descriptive categories, but on ethical criteria, in particular those ideals of self-knowledge and self-representation which a critic believes to be most valuable in human experience. Such ethical evaluation may be expressed in various terms, such as truthfulness or self-deception, authenticity or bad faith, honesty in contrast to hypocrisy, or some other standard the critic adopts. In spite of their actual practice, however, literary critics have so far given little theoretical attention to the ways in which either writing about one's own life or interpreting an autobiography involves moral considerations. When critics do address ethical aspects of autobiography, it is usually with limited knowledge of how such concepts as virtue, shame, or character are understood and explicated by philosophers and theologians.

Some of the central assumptions of my approach have been

attacked by the recent critical theories of deconstruction and post-structuralism. French critics such as Jacques Derrida and Michel Foucault and their American followers criticize common ideas of a coherent text or self; they would surely challenge my focus on the conscience of the autobiographer and my interest in such values as integrity, coherence, and truthfulness. Although in Chapter 3 I address some implications of the emphasis on textuality for approaching characterization in autobiography, a refutation of deconstruction falls outside the scope of this book. Literary critics who have challenged deconstruction's self-aggrandizing and inconsistent tendencies seem to me far more compelling than this theory's advocates.[1] While deconstruction may suggest new readings of certain texts and raise interesting issues as a philosophy of language, I know of no major ethical thinker today who does not consider the ethical implications of deconstruction to be either nihilistic or incoherent. I share this assessment, although I do not develop an argument to that effect in this book. The interesting issues for me are not generalizations about *a priori* abstractions such as 'textuality' or 'the subject', but what alternative critical approaches reveal about particular texts. I think focusing on the conscience of the autobiographer reveals crucial aspects of certain texts' meaning, and the best argument for this claim will be the ethical criticism in the chapters that follow.

A reader's response to an autobiography is a form of ethical criticism because it involves assessing the character (*ethos*) of the author. I hope that literary critics will gain from this book increased understanding and appreciation of the centrality of ethical concerns in the writing and interpretation of autobiography. Ethical criticism as I understand it is not a single theory or method to be applied to every text, but a practice; it is detailed, specific, and various, reflecting the interests of the individual critic and the nature of the works discussed.

I offer an integrative approach to some of the ethical and religious dimensions of autobiography, an approach that is grounded in literary theory as well as ethical theory, and that considers particular texts in depth. In the chapters which follow, moral theory informs interpretation of the autobiographies. At the same time, analysis of specific narratives shapes my reflections on moral issues. The autobiographies examined test the adequacy of ethical theories to moral experience, and they also generate new insights. The 'fit' between narrative analysis and conceptual formulation is not and indeed should not be exact, for each kind of thought has its own integrity, limits, and value as an attempt to comprehend moral experience. Since conscience does not function in the same manner in all autobiographies, no single method or approach is appropriate for every work. In this book I explore dimensions of particular autobiographies as their ethical and religious significance presents itself to me.

Chapter 2, 'Conscience and Truthfulness', presents my basic theory of how conscience may serve as an incentive to autobiography, and how the attempt to depict one's own character truthfully poses certain difficulties, temptations, and challenges for the autobiographer's conscience. Drawing on Paul John Eakin's critical approach, I present the writing of an autobiography as an extension and development of the author's conscience. My ideas about truthfulness are demonstrated in several works, especially in the contrast between Rousseau's classic example of self-deception and the practices of Augustine and Mary McCarthy.

Chapter 3, 'Character and Characterization', examines how the autobiographical act may challenge and nurture an author's conscience as he both assesses his own moral character and employs the literary techniques and tropes of characterization. I analyze theories of character of theologians and literary critics, turning then for further insights to Malcolm X's narrative and to fictional autobiographies by Robertson Davies. I show how character assessment and characterization are closely related in the activity of the conscientious autobiographer.

In Chapter 4, 'Conscience in the Essays of Montaigne and Johnson', I explore the central moral concerns and characteristic patterns of reflection found in the essays of these two authors. I explain why the essay form is peculiarly appropriate to express certain ethical and religious interests, and suggest the distinctive acheivements that are possible in this form of discourse. Montaigne's and Johnson's essays demonstrate the crucial role of conscience in this form of autobiographical writing.

Chapters 5, 6, and 7 consider the autobiographies of Benjamin Franklin, of Malcolm X, and of Mary McCarthy, each in terms of a crucial issue for conscience. In each case I first delineate a theoretical framework for understanding the ethical issues at stake. I wish to emphasize for literary critics the importance of theoretical rigor in ethical criticism, as well as to demonstrate to scholars of ethics the value of narrative texts in elucidating issues usually considered only in more abstract terms.

The central issues for my interpretation of Franklin's work are his understanding of the relationship between his own interests and the welfare of others, and the ethical implications of this self-conception. I discuss critics who have attacked Franklin's individualism and then analyze his autobiography for evidence of how he himself understood this question, concluding with an assessment of his model of the individual.

In Chapter 6, on Malcolm X, the concepts of *ressentiment* and public virtues are used to interpret central concerns of his auto-biography. *Ressentiment* refers to the problem of animosity towards human otherness, while public virtues are moral qualities affirmed to be normative for the members of every community. These concepts define the role conscience plays in Malcolm's narrative as well as my view of the religious significance of his final changes.

In Mary McCarthy's two autobiographies a primary theme is her experiences of shame. A crucial component of the autobiographical act for this writer is the assessment of shame in order to clarify the proper grounds for shame and self-esteem. Conscience plays a crucial role in this process, and also in healing or transcending the destructive effects of shame.

The religious dimensions of conscience are manifested in two general ways in works of autobiography. First, all of the principal writers discussed – Montaigne and Johnson, Franklin, Malcolm X, and McCarthy – were profoundly influenced by Christian traditions, both moral and literary ones. At the same time, all of these writers stand at some critical distance from the Christian tradition. Even Samuel Johnson takes a secular stance in his essays, in contrast to his sermons and religious writings. I will explore the ways in which each writer's understanding of autobiography and of conscience is related to Christian traditions and texts, although this topic obviously invites much more extensive treatment in each case. This book describes how writing about the self has been shaped by Christian conventions and modes of thinking, including patterns of conversion, Biblical themes and metaphors, and the Augustinian mode of confession. It examines, too, why concerns of conscience have sometimes demanded the revision or rejection of aspects of Christian thought, practice, or identity.

We may discern a second form of religious dimension in auto-biography in the very nature of this self-critical act. In my view conscience is neither autonomous nor entirely determined by religious and cultural norms. Although a person's conscience is formed by a particular culture, the developed conscience has a capacity for transcendence which allows for the evaluation of its original religious community or tradition. A reorientation of conscience is based on a new understanding and acceptance of the deepest sources of one's identity, those ultimate powers, values and standards which a person trusts and seeks to live by. This sort of ethical reorientation and regrounding is often, I think, both a primary incentive for and a consequence of the autobiographical act. An autobiographer may assess the judgments of his or her conscience and aspire to a moral standard better than that envisioned in the past. Although the capacity for moral revision is certainly not always linked to explicit and self-conscious religious belief, the process of self-correction and reformation of conscience that can be evidenced in autobiography demonstrates one of the most significant human acts of spiritual or religious development.

2
Conscience and Truthfulness

The conscience of the autobiographer may be seen at work both in the past and the present character of the writer, that is, in the author as protagonist and as narrator of his autobiography. Here I discuss the operation of conscience in the author's present as it shapes the writing of autobiography, that is, conscience as a component of what theorists call 'the autobiographical act'.[1] Particular attention will be given to the autobiographies of Augustine, Rousseau, and Mary McCarthy as I seek to generalize about some of the ways conscience can shape the writing of autobiography. The discussion is organized in terms of three rubrics. First I suggest ways that conscience can be a vital incentive or motivation for writing an autobiography. Second, I analyze certain difficulties and temptations for conscience which are posed by the attempt to present truthfully one's own character. Thus the first two sections discuss in turn the ways conscience sponsors and monitors the autobiographical act. Finally, I elaborate my understanding of what truthfulness in autobiography means. The most conscientious autobiographers – those, such as Augustine and McCarthy, to whom we attribute a truthful conscience – are both committed to and yet skeptical about achieving a truthful moral judgment of the self.

I CONSCIENCE AS AN INCENTIVE FOR AUTOBIOGRAPHY

Although various more restrictive definitions of conscience have been proposed, in this book I define conscience simply as moral self-assessment. Conscience refers not to a discrete faculty but to 'the whole person passing moral judgments on issues of right and wrong'.[2] Most thinkers limit the term to assessments of the self; a person does not usually say it is his conscience which evaluates the actions of other people. In accord with common usage, I take conscience to mean a person's moral judgment of his or her own actions and character. Conscience can be retrospective or prospective, and judge positively as well as negatively. Conscience is intimately connected with an individual's sense of identity, for it monitors behavior and determines that for which one holds oneself responsible. Conscience assesses which aspects of one's actual character are consistent with one's deepest aspirations and commitments, and judges character accordingly. These positive and negative judgments about one's conduct and character reflect basic and deep-rooted beliefs about personal identity. The business of conscience is thus to protect the integrity of the self, and to maintain the self's continuity and identity.

The discernment of the self's identity, integrity, and consistency is equally central in autobiography. In constructing a narrative of the self, even the most volatile and fragmented person must outline some basic contours of his or her character, defining its limits in duration and identity. Even a writer who calls in question the traditional notion of the self distinguishes between the bundle of contradictory impulses he experiences and something else, something other, something beyond. Conscience and autobiography are each vitally concerned, then, with judging the self's identity, consistency, continuity, and integrity, although a probing analysis usually discloses that a person is deficient in terms of one or more of these values.

The exercise of conscience is an essential component of the auto-biographical act itself. The writing of an autobiography is not simply mimesis or description of earlier periods of conscience-formation, but an exercise and extension of the writer's still-developing conscience. This thesis, the central principle of this book, is analogous to the understanding of autobiography proposed by Paul John Eakin. Focusing on the development of the self's identity, Eakin presents the writing of an autobiography as a symbolic re-enactment and extension of two earlier phases of identity formation. Autobiography recapitulates the unrememberable 'coming together of the individual and language that marks the origin of self-awareness', and also the 'I-am-me experience' in which a child for the first time has a 'self-conscious experience of self-consciousness'. The autobiographical act emerges for Eakin as 'a third and culminating moment in the history of self-definition'.[3] An important motivation for writing autobiography is a person's need for further 'self-invention', an activity practiced in the lives of all who share the modern Western concept of the self, and occasionally articulated publicly in the writing we call autobiography:

> The act of composition may be conceived as a mediating term in the autobiographical enterprise, reaching back into the past not merely to recapture but to repeat the psychological rhythms of identity formation, and reaching forward into the future to fix the structure of this identity in a permanent self-made existence as literary text. This is to understand the writing of autobiography not merely as the passive, transparent record of an already completed self but rather as an integral and often decisive phase of the drama of self-definition.[4]

While Eakin is interested in the psychological basis of identity, this book focuses on how moral values and principles shape a writer's sense of self. (The moral and psychological bases of identity are of course deeply interdependent, both resting on a conception of the person, on ideas about what it means to be a self.) I wish to extend Eakin's model of autobiography to encompass the continuing process of conscience-formation. Autobiographical writing, in my view, is a heightened and extended example of the ordinary workings of conscience, an unusually articulate depiction of a person's moral reflection on her own life. It is not only a record of conscience; it is an act of conscience, a critical event which shapes personal identity.

Many strategies and structures of autobiographical writing are shaped by the moral stance the author takes towards the past. The confession is a common form of autobiography, and many people believe that all autobiography is in some sense confession. The influence of the confessional form on the history of autobiographical writing reflects some of the ways that conscience has served as an incentive to self-examination. For example, an autobiographer may be impelled by longing for relief from the burden of guilt, or believe that contrition and remorse partially atone for earlier wrongdoing. Augustine and countless later writers link autobiographical truth to confession of the self's past sins (although confession means more than this to Augustine: praise and thanksgiving for God's grace are also 'confessed'). Confession is our primary metaphor for the analysis and public articulation of conscience, and we immediately assume (sometimes mistakenly) that a serious examination of conscience will take the form of a confession. The writer's conscience struggling to recognize and admit error or evil produces most of the elements we expect in a confession, whether oral or written: intense internal conflict, emotional unburdening, the form of an imagined dialogue with God and/or a human audience, contrition, and either praise to God for release or some other resolution to the writer's sense of guilt, often expressed by metaphors of unchaining or catharsis. The narrative form taken by a confession discloses the moral structure of a person's scrutiny of his conscience.

As its origin in the Greek *apologia* ('defense') indicates, in an apology the author defends his past conduct against moral criticisms. As did Plato's Socrates, the author asserts that he is not troubled by his conscience, for he believes he has acted rightly. Newman's *Apologia Pro Vita Sua* is one of the clearest examples of an autobiography motivated and shaped by the writer's desire to vindicate his moral character.

Confession and apology, as abstract concepts of genre, seem to be mutually exclusive in character, involving as an incentive to autobiography either moral rebuke or vindication of the writer's character. In fact, however, any particular autobiography, like any complex human life, will probably involve a mixture of confession of guilt, excusing of apparent errors, and approval of virtuous actions. Furthermore, the interest and power of an autobiography often arise from the dramatic tension between differing moral perspectives on a particular event, each of which has some validity for the writer. An autobiographer may also use a conventional form of moral rhetoric for unexpected ends. For instance, Rousseau's *Confessions* is an apology disguised as a confession, turning to the author's credit every instance of wrong-doing he performed. Since Rousseau believes that his intentions were always pure, and he recognizes no moral standard beyond good intentions and sincerity, he defies his readers to condemn him, or to believe that anyone could have done better. Rousseau therefore challenges his readers and his 'Sovereign Judge': 'Let each one of them reveal his heart at the foot of Thy throne with equal sincerity, and may any man who does, say "I was a better man than he."'[5] Thomas De Quincey's *Confessions of an English Opium Eater* mingles both confession and apology, revealing the struggles of his conscience to justify his addiction. De Quincey basically excuses his use of opium as being not a form of sensual indulgence but an anodyne necessary to cope with unbearable pain. His work, like most autobiographical writing, reflects a structure of moral self-examination which is more complex than can be summarized in an abstract conception of genre.

As an incentive to autobiography, many writers speak of their desire to pursue truth for its own sake. Conscience is often at work in such a case, as the writer struggles to face something that has been denied or repressed for many years. For Saul Friedländer, his book *When Memory Comes* represents 'a need for synthesis, for a thoroughgoing coherence that no longer excludes anything', especially the Jewish traditions he 'forgot' or repressed during his years in Nazi-occupied France.[6] Telling the truth about himself – to himself as much as to others – is a test of conscience, for he has strong motivation to deny painful memories. Another autobiographer who speaks of truthfulness as an incentive is Gandhi, who conceives of his autobiography as an account of 'experiments in truth'. His autobiography is a self-conscious endeavor to test his capacity for the truth. 'My purpose is to describe experiments in the science of Satyagraha, not to say how good I am. In judging myself I shall try to be harsh as truth, as I want others also to be.' It is painful for Gandhi to have to write about his marriage as a child, or about his shameful absence when his father died. 'I know that I shall have to swallow many such bitter draughts in the course of this narrative. And I cannot do otherwise, if I claim to be a worshipper of the Truth.'[7] For Gandhi, narrating his experiments in truth is an act of conscience which constantly teaches the lesson of humility.

The ideal of the truthful conscience decisively shapes the goal of truth-telling in autobiography. Truth has various meanings for writers: the capacity to face evil, accurate reporting of past events, disclosure of the motives and intentions that explained public actions, or discernment of a pattern or significance in apparently random events. However understood, truth is usually linked to conscience. The writer feels not only an interest in but a moral obligation to search for and define his inner value or standing in relation to ideals. Invoked as the goal of autobiography and the standard for the writer's conscience, truth-telling is an incentive to discerning the self's identity and integrity or their lack.

There are other ways that conscience may provide an incentive to write an autobiography. For some writers there may be a duty, a challenge, or even pleasure in providing conscience with one of its greatest tests. The exercise of conscience is not only the subject matter, but an integral part of Augustine's activity as he writes his *Confessions*. Such an examination of conscience deeply affects his relationship with God:

O Lord, the depths of man's conscience lie bare before your eyes. Could anything of mine remain hidden from you, even if I refused to confess it? I should only be shielding my eyes from seeing you, not hiding myself from you. But now that I have the evidence of my own misery to prove to me how displeasing I am to myself, you are my light and my joy. It is you whom I love and desire, so that I am ashamed of myself and cast myself aside and choose you instead, and I please neither you nor myself except in you.[8]

Examining his past provides Augustine with evidence of his past misery and turns him – again, in the present – to God. Karl Weintraub interprets Augustine's *Confessions* as the exercise, testing, and conditioning of the soul for life's spiritual pilgrimage. 'The analysis of the past is never simple remembrance. Each component that he lifts into consciousness becomes an appropriate occasion for such an *exercitatio animi* . . . . For Augustine life itself is such a never-ending process of conditioning the soul and the mind and the whole being for the ultimate contemplation of truth in the *vita beata*.'[9] The autobiographer, then, may survey his moral history not only to see how his conscience developed, but to develop it further. This project, evident throughout Augustine's *Confessions*, focuses explicitly on the present moment in chapters 30 to 41 of Book X, which analyze the forms of temptation to which Augustine remains susceptible in his present condition. Augustine discloses continuity between past sins and his persisting attraction to the lesser goods of the world, though he also affirms that faith has made a difference, enabling him to resist temptations.

For later writers, too, the task of truthfully understanding and articulating one's past is not always a painful burden, but may be welcomed as beneficial or challenging for conscience. An autobiographer may wish to stress either essential continuity or discontinuity between the workings of conscience in past experience and in the present. He may imaginatively relive a conscience-forming experience, reject a former scruple, recommit himself to some crucial principle, or reflect on what new ideals have replaced old ones. The autobiographer may make a partial amendment for an early error by judging rightly what was wrongly assessed in the past. He may find a kind of atonement for his sins in the shame or humiliation of publicly exposing his misconduct. In all of these instances, conscience motivates or sponsors the writing of autobiography.

A particularly significant aspect of autobiography as an exercise of conscience is the reconstruction of what may be called the 'moment of truth'. This critical passage in an autobiography presents a person's earliest (or first significant) memory of conscience. The term refers doubly to a formative event in a person's moral development and also to a 'moment' we can construe within the autobiographical act when the writer discerns the paradigmatic place of this incident in his life. In the representation of this moment, the writer's conscience first 'pronounces judgment' or 'bites' with remorse or 'whispers the truth'. The metaphor used for conscience often determines the quality and significance of later moral experiences. Augustine's vandalism of the pears was just such a critical moment in moral development, and his explanation of this senseless action sets the tone for his treatment of sin throughout the *Confessions*. Most of the elements in Augustine's mature understanding of moral agency first come together in his analysis of the pear-tree incident: the attraction to 'lesser goods', the determination of human destiny by what one loves, the chain of habit (in this case in the form of concern for others' opinions), and the utter lack of prudence or foresight that characterize so many human decisions. The self-understanding of the seventeen-year-old boy was certainly rudimentary, yet Augustine must have made some inchoate reflections at the time of the vandalism which stayed with him and were developed two decades later. The deepest significance of the incident, however, lies not in the past, but in what is discerned by the trained and relentless conscience of the Bishop of Hippo.

The moment of truth is a paradigmatic event in an autobiography, when a writer dramatizes how his conscience first made significant moral judgments and presents this moment as a key to understanding later experience. We can construe as moments of truth the 'errata' Benjamin Franklin attributes to youthful inexperience and passion, C. S. Lewis's seduction by 'the World' in his English boarding school, and Jung's account of how he reacted to a dream of God defecating on a golden cathedral. In each case the writer presents a foundational moment of moral self-consciousness as a paradigm for later experience.

The first moral crisis – the moment of truth – in Mary McCarthy's *Memories of a Catholic Girlhood* prefigures all of her later dilemmas. On the morning of her first communion, McCarthy unthinkingly takes a drink of water, and thus accidentally breaks her fast. She agonizes about whether to take communion in this state of sin, and when she does receive the sacrament 'in a state of outward holiness and inward horror', believes she is damned. 'The despair I felt that summer morning (I think it was Corpus Christi Day) was in a certain sense fully justified; I *knew myself*, how I was and would be forever; such dry self-knowledge is terrible. Every subsequent moral crisis of my life, moreover, has had precisely the pattern of this struggle over the first Communion; I have battled, usually without avail, against a temptation to do something which only I knew was bad, being swept on by a need to preserve outward appearances and to live up to other people's expectations of me.'[10] In this instance, too, conscience's moment of truth is not merely the record of a past insight, but the autobiographer's perception of an overall pattern and coherence in her moral development. McCarthy is unusually perceptive in exploring analogies between past dilemmas and her present temptation as an autobiographer to 'preserve outward appearances' at the expense of truth.

For Rousseau the founding moment of conscience was his refusal to confess to a crime he did not commit: breaking the teeth of Mlle. Lambercier's combs. When he is wrongfully punished, the pattern is set for the *Confessions*: reiterated appeals for exculpation from public condemnation. Rousseau traces his lifelong hatred of injustice to this experience:

> That first meeting with violence and injustice has remained so deeply engraved on my heart that any thought which recalls it summons back this first emotion. The feeling was only a personal one in its origins, but it has since assumed such a consistency and has become so divorced from personal interests that my blood boils at the sight or the tale of any injustice, whoever may be the sufferer and wherever it may have taken place, in just the same way as if I were myself its victim.[11]

With this experience Rousseau is also initiated into wrongdoing, secretiveness, and rebellion, so that 'there ended the serenity of my childish life'. The die is cast; from this point on, even when Rousseau admits to wrongdoing, he presents himself as an innocent victim of a corrupting environment. This early incident establishes the basic pattern of Rousseau's conscience; it represents a moment of truth in the writing of the *Confessions*, when Rousseau perceived how conscience played a determinative role in forming his personal identity.

Since conscience is a person's assessment of his own character, many of these formative moral experiences are precipitated by a discrepancy between the writer's self-knowledge and his awareness of how a parent or external authority judges him. We are most keenly aware of conscience in situations of moral conflict, especially when we deviate from conventions, rules, or others' expectations. Because of the perceived conflict between external sources of moral authority and the inner moral sense, a child remembers being punished unjustly, or guiltily escaping the detection of a delinquency, or secretly despising someone whom she is instructed to admire. As in Rousseau's case, a person's very sense of self may be rooted in the perception of incongruity between external authority and one's own secret knowledge. In *Father and Son*, Edmund Gosse recounts how 'the consciousness of self' came to him as a result of two incidents in which his supposedly omniscient father did not know something about him as a boy. Gosse's 'I-am-me' experience is intimately linked with the discovery of conscience, presented in this case as a secret companion which does not accuse but sympathizes with the self.

> I had found a companion and a confidant in myself. There was a secret in this world and it belonged to me and to a somebody who lived in the same body with me. There were two of us, and we could talk with one another . . . . It was in this dual form that the sense of my individuality now suddenly descended upon me, and it is equally certain that it was a great solace to me to find a sympathizer in my own breast.[12]

Gosse's conscience was more lenient than his father's stern judgment, and he experienced self-approval rather than guilt. The incident is paradigmatic of his entire relationship to his father and the Plymouth Brethren, foreshadowing the conclusion of *Father and Son*: 'Desperately challenged, the young man's conscience threw off once for all the yoke of his "dedication," and, as respectfully as he could, without parade or remonstrance, he took a human being's privilege to fashion his inner life for himself.'[13] In this incident Gosse first perceived his father's moral judgments as erroneous and recognized the voice of his own conscience as an inner standard which could conflict with external authority.

Such formative moral experiences shape a writer's perception of later incidents in his life, give them a certain emotional tone, and establish a significant pattern to the working of his conscience. In the course of the autobiographical act, assessing a moment of truth may serve as an occasion for the author to re-experience imaginatively and to reinterpret the events that first led him to recognize conscience as a moral authority. A powerful and lasting effect may result from this return to the sources of one's moral being. In any case, a writer's attempt to interpret a moment of truth reveals one role conscience may play in shaping autobiography. The writer's desire for an act of grounding, through remembering the foundations of his sense of moral agency, is another of the several ways in which autobiography may be motivated by a truth-seeking conscience.

II DIFFICULTIES FOR CONSCIENCE

Conscience not only sponsors the writing of autobiography, but monitors this activity. Augustine first discerned some of the ways that writing an autobiography poses certain challenges to and difficulties for conscience. Epistemological problems such as for-getfulness (discussed in Book X, chapters 16–19) and moral vices such as cowardice or sloth may obstruct conscience from accurate judgment about the self. One's proper motive for confession should be thanksgiving at being saved, not pleasure in rehearsing sins:

> I must now carry my thoughts back to the abominable things I did in those days, the sins of the flesh which defiled my soul. I do this, my God, not because I love those sins, but so that I may love you. For love of your love I shall retrace my wicked ways.[14]

When Augustine discusses the temptation to take pride when others praise his goodness (Book X, chapters 36–38), he 'confesses' to a sin which is somewhat hypothetical. 'I cannot easily deduce how far I am cured of this disease, and I have great fear of offending you unawares by sins to which I am blind, though to your eyes they are manifest.'[15] Although uncertain about whether or not he is guilty of such vanity in the past, he expects to face this temptation in the future, partly because he can anticipate the responses that will probably be made to the *Confessions*. Augustine notes a potential danger for conscience inherent in the practice of confession: 'Even when I reproach myself for it, the love of praise tempts me. There is temptation in the very process of self-reproach, for often, by priding himself on his contempt for vainglory, a man is guilty of even emptier pride; and for this reason his contempt of vainglory is an empty boast, because he cannot really hold it in contempt as long as he prides himself on doing so.'[16] As we shall see, Augustine's scruples about being proud of one's own humility point to a constant temptation for the conscience of an autobiographer.

The difficulties writing an autobiography poses for conscience are as various as the ways in which humans err in their choice of moral values and principles and the ways in which they apply these values to their own characters. In addition, the autobiographical process itself engenders certain ambiguities and uncertainties for conscience. Five issues that can arise for conscience will be considered: a writer's misgivings about introspection, the danger of self-deception, the tendency to make the confession of guilt a virtue, uncertainties about the use of conventions, and a writer's scruples about whether his present perspective distorts the true facts about the past.

1. *Introspection.*   For the Christian writer the protracted introspection of the autobiographical act often creates an uneasy conscience, since dwelling at length on the self suggests egoism. Newman asserts that 'it is not at all pleasant for me to be egotistical; nor to be criticized for being so'.[17] At the end of *Surprised by Joy* C. S. Lewis claims that he cannot fully explain his transition from Theism to Christianity because his faith has led him to lose interest in his own development. 'One of the first results of my Theistic conversion was a marked decrease (and high time, as all readers of this book will agree) in the fussy attentiveness which I had so long paid to the progress of my own opinions and the states of my own mind. For many healthy extroverts self-examination first begins with conversion. For me it was almost the other way round.'[18] Lewis's remarks express well the ambivalence felt by many Christian autobiographers about prolonged attention to oneself, given the ideals of self-forgetfulness and concern for the needs of the neighbor. The Christian almost inevitably follows Augustine's example and asserts that she is telling her story not to reveal an interesting personality, but to 'rouse the hearts' of readers and to demonstrate general truths about how God deals with humans. The focus of the work may be displaced onto another person, as when Dorothy Day portrays Peter Maurin as a modern-day saint and the founder

of the Catholic Worker Movement. By various strategies Christian autobiographers try to ease the nagging conscience which often attends concentrated focus on the self.

Secular autobiographers, as well, have sometimes felt that protracted introspection is an unreliable means of attaining self-knowledge, and instead have sought to assess themselves in the context of encounters with other persons or cultures. For example, the travel narrative has been interpreted as an alternative to the traditional crisis autobiography in that it attempts to avoid the flaws of introspection through 'objective' responses to a landscape or other people.[19] What is at stake in some cases is not simply an aesthetic preference but a conscientious concern to present the self truthfully.

2. *Self-Deception.* Self-deception is a constant danger for the autobiographer. As Augustine's remarks indicate, truthtelling in autobiography is not only a matter of honesty in communication with others, for it concerns also honesty with oneself. An autobiographer may sincerely believe he is telling the truth and yet be guilty of self-deception. Self-deception is a somewhat awkward metaphor for the refusal to face the truth about oneself, based on the analogy of one person deceiving another.[20] Just as not every fact about an autobiographer's life qualifies as significant truth, so not every omission, exaggeration, or inconsistency counts as self-deception. Self-deception is the vice of a conscience which cannot admit unpleasant truths to itself. Its opposite is the truthful conscience, the kind of moral self-consciousness which is capable of honestly facing those inconvenient or disreputable things which persons usually prefer not to recognize about themselves.

The classic case of self-deception in autobiography is Rousseau's work. Rousseau's peculiar pattern of confession is directly linked to the problems his conscience confronts as he writes about the past. One senses a deep guilt underlying Rousseau's confession of what seem very trivial matters. At the same time, rationalization and exculpation of his behavior always characterize his discussion of weightier moral issues, such as his allowing the servant Marion to be ruined, abandoning his friend Le Maitre during a fit, and, most significantly, giving five children to the Foundling Hospital. Rousseau is aware that a guilty conscience has motivated his autobiography: 'The burden, therefore, has rested till this day on my conscience without any relief; and I can affirm that the desire to some extent to rid myself of it has greatly contributed to my resolution of writing these *Confessions.*'[21] In spite of his confessions of guilt, however, one cannot help feeling that Rousseau has not adequately interpreted his moral experience. He compulsively reiterates the sincerity of his benevolent feelings – for instance in relation to his children: 'Never for a moment in his life could Jean-Jacques have been a man without feelings or compassion, an unnatural father.' He wants to be judged only by his intentions, and rarely considers the objective consequences of his actions – such as the probable fates of his children. Rousseau thus avoids the real sources of his guilt. The pattern is one of inordinate attention to rather minor moral issues, along with trivialization, minimalization, and avoidance of what seem the truly significant matters. His partial awareness of unacknowledged guilt continues to haunt him, prompting further confessions that fail to set his conscience at rest. Rousseau's work demonstrates both what philosophers usually mean by self-deception and what Christian manuals of moral casuistry discuss under the rubric of the overscrupulous conscience.[22] My point is not that Rousseau's *Confessions* lacks literary merit or that it does not provide a revealing view of the author. Although Rousseau's autobiography is a text which reveals in extraordinary detail the mind of its maker, that mind does not possess a truthful conscience, for Rousseau is an incorrigible self-deceiver when it comes to judging himself.

3. *Guilt as a virtue.* The history of autobiographical writing reveals a repeated tendency to make the confession of sin or guilt the basis for a claim of virtue. This tendency has roots in an interpretation of the apostle Paul which sees him as having required a broken conscience as the only gateway to salvation. According to Krister Stendahl, Augustine was the origin and Luther the climax of this misinterpretation of Paul's letter to the Romans. The 'introspective conscience of the West' expressed paradigmatically by Augustine and Luther was concerned for vital religious reasons to attack the 'good conscience', the self-satisfied moral consciousness. Stendahl points out that, whatever its theological insight, this view misinterprets Paul's real concerns and ignores the 'robust conscience' of this founder of the Church: 'We should not read a trembling and introspective conscience into a text which is so anxious to put the blame on Sin, and that in such a way that not only the Law but the will and mind of man are declared good and are found to be on the side of God.'[23] However, the Augustinian interpretation of Paul became dominant in the West, especially in Protestant forms of Christianity, and Paul was understood to have said that God not only welcomes

but requires a broken heart, utter contrition, and an overwhelming sense of guilt. The only legitimate entrance into the life of faith was supposed to be through increasingly introspective and remorseful consciousness of sin. This understanding of conscience has been one of the deepest motivations behind autobiographical writing. Most of the great examinations of conscience, including fictional auto-biographies by Kierkegaard, Dostoevsky, and Camus, have been first-person confessions, public articulations of a guilty conscience.

We may discern in this historical development a permanent temptation for the conscience of the autobiographer: the hidden claim to virtue that may underlie professions of a guilty conscience. The genuine insights of this view of conscience may be seen in the work of Dietrich Bonhoeffer, whose resistance to the Nazis led him to believe that Christian responsibility requires one to assume a bur-den of guilt as an act of responsibility to one's neighbor.[24] The same view of conscience has also produced less commendable versions of the 'greatest sinner' genre. Although Augustine pointed out the danger of pride lurking in confessions of sin, this very recognition of temptation or guilt can lead to an attitude of moral superiority to contemporary 'Pharisees', those with a good conscience. Although Paul warned that Christians should not continue in sin 'that grace may abound' (Romans 6:1), some Christian autobiographers have succumbed to the danger of a subtle spiritual competition to be the greatest sinner, the most utterly damnable recipient of miraculous grace.

Secular writers, too, such as Rousseau, have attacked the good conscience – the person who claims to have an untroubled moral self-consciousness and to be free of guilt and shame. In the cor-rupted forms of this ethic, a guilty conscience becomes the basis of a claim to virtue, and even a means of dominating others. The history of autobiography documents the persistence and the secularization of the idea that a guilty conscience is necessary for true virtue. This development is brilliantly criticized in Camus's fictional confession *The Fall*, which demonstrates how Jean-Baptiste Clamence's relentless examination of conscience and professions of guilt assume a covert claim of superiority to others, and become a means of manipulating and exploiting them. For some auto-biographers introspection and self-accusation are elevated to the supreme virtues, more important than kindness, justice, or loyalty to any conviction or person. The conscience of the autobiographer in the confessional tradition is always in danger of succumbing to this temptation, this paradoxical combination of compulsive self-humiliation, contempt for those less introspective, and underlying moral smugness. This tendency discloses how closely related are the ways in which conscience may both motivate an autobiographer and entangle him or her in moral confusion, ambiguity, or vice.

4. *Conventions.*   A writer's awareness of her dependence on conventions poses other issues for conscience. Just as the sacrament of confession demands a ritualized pattern of action, so the confessional autobiography in particular entails a set of conventional expectations. As public behavior, the outward act of confession in both its religious and literary forms may or may not correspond to inner intentions and dispositions. Questions about his own sincerity may arise for the autobiographer. Is his professed contrition for past sins genuine, or is the autobiographer deceiving the reader, and perhaps himself, by simply conforming to an established model? The self-reflective autobiographer may express doubts about the capacity of conventions to express fully the meaning of his life. Conscience is at work here, monitoring the distance between public performance and private disposition.

Thus an autobiographer may reveal an uneasy conscience when he complies only partially with the conventions of a genre. He may need to distinguish his goals from readers' probable expectations. For example, C. S. Lewis states that 'this book aims at telling the story of my conversion and is not a general autobiography, still less a "confession" like those of St. Augustine or Rousseau'. Lewis enigmatically warns his readers several times about the selectivity of his account (sending them, perhaps, to biographical studies to infer the missing events). For instance, at one point he admits that he omits a 'huge and complex episode' in which 'my earlier hostility to the emotions was very fully and variously avenged'.[25] Why does Lewis call attention to omissions in this way? His warnings are necessary not only to shape the reader's expectations, but also to release Lewis from the duty to go into certain aspects of his life which he sees as morally significant but peripheral to the story of his conversion. Lewis's conscience requires that he distinguish his autobiographical purposes from complete adherence to the Augustinian model of confession, which would entail a scrupulous account of all sins.

Articulations of conscience in autobiography are constrained by the conventions which shape writing about the self in different historical periods. The language of conscience reflects not simply a writer's solitary meditations upon his deepest values, but rhetorical strategies in relation to an audience. Awareness of an audience's expectations and interests focuses the public articulation of conscience in highly selective and formalized ways. For example, Victorian England produced few unabashed confessions as revealing as Rousseau's. Silences and oblique references often obscure our understanding of matters which were undoubtedly of central importance, such as troubled marriages or conflicts with loved ones. 'Where was Rousseau?' wonders one critic, surprised by the apparent lack of influence of the great French confessor. The Victorians were not prepared to imitate Rousseau's candor, and could only face the darker and puzzling aspects of human nature in the form of 'distancing fiction . . . . The milieu of nineteenth-century England, in short, made it impossible to write an autobiography which would also have been a true confessional. Perhaps only the novel provided that.'[26] A Victorian autobiographer's credibility was linked to his demonstration of a concern for honesty. Victorian writers needed to defend or apologize for introspective reflection and to establish a relation with their audience which avoided doubts and anxieties about the writer's honesty. The writer's task is conceived of by one critic as 'convincing us of the congruence of style and character' by making rhetorical gestures intended to convince readers of his credibility.[27] From such a critical perspective, appeals to conscience are only a public performance, a means of attaining credibility by conforming to whatever norms govern the expression of self-examination. To take an autobiography as the direct result of a writer's conscientious struggle to be truthful with himself would seem at best naive about the realities of the relationship between author and audience.

However, the use of traditional conventions should not be understood as antithetical to a person's search for the truth about the past, and about his present relation to that past. All writers depend upon what Avrom Fleishman calls 'figures' of autobiography: those literary formulas, motifs, and conventions that shape writing about the self. Augustine's conversion scene in the garden at Milan, for instance, uses four figures from ancient literary tradition: 'the sudden apparition (in this case a voice), as found in African "vision" literature; the admonition by a children's game, as in a host of classical didactic works; the *sortes*, or opening at random, practiced on a variety of privileged texts in both Jewish and pagan as well as Christian culture; and the formula "Take and read," widely used to encourage scholars in both Christian and pagan writings.'[28] The historicity of Augustine's experience and the truthfulness of his conscience are not discredited when we recognize his dependence on conventions. Nor is their interpretation of personal experience by later autobiographers dubious simply because they interpret it with 'Augustinian figures' such as three figures of movement (wandering, journey, and pilgrimage) or a crisis stage expressed in medical imagery. Augustine is the inventor of autobiography not because his experience was absolutely original but because he demonstrated how to interpret one's own life figuratively. 'The *Confessions* became a model for Western autobiography because Augustine knew how to model his life on the lives of Adam, Moses, Jesus, and Paul.'[29] There is no necessary contradiction between reliance on conventions and conscientious pursuit of autobiographical truth, since all writers rely on and are formed by communities of discourse, and by both literary and moral norms. There is no direct access to a person's life unmediated by rhetoric, style, and conventions.

While we need to interpret the ways in which the articulation of conscience is constrained by the conventions shaping autobiographical writing, we need not assume that the language of conscience is only a means of manipulating readers. An autobiographer's conscience can only attain and communicate a truthful judgment in terms of shared norms to which he and his audience adhere. Conventions (from the Latin *com* + *venire*: to come together) both constrain expression and enable a writer to achieve the standard of truthfulness he shares with readers. As readers we can recognize a writer's use of rhetoric and his relation to conventions, and we may evaluate how these matters affect his insights into and assessment of his life. Indeed, our understanding and assessment of an autobiographer's conscience are greatly influenced by the quality of his awareness of his dependence on conventions. In the next chapter I will examine the autobiographer's use of tropes and figures of character as an instance of this general issue.

5. *Scruples about historical accuracy.* A final difficulty for the conscience of some autobiographers concerns distinguishing between past experience and present perspective. Every autobiographer's past is mediated by a set of present convictions that provides an organizing perspective on experience. The autobiographer must create a meaningful pattern or design out of his experiences, but conscience may require him to admit that in doing this he may be simplifying the actual complexity of past experience, omitting important events, or distorting 'what really happened'. The more

self-conscious the autobiographer, the more aware he will be of his activity as a writer. As we shall explore in detail in Chapter 3, a self-reflexive autobiographer realizes his dependence on literary techniques of plotting and characterization, and sometimes calls attention to his design. He may point out, for example, his choice to portray his life as a series of radical transformations or as the gradual disclosure of a persistent underlying identity, thus acknowledging either discontinuity or continuity as a controlling interest in plotting and characterization. Yet he may seem skeptical of his own design and show its limitations, apparently undermining his attempt to unify his experience or discern a pattern.

For example, even though Malcolm X claims to have discarded his past 'selves', he reveals that his days as a 'mascot', a 'hustler' and a Black Muslim permanently affected his character. C. S. Lewis portrays a persisting romantic temperament searching for elusive 'Joy' in a variety of pursuits and circumstances. Yet he also depicts himself forgetting about Joy for years at a time, and on the last page of his autobiography he asserts that as a Christian he has lost all interest in Joy. Was the search for Joy really the dominant motif of his early life or does *Surprised by Joy* misrepresent the past? The questions Malcolm X and Lewis raise about the adequacy of their overall designs are not only aesthetic ones. Matters of conscience are at stake insofar as an autobiographer worries about whether his overall design falsifies the past. In this way the potential conflict between the need for a meaningful narrative pattern and truthfulness in the form of historical accuracy may pose an issue for conscience.

The ideal of truthfulness deeply influences an autobiographer's scruples about historical accuracy. This concern, like the other issues addressed in this section, shows how the autobiographical act is not only motivated by conscience but at the same time raises problems for conscience. Conscience both sponsors and monitors the autobiographer's quest for the essential truth about himself. The nature of autobiographical truthfulness in relation to conscience, however, is not an easy thing to define abstractly. This difficult topic needs further explanation as well as analysis in the case of specific texts.

III TRUTHFULNESS IN AUTOBIOGRAPHY

Writers and interpreters of autobiography have long puzzled over the nature of truthfulness in this form of writing, which is neither

history nor simply fiction.[30] Many critics have attacked the very
idea of truthfulness as a useful concept for understanding autobiography, for they see it as imposing a narrow and unattainable
standard of resemblance to an irrecoverable past, or as mislead-
ingly posing from the autobiographer's point of view issues that
arise only from the reader's perspective. However, I submit that
truthfulness, although exceedingly difficult to define abstractly, is
a crucial goal of most autobiographers. Furthermore, assessments of
truthfulness or its lack are a crucial element in the distinctive mode
of reading that autobiography engenders. Even those contemporary
critical theories which view as an illusion the idea of an individual
telling the truth about the self are caught up in assumptions about
and assessments of truthfulness – if only to discriminate between
those persons who are mystified and those who discern the actual
functioning of the unconscious, or the struggle between classes, or
the real nature of language.

It is easier to show specific achievements or failures of truthfulness in particular autobiographies than it is to define the nature
of truthfulness. Nonetheless, some generalizations may be offered
before I turn to specific texts. Truthfulness must be distinguished
from truth. Truth is usually thought of as a kind of correspondence
between human thought and reality, or as a matter of coherence
among different ideas and propositions. Truthfulness, in contrast,
is a process or quality of a person, a virtue we ascribe to certain
individuals and not others. In my view, an autobiographer cannot
convincingly claim to present the authoritative account of the reality
of the past. For the autobiographer may err; he is as fallible as
any human being in interpreting reality. The autobiographer may,
however, demonstrate truthfulness, which is an active search for
the most exact and insightful understanding of past experience.
Truthfulness is closely related to the virtue of conscientiousness:
that is, being governed by the dictates of conscience, being careful
and scrupulous about assessing one's conduct and character.

Truthfulness is not a matter of exhaustive factual record or accuracy in every detail; the mere accumulation of facts may produce
triviality or a mass of uninterpreted data. The autobiographer tells
the truth about herself as she imaginatively reconstructs personal
history, creating a narrative with most of the elements characteristic of fictional stories. Self-representation in narrative necessarily
requires the use of fictional techniques and literary figures, as
Eakin and Fleishman demonstrate. An autobiographer may even

tell the essential truth about herself by lying, in the sense of misrepresenting what she knows to have been the actual facts about the past.[31] At the same time, the goal of truthfulness implies a kind of faithfulness to the past, and this ideal creates obligations for the writer's conscience. The writer's moral scruples set limits to and orient the imaginative project of self-representation.

Even if we are as skeptical as are most critics today that a single definitive account of the past can be recovered, as readers of autobiography we constantly make judgments about the truthfulness of writers. The reader's assessment of the truthfulness of an autobiographer's conscience concerns one's sense of his moral honesty and trustworthiness. When a writer's self-assessment differs in certain crucial ways from our own, we sense a lack of truthfulness. It is not that readers have to share all the values of an autobiographer to appreciate his work, but that we hold him to his own standards, among others. Probably the most basic and universally human form of ethical evaluation is the criticism of hypocrisy. We do not have to accept all of another person's principles to believe that he ought to clarify just what his moral standards are, be consistent in practicing what he professes, and apply to his own case the standards by which he evaluates others. We may also judge a writer in terms of values he does not hold but – so we believe – should have held. For instance we may feel that an autobiographer has avoided some central moral issue which he should have addressed. Critics contrast truthfulness with autobiographical defects which they usually characterize in moral language: evasiveness, triviality, hypocrisy, or self-deception. Our response to the conscience of an autobiographer is a basic form of ethical criticism, because it is a response to the writer's character, or *ethos*. Making these inferences about the moral qualities of 'the company we keep' as we read is a basic aspect of our response to an autobiography.[32]

We do not need to know and approve of every characteristic of an autobiographer, but, to be fully engaged in his work, we need to understand how he applies moral principles to himself, and to assess how he does this. Our ideas about the role of conscience in a person's life reflect basic assumptions about moral agency, and in some ways they are more fundamental than many of our beliefs about other aspects of moral behavior. For we apply these ideas about conscience to every person, regardless of his or her more specific beliefs about what counts materially as right or wrong action. That is, assessments of conscientiousness are made independently of whether we share all of another person's moral standards. Conscientiousness, as David Little explains, is subject to public evaluative criteria in a way that the content of conscience is not:

> The content of the conscience is, up to a point, the private responsibility of each individual. Each person has a right to determine the character of his basic convictions, and must take the consequences for so doing. But whether someone is to be called conscientious in obeying his conscience is a matter for public scrutiny and determination; it is something observers properly judge, rather than being simply a private affair.[33]

As Little's analysis demonstrates, conscientiousness is a composite virtue encompassing such qualities as honesty, trustworthiness, impartiality, and courage. These qualities are also components of truthfulness, and they are among the most significant things we assess about an autobiographer's work.

We can best understand truthfulness in autobiography not as a strange hybrid of history and fiction, but in terms of a continual dialogue between a writer's conscience and his imagination. Imagination in the context of autobiography means the mind's capacity to conceive and represent an image of the self. Imagination is both empowered by conscience to seek for this form of truth and constrained by conscience. That is, conscience sponsors the imaginative effort to understand one's past, and it monitors how well the created image accords with certain standards. Truthfulness in autobiography means that a writer strives for fidelity to both his creative imagination and his conscience. These two impulses – imagination and conscience – produce potential conflicts as well as possible linkages in the autobiographical process. The autobiographer creates a truthful portrait when he shows a pattern in his experience that satisfies both his conscience and his imaginative capacities. As readers we assess autobiographers according to whether they reconcile and integrate imagination and conscience, both creative revisioning of the past and concern that the constructed image of the self reflects the actual nature of the past.

Those writers who describe the autobiographical act demonstrate and illuminate this dialogue between conscience and imagination. Mary McCarthy's *Memories of a Catholic Girlhood* discloses some of the tensions and alliances between conscience and imagination which emerge as a person searches for truthful understanding of her relation to the past. In the italicized sections between the chapters of this work, McCarthy analyzes the elements of fiction in her account of the past, and explains her uncertainties about the truth of what she has written. Yet she claims to be writing a historical memoir, and invites others to set the record straight if they can. 'This record lays a claim to being historical – that is, much of it can be checked. If there is more fiction in it than I know, I should like to be set right; in some instances, which I shall call attention to later, my memory has already been corrected.'[34] When she describes the difficulties of being historically accurate, she often uses the language of conscience, referring to temptations, scruples, and excuses. When she speaks of her recourse to fiction, it is usually to justify this as necessary in her quest for essential truth. For example, she says of 'The Blackguard': 'This account is highly fictionalized . . . . In short, the story is true in substance, but the details have been invented or guessed at.' Of 'C'est le Premier Pas Qui Coute', McCarthy comments: 'This story is so true to our convent life that I find it almost impossible to sort out the guessed-at and the half-remembered from the undeniably real.' And on 'The Figures in the Clock': 'This is an example of "storytelling": I arranged actual events so as to make "a good story" out of them. It is hard to overcome this temptation if you are in the habit of writing fiction; one does it almost automatically.'[35] Conscience warns her to acknowledge historical inaccuracies or uncertainties, and to 'confess' to infidelities to her memory of the facts. At the same time, her quest to express the essential truth (the truth 'in substance', the 'undeniably real') about her past experience requires the use of fictional techniques such as plotting ('rearranging' events) and inventing imaginary conversations. McCarthy provides a scrupulous account of how memory and imagination and historical guesswork were woven together and, guided by conscience, formed into an account of the essential truth of the past.

How may fiction or even conscious 'lying' tell the essential truth about the self? Commenting on 'A Tin Butterfly', McCarthy discusses whether Uncle Myers really did steal a butterfly and incriminate Mary by placing it under her plate. 'After a struggle with [her] conscience (the first Communion again)', she consults her brothers Kevin and Preston, who cannot confirm her account. So she 'pleads guilty' to probably having taken from a drama teacher the idea that Uncle Myers put the butterfly at her place. 'The most likely thing, I fear, is that I fused two memories. *Mea culpa.*' Yet this confession of the probability of her memory's creativity in imagining this scene does not undermine the truth of 'A Tin Butterfly'. It is consistent with what we see of Uncle Myers' character that he might well have done this, even though McCarthy has no firm evidence. 'Who did put the butterfly by my place? It may have been Uncle Myers after all. Even if no one saw him, he remains a suspect: he had motive and opportunity.'[36]

Here, then, McCarthy conscientiously compares her memories of the past to external sources (which are not fully reliable), and reflects on the indispensability of imaginative fiction in reconstructing and recreating her past. Fictional elements do not discredit the truth of the narrative, but they must be approved by her conscience. In McCarthy's account of the autobiographical act, conscience and imagination can either conflict or co-operate. The plot and the theme of *Memories of a Catholic Girlhood* center on McCarthy's struggles – in both her early life and in the writing of that book – to reconcile conscience and imagination by finding a form of acting or writing that expresses both demands. McCarthy is unusually self-conscious and articulate about the dialogue between conscience and imagination, and unusually scrupulous about explaining the quest for essential truth in her stories. I submit that a form of this dialogue is intrinsic to the writing of every autobiography, although it is rarely formulated theoretically or rendered so vividly.

Malcolm X's *Autobiography* presents a case where an autobiographer admits to telling a lie in the service of the truth. To dramatize his desperate and suicidal character as a hustler, Malcolm recounts how he played Russian roulette with his gang. In his epilogue, Alex Haley indicates that Malcolm admitted that in fact he had secretly removed the bullet. Malcolm X did not want this admission to be included in the text of the autobiography:

> 'You know this place here in this chapter where I told you how
> I put the pistol up to my head and kept pulling the trigger and
> scared them so when I was starting the burglary ring – well,' he
> paused, 'I don't know if I ought to tell you this or not, but I want
> to tell the truth.' He eyed me, speculatively. 'I palmed the bullet.'
> We laughed together. I said, 'Okay, give that page here, I'll fix it.'
> Then he considered, 'No, leave it that way. Too many people
> would be so quick to say that's what I'm doing today, bluffing.'[37]

What are we to say of this confession of a lie in the service of the truth? (And what are we to make of this passage from Haley's epilogue as being – ambiguously – a part of Malcolm's autobiography?)

Malcolm wanted to tell the truth about his essential character – in this case that he could sway others to his purposes and that he often risked death. His conscience was troubled by his knowledge of a factual inaccuracy in his narrative, but he chose to lie about this detail in order that his entire story not be discredited. The lie is intended to further Malcolm's credibility, but it also reflects Malcolm's basic self-image; it fits his character. Perhaps when Haley included this passage in his epilogue he diminished Malcolm's credibility for some readers. I suspect, however, that most readers' view of Malcolm's essential truthfulness is not significantly affected by this incident. In fact, the acknowledgment probably increases our trust in his reliability throughout his autobiography, as well as our confidence in Haley's editorial work. Confessions of lying, either within or outside the text of an autobiography, are indirect testimony to the quest for essential truth about the self. Homage is paid to conscience when a writer explains the need for distorting the literal facts about the past in order to be truthful about his present understanding of the past. Conscience is honored in the explanation of how a conventional moral scruple about literal accuracy was overridden by a larger concern with truthfulness.

Suppose, however, that a consistent pattern of distortion was either confessed or detected by external evidence. How would the texture of Malcolm's narrative have been affected? Would the reader perceive signs of self-deception? How many such lies in other autobiographies are we unaware of because the autobiographer does not acknowledge them either within his or her life-story or in external commentary upon it? How can we tell the difference between a lie in the service of the truth and a lie told to deceive others or oneself? These important questions, which are probably impossible to answer in the abstract, often arise in our assessment of particular autobiographies. Although most recent theories of autobiography assert that an invented self-portrait need have little to do with 'what really happened', concern for historical accuracy raises crucial issues of conscience for many writers, and enters into the critic's interpretation of such works. Whether to omit, exaggerate, or understate certain incidents in narrating one's story raise issues that are resolved partly according to one's scruples about falsehood and truth. The nature of the dialogue between these scruples of conscience and the imaginative revisioning of the past is one index of an autobiographer's truthfulness.

An autobiographer seems to me most trustworthy when he aspires to a truthful conscience but remains somewhat dubious or skeptical about his achievements. This is not to make a guilty conscience the norm for all good autobiography. My assessment of truthfulness in an autobiography, however, is more than an aesthetic judgment of a text; my evaluation indicates what I value most in self-knowledge and moral consciousness. I submit that a sensitive and healthy conscience is self-critical, aware of mixed motives, and skeptical of the best intentions. And yet skepticism need not undermine commitment to the basic project of seeking truth.

Truthfulness seems to require a testing of the verdicts of conscience against external perspectives and assessments of the self. For the religious autobiographer, conscience is never the final judge. In what is meant *not* to be an ironic comment, Augustine, in the midst of his unrelenting soul-searching, abruptly cites I Corinthians 4:3: 'I do not scrutinize my own conduct'. He recognizes that, though a person must live according to its judgments, one's conscience may be erroneous. 'It is you, O Lord, who judge me. For though no one can know a man's thoughts, except the man's own spirit that is within him, there are some things in man which even his own spirit within him does not know. But you, O Lord, know all there is to know of him, because you made him.'[38] Faith in God is not requisite, however, to recognize one's capacity for moral error, and to strive for truthfulness by comparing one's conscience with the verdicts of external judgments. We have seen how Mary McCarthy discloses her scruples about whether her best efforts and intentions have conveyed the truth about her past.

This pattern of conscientious reflection indicates a very different kind of conscience from that revealed in the ordinary unreflective autobiography. It differs, too, from the work of a person who sees his conscience as the sole moral authority and as an autonomous determiner of value. Such a belief characterizes Rousseau's *Confessions*. For Rousseau, autobiographical truth means the demonstration of the sincerity of his present feelings as he writes:

I have only one faithful guide on which I can count; the succession of feelings which have marked the development of my being, and thereby recall the events that have acted upon it as cause or effect . . . . I may omit or transpose facts, or make mistakes in dates; but I cannot go wrong about what I have felt, or about what my feelings have led me to do; and these are the chief subjects of my story. The true object of my confessions is to reveal my inner thoughts exactly in all the situations of my life. It is the history of my soul that I have promised to recount, and to write it faithfully I have need of no other memories; it is enough if I enter again into my inner self, as I have done till now.[39]

Jean Starobinski argues that Rousseau was the originator of a new conception of truth in first-person writing: 'What is of primary importance is not historical veracity but the emotion experienced as the past emerges and is represented in consciousness. The image of the past may be false, but the present emotion is not. The truth that Rousseau wishes to communicate is not exactitude of biographical fact but accuracy in depicting his relation to his past.'[40] Rousseau locates autobiographical truth not in the reproduction of some historical referent, but in the authenticity of his feelings as rendered in the style of his language. According to Starobinski, Rousseau's new ethic of authenticity deeply influenced the course of autobiographical writing:

No longer does the literary work call forth the assent of the reader to a truth that stands as a 'third person' between the writer and his audience; the writer singles himself out through his work and elicits assent to the truth of his personal experience. Rousseau discovered these problems; he truly invented a new attitude, which became that of modern literature . . . He was the first to experience the dangerous compact between ego and language, the 'new alliance' in which man makes himself the word.[41]

Whatever its value in demonstrating and influencing a new honesty in the expression of emotion, the ideal of authenticity of feeling leaves much to be desired as a standard of moral truthfulness. When sincere intention becomes the only criterion of moral judgment, a person is insulated from direct challenge by other points of view, and blinded to the actual consequences of his actions. Rousseau's fascinating and invaluable testimony is that of a conscience which denies the possibility of a truth not of its own making or a moral reality beyond its own wishes. Rousseau does not realize that conscience does not itself create standards of rightness and goodness, but relies on moral principles which were learned in a human community and transcend the self.[42] Truthfulness eludes Rousseau, I think, precisely because he believes there is no objective standard of truth and no evidence or witnesses who might call into question his current version of his life. His skepticism and suspicion apply to everyone and everything but his own conscience. Unwilling to compare the inner verdict of his conscience with any external judgments, Rousseau is trapped in a solipsistic moral world. To what can he appeal for confirmation of his truthfulness, except his own feeling that he would like to be truthful? And yet he is plagued with doubts and anxieties whose source continually eludes him. Judged by his own standard of authenticity, Rousseau succeeds brilliantly at expressing his confused feelings of guilt, shame, and wounded innocence as he reflects on the past. But that standard is an inadequate criterion of truthfulness when it comes to moral assessment. His focus on his own feelings leads him to moral self-deception, in the form of a studied aversion to considering either the consequences of his actions or the perspectives of other persons. Rousseau wrote a fascinating history of his good intentions and sincere feelings but, I submit, he did not reveal a truthful conscience; he did not demonstrate conscientiousness. The antidote to self-deception is not simply more intensive self-examination or subtler portrayal of the nuances of emotion; concern for the perspective of the other is essential.

We want to know not only what a writer feels as he writes, but the nature of the past events and actions which evoke those feelings. In fact there is a reality beyond the autobiographer and his reader: the writer's past self, about whom the narrator offers what he proposes as the most convincing interpretation. While as readers we have no direct access to this past reality, the author as protagonist, we constantly make judgments about the writer's truthfulness in reconstructing an image of his past character. We judge an autobiographer's trustworthiness and honesty in this regard in many of the same ways that we assess reliable and unreliable narrators in fiction. We do not need to go outside the text for external evidence; our inferences about motivation, special pleading, inconsistency, or patterns of avoidance provide the materials from which we construct an interpretation of how the writer's conscience operates.

In contrast to Rousseau, the autobiographies of Augustine and Mary McCarthy reveal very different assumptions about truthfulness. Both writers believe that truth refers to something beyond what they create in language and to a reality outside their feelings, and they see conscience as calling the autobiographer to account for that truth. Each writes a narrative of corrected self-deception: a story which incorporates an experience of self-deception as central to personal identity. That these writers recognize that they have been guilty of self-deception in the past strongly affects their identities and their ideas about conscience. Augustine's analysis of his reasons for denying human sin and his own errors and McCarthy's interpretation of her compulsive lying explore how each writer refused to face the truth. Each detects in an earlier self characteristic patterns of evasion, motivated forgetfulness, and systematic excuse-making. Augustine and McCarthy are alert for similarities between past self-deception and present temptations. Their awareness of the danger of self-deception, as discerned in the patterns and proclivities of past actions, and their deep desire to avoid that danger in the present, convince us that in each case a truthful conscience is at work. That a person is willing to revise or educate his conscience, and has done so in spite of temptations not to do so, is one of the most basic conditions of a truthful conscience. McCarthy's scrupulous wish to corroborate her memories with whatever external evidence she can find, and Augustine's desire to have his moral judgments corrected by God, each witness to a conscience aware of its fallibility and seeking clarification and validation outside itself. We may or may not share all of the moral standards by which they assess the past, but we cannot doubt their essential truthfulness, their commitment to the task of fair and accurate moral judgment.

The works of Augustine and McCarthy demonstrate the arguments of this chapter regarding conscience as an incentive for autobiography, the difficulties the autobiographical act may pose for conscience, and the nature of truthfulness. Their works show conscience at work both sponsoring and monitoring the autobiographical act. Although conscience is both their central subject matter as they reflect on the past and an essential component of autobiographical writing as they conceive of that task, neither McCarthy nor Augustine claims to have achieved with certainty one of their highest aspirations, a truthful conscience. In contrast to Rousseau, they do not claim to offer the single authoritative version of the past ('the truth'). Tentativeness and educability characterize their striving for truthfulness. As narratives of corrected self-deception, their autobiographies demonstrate a capacity and a vital concern to discover the truth about their past and present characters. The nature of truthfulness in autobiography is demonstrated by Augustine's and McCarthy's commitment to accurate assessment of the past, skepticism about their own moral veracity, and willingness to submit the verdicts of conscience to comparisons and possible correction.

3

Character and Characterization

Character is a traditional word for a person's consistency, integrity, and fidelity to their deepest commitments. Conscience monitors and safeguards the consistency of character, warning of inconsistencies between a person's established priorities and his actions, detecting failures to integrate belief and conduct.

The significance of character in autobiography has been asserted by a number of theologians and scholars of religion. This interpretation of autobiography is now in doubt, however, because the central notions of self and character are being questioned or attacked by recent narrative theory. Many theories of narrative collapse traditional humanistic notions of self, character, and author into 'text' and see in autobiography not the representation of character but a process of fictional characterization. These contrasting emphases on character and characterization raise crucial issues for understanding autobiography. This chapter first analyzes theories of character in the fields of religious studies and literary criticism. I will then argue that character and characterization should not be thought of as two alternative interpretations of the activity of the religious autobiographer, but as inseparable concerns. Two important sources of narrative theory – autobiographies themselves and the genre of fictional autobiography – will suggest further insights into the relationships between character and characterization.

I THEORIES OF CHARACTER AND CHARACTERIZATION

According to many contemporary theologians and scholars of religion, narrative is significant because it shows how religious beliefs, values, and commitments shape a person's character. Autobiography is often assumed to illustrate the connections between

37

narrative and character, for in autobiography the writer describes and evaluates the development of his or her character from the perspective of present religious convictions. In a religious auto-biography the self's character is interpreted as a response to the formative and shaping action of God or whatever the writer holds sacred.[1]

Books by McFague, Novak, McClendon, Gunn, Dunne, Hauerwas, Stroup, and Goldberg interpret in diverse ways the significance for religious studies of autobiography (and/or biography).[2] They agree, however, about its significance in two areas. First, autobiography shows the necessity of narrative in religious self-understanding. Narrative is essential because, in contrast to abstract or theoretical ways of thinking, it dramatizes the temporal and historical qualities of human experience. Many of the works on narrative in the field of religious studies depend on Stephen Crites' claim that 'the formal quality of experience in time is inherently narrative'.[3] Narrative form is necessary to show the 'tensed unity' of past, present, and future in every moment of life. In various ways, all the authors mentioned above use autobiographical works to explain how religious myths and symbols shape character by orienting an individual's sense of time and understanding of personal history.[4]

A second common assumption of these works is the significance in autobiography of the moral evaluation of character. Each of these authors depends upon a concept of character or some func-tional equivalent (such as 'personal identity' for Stroup or 'self' for McFague). The question of the truthfulness of autobiography is cen-tral; autobiography is taken to exemplify basic problems of religious self-knowledge and moral judgment. The theologians recognize that truthfulness is not necessarily the same as truth in the sense of literal factual accuracy. Truth in the most exhaustive and exact factual sense is not required for the project of self-evaluation, for the autobiographer's omission of certain facts, erroneous memory, or even conscious distortion of the past may still reveal what is most central in his character. Rather, truthfulness is a question of whether a person is able to avoid self-deception, particularly by facing up to past evil actions. (Unfortunately, none of these writers deals sufficiently with the relevance to 'truthfulness' of accuracy in matters of factual detail, an issue for conscience discussed in the previous chapter.) Stroup and Goldberg, like Hauerwas and Burrell, contrast truthfulness with self-deception, relying on Herbert

Fingarette's psychological analysis. According to Fingarette, a self-deceiver achieves consistency and coherence in her life by failing to acknowledge what she has in fact done. The theologians assert that the religiously committed self has a 'story' which gives her the skills to 'spell out her engagements' in such a way that evil is not evaded but acknowledged and confessed. Stroup uses the metaphor of a 'collision' between an individual's personal narrative and the narratives of the religious community to describe how religious faith can help minimize self-deception. The autobiographies of Augustine and Malcolm X document such a collision and show the writer coming to a more truthful understanding of his past life and character. For the scholars of religion, in sum, autobiography is significant because it demonstrates how narratives articulate a distinctive sense of temporality and because autobiographical writing forces a person to engage with honesty and courage in an evaluation of character, especially one's capacity for evil.

Character receives quite different treatment in the theories of narrative growing out of recent literary history and criticism. To be sure, some critics reaffirm the traditional ideas that a self pre-exists autobiography, and that autobiography represents and judges the character of this self.[5] Such a humanistic critic analyzes the ways that metaphors and fictional techniques shape the presentation of self in an autobiographical text, but does not doubt that the textual self corresponds to the writer's historical existence. Many recent studies of autobiography, however, question or dismiss the traditional notion of character. Autobiography is treated as a process of fictional characterization in which there are, at the very least, crucial differences between the textual version of a self and a writer's actual experience. Extratextual fact, truth-as-correspondence to the author's life, and even the notion that there is a persisting self are dismissed by radical literary critics as the tokens of an outmoded and wrongheaded historical approach to autobiography. As James Olney has noted, the focus of autobiography criticism first shifted from an interest in 'bios' (the life) to one in 'autos' (the self), defined as 'the "I" that coming awake to its own being shapes and determines the nature of the autobiography and in so doing half discovers, half creates itself'.[6] The older historical approach was displaced by philosophical, psychological, and literary treatments of the self behind – or rather created by – autobiography. More recent developments in autobiography criticism have turned to the third element in autobiography – the writing – as the key to understanding this genre; without 'textualization' there is neither life nor self. Yet questions about the self – its character and the possibility of its knowing itself – still set the agenda.

> However much they talk about genre or linguistics or deep-lying structures, what they are still troubling about is the self and consciousness or knowledge of it, even though in a kind of bravura way some of them may be denying rather than affirming its reality or its possibility. And this is the crux of the matter, the heart of the explanation for the special appeal of autobiography in recent times: it is a fascination with the self and its profound, its endless mysteries and, accompanying that fascination, an anxiety about the self.[7]

This critical theory raises two issues for the understanding of autobiography in the fields of theology and religious studies. The first concerns the implications of this view of language for the ideal of truthfulness in judging character. Recent criticism challenges the notions that the character created in a text corresponds directly to the writer's historical self, and that the writer can use language as a tool directly to express himself. To be sure, traditional approaches to autobiography recognized that autobiography is not simply a matter of recording memories, but a process of selection, imaginative recollection, and ordering that reflects the present perspective and language of the writer. However, recent critical theory is not only more highly aware of the ways that the writing process shapes perceptions of the past, but is also skeptical that either historical accuracy or truthfulness about one's character can be achieved. In its most radical form, recent critical theory formulates as doctrine the impossibility of the autobiographical project of self-representation. For Louis Renza, autobiography means translating the events of a life into a public event of language. Autobiography can not fully communicate the privateness of the self or the feeling of pastness; it forces the writer to adopt a persona, and to 'make his language refer to himself allegorically'.[8] The very conditions of writing 'veto' the autobiographer's imaginative project of self-portrayal. Similarly, Michael Sprinker brings to bear on traditional notions of author and self the theories of Lacan, Foucault, Barthes, and Derrida, and concludes that 'autobiography, the inquiry of the self into its own origin and history, is always circumscribed by the limiting conditions of writing, of the production of a text . . . . No autobiography can take place except within the boundaries of a writing where concepts of subject, self, and author collapse into the act of producing a text.'[9]

These critics rightly deny that the past can be retrieved without mediation, and they astutely challenge the idea that character can be known and expressed in some other terms than a particular culture's available figures and fictions of the self. There is no access to 'actual experience' unmediated by language and literary tradition. Given this recognition of the power of language, the problem of truthfulness in characterizing the self changes in form, becoming an epistemological issue as well as a moral one. It is not only a matter of truth-telling as opposed to falsity, or even truthfulness rather than self-deception, but a matter of finding the right metaphors and figures to express essential character. By what criteria does a writer judge the adequacy of metaphors to characterize herself or himself? As we shall see in the case of Malcolm X, the conscientious autobiographer is often haunted by the ambiguity and uncertainty of self-knowledge expressed metaphorically.

A second challenge suggested by recent critical theory concerns the link between narrative and temporality as the hermeneutical lens through which autobiography is viewed. Some contemporary approaches to autobiography see the creation of the author's self as dependent on narrative, but they free narrative from any obligation to record memories or to describe accurately historical events. From this perspective, narrative is not tied to the experience of temporality. For Barret Mandel, the form of the writing, the shape of the narrative, figures a self that may not correspond to the writer as a historical agent in the past. Autobiography is not denied all reference by this view; however, its truth is not based on recollection of the past, but on the way narration reveals the self's 'deeper being' in the present, at the moment of writing: 'We mistakenly assume that this consciousness is coterminous with who we are. Actually the conscious mind is rooted in the unseen (but not unseeing) being – the source of consciousness.'[10] For Jean Starobinski, it is not whether Rousseau reports the past accurately but his narrative style that reveals his character: 'The originality in the autobiographical style – far from being suspect – offers us a system of revealing indices, or symptomatic traits . . . . No matter how doubtful the facts related, the text will at least present an "authentic" image of the man who "held the pen."'[11] James Olney analyzes as autobiography works by Valery and Yeats which make little if any reference to the writer's memory of the past. Olney holds that more important than the historical self is a writer's sense of *bios*, which 'extends down to the roots of individual being; it is atemporal, committed to a vertical thrust from consciousness down into the unconscious rather than to a horizontal thrust from the present into the past'.[12] And for Christine Downing, modern autobiographers informed by psychology may write their life histories not in terms of a chrono-logical arrangement of outward events, but as a series of dream images. The work of Freud and Jung shows that the associations of the unconscious form both the basis of the self and the structure of autobiographical works. Downing argues that the discovery of the unconscious mind forces autobiographers to abandon the traditional or classical historicist approach to autobiography in favor of an act of *poesis* based on dreams, myth, and identification with archetypal figures.[13] For these critics, autobiography reveals the writer's character, but character is not tied to the historical agent who performed certain actions in the past. The issue at stake is not the self's existence outside the text, but rather the nature of the self: what gives it identity and character. While not denying that temporality is an important element in human experience, these critics stress another factor as determinative in forming personal identity. They hold a psychological theory of the self which posits that beneath consciousness lies a deeper and 'timeless' self. It is not the autobiographical subject's memories of historical events that provide identity, but some kind of deep-rooted psychic structure which expresses itself primarily through images and metaphors.

This approach to autobiography thus challenges the assumption that the narrative structure of autobiography is based first and foremost on the chronological development of the writer. These writers would agree with the view that narrative forms correspond to fundamental structures of human experience, but they differ as to just what is most fundamental in experience. This critical approach denies the assumption that the structures of narrative necessarily reflect and express the basic human experience of temporality – and that the 'narrative quality of experience' is essentially one of living in time. More fundamental for them than the experience of temporality is the human mind's capacity for metaphor. From this point of view, both the self and its narratives are structured by the associations and desires of the unconscious mind, which are not regulated by the normal consciousness of temporality. This critical perspective, then, challenges us not only to revise our understanding of truthfulness, but to enlarge our model of how autobiography as narrative reflects basic patterns of human experience. There may be several distinct 'narrative qualities of experience' that shape an autobiographer's self-characterization.

II THE INSEPARABILITY OF CHARACTER AND CHARACTERIZATION

The approaches of the theologians and the literary critics focus respectively on character and characterization. Yet within autobiography there is clearly a relationship between character and characterization. Not all autobiographies are explicitly self-conscious about this relationship, but they all demonstrate it, and the most articulate ones often postulate it. Autobiography involves both the conscious artistry and fictional techniques of characterization and also the endeavor to know, depict, and judge truthfully the self's moral character. The most perceptive and convincing writers know and show that character assessment and characterization are neither synonomous nor unconnected nor antithetical, but distinct and yet mutually dependent elements in autobiography. The assessment of character in autobiography necessarily involves various techniques of characterization. And the series of characterizations in any autobiography is organized as a hermeneutic of character, a testing of various metaphors for the self against the author's memories and conscience.

To hold that in autobiography character is inseparable from characterization is to say first that insofar as a person's character is accessible to scrutiny it must be given verbal expression as a characterization of the self at a particular time. Every individual has a character: a combination of personality traits, continuities of thought, and habits of feeling and behavior that distinguish him or her from every other individual. One knows this character through conscious efforts to articulate its identity. My projection of myself in a story necessarily involves fictional elements, because my actual memories of the past are too meager to do it justice, and because imagination and desire shape the project of characterizing the self in autobiography. Characterization is necessary to portray character, but is never identical with it; it is a person's own interpretation of his or her self, as selective, fallible, and debatable as any other view.

To hold that characterization is inseparable from character is to say that as we read an autobiography we never doubt that the characterizing is always *of someone*, a person searching for (or in modern works sometimes denying) consistency, integrity, or purpose in a life. The way a writer characterizes herself inevitably reveals a great deal about her character. The various characterizations of an autobiographer, even if they are inconsistent or admittedly fictive, depend on certain recurrent metaphors or themes and express persistent concerns and desires. Whether or not the author convincingly interprets her past, characterization displays the writer's character at the moment of writing. Characterization reveals character, although what is revealed may or may not correlate with the author's own understanding of his character, either in the past or the present. From this perspective, too, characterization and character are perhaps never synonomous, but they are closely related. Characterization of a past self is probably never exactly accurate about the actual character of that self, because the imaginative element in autobiographical creation and the present perspective of the writer produce unintentional distortion, misplaced emphasis, rationalization, and self-deception. Yet character – the moral condition of the writer both in the past and at the moment of writing – sets limits to the imaginative and creative license of characterization. For conscience is exercised in the writing of autobiography, and a person's memories of past experience orient the process of characterization.

Understanding autobiography in terms of a relationship between character and characterization suggests a different perspective on four questions raised by the theories of narrative discussed in the first section of this chapter. Two issues are most pertinent to the theologians, and two others to literary critics.

(1) To attend more closely to the various techniques of characterization would enrich what the theologians have seen as the significance of autobiography. When scholars of religion conceive of this significance in terms of 'the narrative quality of experience', this is loosely construed to mean a distinctive sense of temporality. As the lens through which autobiography is viewed, this preoccupation leads to a focus on the plot of autobiography, usually understood as the chronological development of the author. Despite the ethical and religious significance of the concept of character, characterization is given little attention and reduced to a function of the plot.[14] In effect, the concept of narrative is reduced to chronology, while what Paul Ricœur calls its 'configurational dimension' is ignored. I think that in autobiography it is the attempt to define character

that organizes the work's configurational dimension, 'according to which the plot contrives significant wholes out of scattered events . . . . eliciting a pattern from a succession'.[15] We need to recognize that many aspects of characterization will be ignored or seem only digressions or distractions from the work's plot, if this is conceived of too narrowly as merely a succession of events. My point is not that character is more important than plot, for, as Frank Kermode suggests, plot and character are inseparable and mutually dependent.[16]

There are many ways in which character can be articulated in autobiography besides the chronological narration of one's history. Significant feelings can be evoked: for example, Dorothy Day's 'long loneliness', C. S. Lewis's 'joy', and Jung's feeling of excitement and dread whenever he sensed the eruption of images from the unconscious. Natural settings and buildings that shaped character may be described: Day's Staten Island beach home, Lewis's Irish and English landscapes, or Jung's tower at Bollingen. Character is revealed in the unique tone of voice of the autobiographer: bitter, wry, self-deprecating, evasive, loftily dignified, or defensive. Systematic beliefs and convictions given extensive development in autobiography are most significant because of their role in forming character. Desires, dreams, fantasies, influential books, and conscious and unconscious identifications with real or fictitious persons are included not simply because they happened at a certain time, but to interpret character. Our understanding of autobiography increases when we see the purpose of all these elements not simply in terms of their place in a chronological succession, but as 'metaphors of self' expressive of character.

In the project of self-characterization, the autobiographer articulates several 'narrative qualities of experience'. Some scholars believe that personal identity is based on a sense of temporality and some think the self's identity is founded on metaphor. But why should we have to choose between a principle of chronology or temporality and a principle of association? It is hard to imagine either a self or a narrative that is not structured by both of these organizing principles of the human mind. Our understanding of autobiography needs to focus on how both of these elements – temporality and metaphor – help constitute the experience that gives identity to and makes mutually dependent the self and its narratives. Furthermore, we need to see the connections between metaphor and temporality. Since a determinative metaphor of self persists and recurs, narrative is required to show its role in the self's temporal experience. And all experience of temporality is profoundly shaped by metaphors. I experience a period of time *as* a suspenseful episode, an anti-climax, a boring interlude, a tragic crisis, etc. Many of the metaphors used to describe the sense of time are, of course, drawn from narratives.

(2) The dynamic between character and characterization also complicates a second issue for the theologians, that of truthfulness. The tasks of self-knowledge and self-evaluation are difficult not only because of the danger of self-deception, but because the perceptive autobiographer realizes the crucial role of metaphorical 'figures' in characterization. A person interprets himself, in the past and in the present, with the use of a figure which is often both a commanding personal presence or role model and a literary type or trope. Identification with, admiration for, and emulation of other persons are basic sources of personal identity, shaping the way an individual perceives and articulates experience. But with awareness of how a figure serves as a metaphor for the self comes uncertainty and ambivalence about the extent of the analogy. Augustine sees similarities between himself and the Egyptian monk Antony; Abelard compares his character to Origen and Jerome; and Dorothy Day admires and imitates St. Teresa, William James, and Peter Maurin. Yet each of these writers also discloses essential differences between the self and its role models. The analysis of points of similarity and difference between the author and his model is a shaping principle of autobiography. The self-critical autobiographer knows how crucial other persons have been as metaphors of self, and how these figures have shaped his language about his identity, but he also sees that metaphors express not identity but analogy. The degree of resemblance and the exact nature of the analogy to a model may be uncertain, or change during the course of years, or be a source of ambivalence because of undesirable elements in the model's character. Thus the autobiographer may be led to reflect on problems of truthfulness that arise when self-characterization necessarily relies on metaphors which are only partially adequate to explain character. *The Autobiography of Malcolm X* will be discussed below in this light.

(3) As we have seen, much recent literary criticism explores the inventiveness and fictionality of autobiographical characterizations, and shows little interest in whether such constructions correspond to the author's character. This perspective offers a

valuable corrective to simplistic ideas about how autobiography assesses character. At the same time, however, most of this criticism fails to recognize two ways in which character is a necessary condition of both autobiography and interpretations of autobiography. First, when the radical critics ignore or deny the differences between autobiography and fiction, they blur a generic distinction necessary to the existence of both autobiography and their own critical practice. Autobiography is always recognized and defined in terms of a concept of the author's role and purpose in writing this kind of text. There is no single textual feature which can always be correlated with autobiography.[17] A critic depends on assumptions about intentionality, or authorial sincerity, or truthfulness, or some other component of the autobiographical act; this distinctive function or purpose makes a text count as autobiography. These definitive attributes of autobiography are not formal qualities of texts, but human acts with epistemological and moral dimensions. Conceptions of autobiography are thus linked to ideas about the self's agency, and very often to an unexamined theory of character. Literary critics continue covertly to depend on concepts of the self and of character even though they reject them theoretically in the name of the autonomy of 'writing' and 'textuality'.

Furthermore, this critical perspective ignores the concern with the moral evaluation of character that is essential in both autobiography and their own practice as critics and interpreters. The assessment as well as the recognition of autobiography depends on a concept of character. The critics' blurring of the genres of fiction and autobiography leads to misconceiving the specific nature of readers' experience. This experience involves the interpretation and evaluation of moral character. Readers evaluate autobiographies as verbal performances expressing self-knowledge and self-judgment. Autobiographies often call explicitly for such evaluation and inevitably elicit it on the part of readers, even those critics most determined not to be didactic or moralistically judgmental. Questions about the relative merits of autobiographies involve not only aesthetic considerations but also issues of truthfulness and self-deception, authenticity and bad faith, or insight vs. hypocrisy (for the critical language varies) in understanding and representing the self. Both in their judgments about what makes a literary work an autobiography and in their assessments of when a 'text' displays their desired ideal of self-knowledge or insight, even the most radical literary critics presuppose the existence of the self they wish to deconstruct. In short, the concept of character is a necessary condition of the autobiographer's characterizations and of the critic's analyses and evaluations of autobiography.

(4) The final point following from my argument about the inseparability of character and characterization concerns self-conscious acknowledgements of fictionality within an autobiography. Such self-reflexive statements appear in quite a different light when seen in terms of an interaction between character assessment and characterization, rather than in terms of either one of these concerns in isolation. Instead of being proof that the autobiographer is consciously writing fiction and is not concerned with a truthful portrayal of his character, such passages can be taken as warnings about his uncertainties in self-representation. The writer's conscience is alert to elements of ambiguity and potential self-deception that may remain in even the most sincere and truthful person. As we saw in the case of McCarthy's *Memories of a Catholic Girlhood*, explicit recognition of the fictional elements in autobiography reflects consciousness of real and serious epistemological and moral problems in self-knowledge. A mimetic concern to portray character accurately may lead a writer to acknowledge her necessary reliance upon literary techniques and tropes, imaginative revisioning of the past, and construal of past actions and motives in terms of the conventions and formulas of historical and fictional writing. Here, too, character assessment and characterization are not two alternative conceptions of the autobiographer's activity, but inseparable in practice.

While there is no assessment of character without imaginative characterization, in reading autobiography we never lose our sense that the techniques of characterization are always devised by and focused on a certain character. Characterization is motivated by and oriented towards the overall project of discovering, articulating, and judging character.

III   THEORETICAL INSIGHTS FROM NARRATIVE TEXTS

The relationships between character and characterization are illuminated by two further sources of narrative theory: autobiographers themselves and the genre of fictional autobiography.

Certain autobiographers – such as Augustine, Montaigne, and

Rousseau – constantly interpret their activities of character assessment and characterization as they engage in them. 'Autobiography is a self-reflexive, a self-critical act, and consequently the criticism of autobiography exists within the literature instead of alongside it.'[18] Recent critics imply that they have discovered issues that in fact have been central to autobiography for centuries. For example, Augustine dramatized problems of the self's unity and limited knowledge of itself and he focused attention on the power of language long before the modern theories which have made so much of these issues. Self-knowledge is always uncertain for Augustine, for finally only God truly knows the self. The famous analysis of time in the *Confessions* expresses Augustine's sense of being divided and dispersed in time (Bk. XI, ch. 28–29). Augustine calls attention to the constant danger of self-deception, for instance in his analysis of his uncertainty as to why he is gratified by praise of his character (Bk. X, ch. 37). Few writers have been as sensitive as was this professional rhetorician to the role of language in the communication and distortion of meaning.

The great autobiographers' self-critical reflections and actual practice can help us evaluate the adequacy of different narrative theories, and can suggest new insights. *The Autobiography of Malcolm X* demonstrates some of the relationships between character and characterization. Malcolm X saw his autobiography as a series of characterizations of his past roles. Each of the many names and nicknames he assumed corresponds to a distinct interpretation of his character at a stage of his life: Malcolm Little, 'Homeboy', 'Detroit Red', 'Satan', Malcolm X, and El-Hajj Malik El-Shabazz. Malcolm X often reflects on the foreignness to his present self of these earlier versions of his identity, for they seem not to have reflected his enduring character at all: 'I still marvel at how swiftly my previous life's thinking pattern slid away from me, like snow off a roof. It is as though someone else I knew of had lived by hustling and crime. I would be startled to catch myself thinking in a remote way of my earlier self as another person' (170).[19] Characterization of several distinct past selves is necessary in this autobiography because of the basic transformations in the author's character. The changes Malcolm X went through even while working on his autobiography challenge the traditional view of a stationary self surveying its past from a consistent perspective. This is why Malcolm X asks Alex Haley: 'How is it possible to write one's autobiography in a world so fast-changing as this?' (408).

For Malcolm X, telling the truth means exposing lies, showing the false ways each race characterizes members of another race:

> I'm telling it like it *is*! You *never* have to worry about me biting my tongue if something I know as truth is on my mind. Raw, naked truth exchanged between the black man and the white man is what a whole lot more of is needed in this country – to clear the air of the racial mirages, cliches, and lies that this country's very atmosphere has been filled with for four hundred years. (273)

Malcolm analyzes masks, public roles, stereotypes, and false identities because he thinks that these are the actual conditions of life in America. 'My own life *mirrors* this hypocrisy' (271).

A racist society forces a black person to characterize himself falsely and to wear a mask in order to survive. Yet the discrepancy between character and characterization is also rooted in a person's need to perform a public role. Even as a minister of the Nation of Islam, Malcolm X found his essential character confined and frustrated. Alex Haley's epilogue dramatizes the growing inner conflict between two sides of Malcolm and reveals how the private, subversive self, scribbling absent-mindedly on napkins, was slowly drawn out. Part of the difficulty of writing the autobiography lay in not 'telegraphing' to readers future changes in Malcolm X's values and beliefs, such as the radical transformations which occurred after his trip to Mecca. 'Telephoning Malcolm X, I reminded him of his previous decision, and I stressed that if those chapters contained such telegraphing to readers of what would lie ahead, then the book would automatically be robbed of some of its building suspense and drama' (414). Even in the last weeks of his life Malcolm X was conscious of role-playing, discussing his public persona in the media as a 'demagogue' (381) and 'the angriest Negro in America' (366), and predicting his next role as a martyr 'in the cause of brotherhood' (429). He reflected constantly on strategies of self-characterization using the popular media, and felt frustrated by the way the media's portrayal of him prevented him from expressing changes in his character: 'My earlier public image, my old so-called "Black Muslim" image, kept blocking me. I was trying to gradually reshape that image. I was trying to turn a corner, into a new regard by the public, especially Negroes' (374). To a degree, then, the 'real' Malcolm X transcends all his roles, describing them as masks and sloughing them off as a snake sheds its skin.

Although his character transcends each role he has played, it is shaped by them. Past versions of the self persist into the present. 'People are always speculating – why am I as I am? To understand that of any person, his whole life, from birth, must be reviewed. All of our experiences fuse into our personality. Everything that ever happened to us is an ingredient' (150). The experience of being a hustler, for example, is not just a discarded metaphor for Malcolm. This past identity serves to help Malcolm interpret his situation when he is silenced by the Black Muslims: 'I hadn't hustled in the streets for years for nothing. I knew when I was being set up' (302). Having been a ghetto hustler provides Malcolm with stratagems for countering the 'tricks' of the media. Whenever he is deeply threatened, Malcolm falls back on this old metaphor for his self.

It is interesting to compare theologians' and literary critics' differing interpretations of Malcolm's self-characterization. For Stroup the book shows Malcolm X's successful quest for a coherent personal identity. For Paul John Eakin, in contrast, Malcolm X's dramatized succession of provisional identities serves to 'defend himself against the fiction of the completed self that his interpreters – both black and white, in the event – were to use against him'.[20] While the theologians are most interested in continuity of character, and in the achievement of wholeness and order, literary critics usually focus on the dramatization of change, and on the fragmentation, alienation, and disorder of the self. Malcolm's autobiography can illustrate either character assessment or characterization. What is needed is an interpretation that shows the connections between these concerns.

This large topic will be broached here only in terms of how Malcolm deals with the problem of truthfulness that arises in characterizing oneself with metaphors. Two passages in which Malcolm X compares himself to the apostle Paul and to Icarus show his uncertainty and ambivalence about the analogies between his own character and these two figures. The striking thing about these two passages is that in both cases Malcolm X first suggests, then denies, his similarity to a figure whose experience in significant ways resembles his own.

I remember how, some time later, reading the Bible in the Norfolk Prison Colony library, I came upon, then I read, over and over, how Paul on the road to Damascus, upon hearing the voice of

Christ, was so smitten that he was knocked off his horse, in a daze. I do not now, and I did not then, liken myself to Paul. But I do understand his experience . . . . The truth can be quickly received, or received at all, only by the sinner who knows and admits that he is guilty of having sinned much. (163)

In the very chapter recounting his sudden conversion to the Nation of Islam, and examining how his past 'guilty' behavior reflected the self-hatred of the 'Negro', Malcolm X says that he does 'not liken' himself to Paul. He merely 'understands his experience'. As a Black Muslim minister he cannot wholly identify himself with the Christian apostle, and yet in this passage Malcolm X clearly calls attention to similarities between his own conversion and Paul's.

Similarly, Malcolm X holds that 'not for one second' has he forgotten his determination not to succumb to Icarus's sin of pride:

Icarus' father made some wings that he fastened with wax. 'Never fly but so high with these wings,' the father said. But soaring around, this way, that way, Icarus' flying pleased him so that he began thinking he was flying on his own merit. Higher, he flew – higher – until the heat of the sun melted the wax holding those wings. And down came Icarus – tumbling. Standing there by that Harvard window, I silently vowed to Allah that I never would forget that any wings I wore had been put on by the religion of Islam. That fact I never have forgotten . . . not for one second. (287)

Could Malcolm have helped wondering whether there might not be some parallels between himself and Icarus, as the Black Muslim leadership and Elijah Muhammad would certainly have held? Alex Haley must have sensed the centrality of this mythological figure in Malcolm X's imaginative life, since he chose 'Icarus' as the title of the last chapter before Malcolm X recounts how he broke with his spiritual 'father' Elijah Muhammad and left the Nation of Islam.

Paul and Icarus are explicitly rejected as metaphors for Malcolm X's basic character at the same time that these figures are invoked to interpret his experience to himself and the reader. Malcolm X seems to be struggling with a problem of truthfulness in using Paul and Icarus as metaphors, for these figures both do and do not reveal his sense of his own essential character. These passages show how the ideal of truthfulness involves a person in ambiguities and uncertainties inherent in the fact that the metaphors necessary for self-understanding are never fully adequate to characterize the uniqueness of experience. Telling the truth about character thus means that an autobiographer may need to reveal his ambivalence about being identified with the typological figures that have captured his imagination.

Another source of insight into character and characterization is the genre of fictional autobiography, for instance Robertson Davies' Deptford Trilogy. In *Fifth Business*, *The Manticore*, and *World of Wonders*, each narrator's memories of his past are contrasted with interpretations of the narrator by others.[21] *Fifth Business* is Dunstan Ramsey's correction of the false impression he feels was created by a story about him in the college paper. In *The Manticore*, which records a Jungian analysis, David Staunton's psychotherapist constantly questions or disputes David's version of his past character and history. And in *World of Wonders*, Magnus Eisengrim's life story is often interrupted and challenged by his audience, including Dunstan Ramsey, who records it. Each autobiographer appears as a 'supporting character' in the other novels, so that we compare his own view of his character with how others see him. Reading this trilogy requires the reader continually to reflect on the validity of the often conflicting interpretations of a particular character by himself and by others. One is also drawn to compare autobiography with many other storytelling forms figuring in the novels. Dunstan Ramsey is at once a professional hagiographer, the autobiographical narrator of *Fifth Business*, the ghost writer of Magnus's 'autobiography', *Phantasmata*, and, in *World of Wonders*, the historian and biographer of Magnus Eisengrim, commenting upon and interpreting Magnus's oral narration of his life story. *World of Wonders* is said to be the 'subtext' of a film in which Eisengrim plays the role of a famous nineteenth century magician. The chief character in *The Manticore* is a lawyer who interprets most events in terms of the narrative structure of a legal brief. All three novels are full of metaphors and imagery from the theatre, revolving particularly around the ideas of role-playing and the truth expressed in illusory appearances. The different ways in which these artistic forms 'tell the truth' about human character are a topic of constant argument.

This complex and intriguing trilogy suggests insights into our central theme of character, and shows how fictional autobiographies constitute a distinctive source for both narrative theory and religious studies. Davies is keenly interested in the ways that a public role, usually related to one's occupation, shapes identity. A person may come to believe that this role encompasses all of his or her character. The person who can grow and develop is the one who realizes that a self-characterization according to occupation is too limited. In the Jungian terms of Dr. von Haller, one must recognize that the persona is a mask:

> We all create an outward self with which to face the world, and some people come to believe that is what they truly are. So they people the world with doctors who are nothing outside the consulting-room, and judges who are nothing when they are not in court, and businessmen who wither with boredom when they have to retire from business, and teachers who are forever teaching. That is why they are such poor specimens when they are caught without their masks on. They have lived chiefly through the Persona.[22]

While a vocational mask expresses a necessary and significant aspect of one's character, the person who is no more than a public role, and who cannot step back and view himself as playing a part in a performance, lacks depth, complexity of character, and a critical perspective on his engagements.

Davies's novels offer a number of fascinating instances of the phenomenon of self-deception in relation to memories of one's past. For example, Boy Staunton forgets for decades about having thrown a snowball with a rock in it which caused the premature birth of Paul Dempster. Ramsey can hardly believe that Boy could forget this, 'but as we talked on I had to accept it as a fact that he had so far edited his memory of his early days that the incident of the snowball had quite vanished from his mind'. This forgetfulness is not merely a failure of memory, but an act – an 'editing' – that says much about Boy's character. Boy himself admits that 'I don't remember what is of no use to me'. Paul Dempster sees a general truth about memory in relation to character in this incident: 'We all forget many of the things we do, especially when they do not fit into the character we have chosen for ourselves.'[23]

It is surprising that in theories of character truthful assessment of other persons receives so little attention. Davies shows that the question of truthfulness in autobiography includes how one characterizes others as well as oneself. David Staunton's psychoanalysis,

his 'battle against the trolls', is a struggle to see the 'cast of characters' in his life, especially his father, for what they really are. The
theory of projection and the Jungian notion of archetypes provide
one explanation of why truthful characterization of others may be
difficult: 'The battle with trolls that Ibsen wrote about is a good
metaphor to describe the wrestling and wrangling we go through
when the archetypes we carry in ourselves seem to be embodied in
people we have to deal with in daily life . . . . Our great task is to see
people as people and not as clouded by archetypes we carry about
with us, looking for a peg to hang them on.'[24] Whether or not one
finds Jungian theory a satisfactory interpretation of this struggle, the
Deptford Trilogy suggests that accurate characterization of others is
a crucial part of truthfulness. Conscience and moral imagination are
called into play as a person interprets not only himself, but those
whom he has mocked, or thrown a stone at, or revered.

One of Davies's chief themes is the need to come to terms with
evil in one's past and in one's present character, especially to
avoid self-deception about one's responsibility for evil. In addition,
Magnus Eisengrim's early self-image as 'a bottle in the smoke' and
his later posture as a master of diabolic knowledge raise the question
of whether a person might also deceive himself by underestimating
the good aspects of his character:

> 'What I can't decide,' said Ingestree, 'is how much of what we
> have heard we are to take as fact. It's the inescapable problem
> of the autobiography: how much is left out, how much has been
> genuinely forgotten, how much has been touched up to throw the
> subject into striking relief: That stuff about Revenge, for instance.
> Can he have been as horrible as he makes out? He doesn't seem
> a cruel man now. We must never forget that he's a conjuror by
> profession; his lifelong pose has been demonic. I think he'd like
> us to believe he played the demon in reality as well.'[25]

An individual may be unable to admit to himself that his life is not
wholly given over to evil. Self-deception takes this form as well as
the more familiar one of denying evil.

All of Davies's autobiographers are said to be egoists, and the
trilogy investigates the ways that egoism influences all narratives in
the form of a point of view. An autobiographer cannot help putting
himself at the center of events. What might the life of Christ look like
as told by the apostle Lebbaeus? Referring to this apostle, Liesl asks

Ramsey, 'If he had written an autobiography do you suppose that
Christ would have had the central position?' Ramsey's knowledge
of Lebbaeus's 'Acts of Thaddaeus' confirms Liesl's hunch:

> 'There is a non-canonical Acts of Thaddaeus – Thaddaeus
> was his surname, you recall – that tells all about him. It didn't
> get into the Bible, but it exists.'
> 'What's it like?'
> 'A great tale of marvels. Real Arabian Nights stuff. Puts him
> dead at the centre of affairs.'
> 'Didn't I say so! Just like a man. I'll bet he wrote it him-
> self.'[26]

The many allusions to religious and literary narratives demonstrate the ways mythic plot formulas and character types structure
every autobiography. Liesl asserts that 'everybody's life is his
Passion, you know, and you can't have much of a Passion if
you haven't got a good strong Judas.'[27] For Davies, the meaning
of one's life cannot be comprehended apart from the question of
which mythic characters a person identifies with. This is hard for
the modern individual to do, for he or she wants so much to be
unique. But for Davies the deepest levels of the self are common
to many persons. His characters must learn to identify themselves
and others with mythic heroes and heroines; ritualized roles (Fifth
Business, the Rich Young Ruler, Trusted Friend); and with literary
figures (in *The Manticore*, Hamlet, Absalom, Candide, Dr. Jekyll
and Mr. Hyde) which 'provide us with an excellent shorthand for
talking about aspects of ourselves'.[28] The necessity of defining the
self with reference to these figures shows another way in which the
delineation of character, whether one's own or another person's,
depends upon a highly stylized process of characterization. Davies's
Deptford Trilogy and other fictional autobiographies, then, are a
distinctive source of insights into the truth-telling and truth-creating
possibilities of narrative.

IV   CONCLUSION

The relationship between character and characterization reflects
the sponsoring and monitoring functions of conscience in autobiographical writing, which I discussed in the previous chapter.

Conscience is both one of the motivating sources of a person's need to articulate and assess his own character, and a primary reason why an autobiographer may reflect on the nature of his activity of characterization.

The dynamic of character and characterization lies at the source of the greatest autobiographies' power. If an autobiographer is not concerned with character assessment we sense a form of triviality and an evasion of a central and crucial aspect of self-knowledge. But the autobiographer who cannot see his self-portrayal as partly a matter of characterization – as involving selective perception, imaginative projection, and imitative patterning according to literary types and figures – seems to lack insight into his own activity as a knower and writer of the self. He seems too confident in his own sincerity, he is naive about the ambiguities of language, and he lacks self-critical skepticism about his own best intentions. Either we don't fully trust him, or we condescend as we read; we think we can 'read him like a book' rather than wondering with him about the mystery of character. To be fully convincing, narratives of the self need to demonstrate both a concern for character and a self-reflexive understanding of the activity of characterization. This combination of interests creates an intriguing tension between the moral demands for consistency and stability and integrity of character, on the one hand, and the constant awareness of psychological complexity, internal conflict, and ambiguity in self-knowledge.

The classic religious autobiography – the one which continues to fascinate a variety of readers speaks both to those whose faith and hope lies in stability of character and to those whose optimism depends on the possibility of basic transformations of character. Such an autobiography appeals strongly to the Western religious consciousness – to our deep desire for an integrated self, based on the ideal of the unified individual and the Jewish and Christian idea of the soul. Such a work addresses, as well, our modern anxieties about the self, and our awareness of the realities of character change, roleplaying, and self-deception. An Augustine or a Malcolm X articulates our desire for a character and a conscience with moral integrity, even as he investigates the difficulty and the possible distortion or dishonesty in every attempt at self-characterization.

4

Conscience in the Essays of Montaigne and Johnson

The classic practitioners of the essay as an exercise of conscience are Montaigne and Samuel Johnson. Johnson and Montaigne differ in their substantive concerns, their ways of proceeding in ethical reflection, and their understandings of the essay form. Montaigne's essays were published together in 'Books' in several editions; Johnson's *Rambler*, *Adventurer*, and *Idler* essays, shorter and more clearly focused on one topic than Montaigne's, were published individually as periodical essays or as regularly appearing sections of a newspaper. The essay developed considerably between the 1580s and the 1750s, and the writing of essays played different roles in the personal and professional lives of Montaigne and Johnson. Although they are rather different in many ways, however, the essays of Montaigne and Johnson also share certain crucial ethical concerns, and they are generally recognized as classic examples of the moral essay. In whatever way the outer boundaries of this genre are defined, their writings are central paradigms which give the moral essay its identity and significance both as a literary form and as a mode of ethical reflection. Indeed, their work shapes our very conception of the nature of the essay. Why this is so deserves interpretation.

There are, of course, many essayists who have little or no interest in ethical matters, but focus rather on aesthetic, scientific, or political concerns. 'The essay can be short or long, serious or trifling, about God and Spinoza, or about turtles and Cheapside.'[1] And Johnson's and Montaigne's essays vary considerably in their attention to ethical matters. Nonetheless, at several points this chapter will generalize about the moral essay, based on the example of this genre's two foremost practitioners. This is not to say that every later essayist – including recent writers such as Joan

Didion, Wendell Berry, Susan Sontag, and Mary McCarthy – simply imitates Montaigne and Johnson. In particular, recent essayists are often more directly autobiographical – more 'confessional' – and less explicitly concerned to generalize about the human condition than the pattern traced in this chapter. The practice of Montaigne and Johnson, however, represents a paradigm or model by which to measure later developments, just as Augustine's *Confessions* is both a dominant influence on the evolving tradition of conversion narratives and a useful reference point for interpreting change.

The conscience of an autobiographer may be as vitally and significantly expressed in the form of a moral essay as it is in a confession, and my focus in this chapter will be on the distinctive role conscience plays in the essay. I explore the central moral concerns and the characteristic patterns of reflection found in Montaigne's and Johnson's works. I seek to explain why the essay form is peculiarly appropriate to express the authors' ethical and religious interests, and the distinctive achievements which are possible in this kind of discourse. The moral essay is most distinctive not because it formulates a theory of conscience, but because it demonstrates conscience in action. The essay is an 'exercise' of conscience: exercise in the sense of practicing a skill or bringing into action a capacity or power in order to demonstrate, further develop, or improve it.

I CONSCIENCE AS THE SUBJECT MATTER OF THE ESSAY

Conscience figures as the explicit subject matter of many of Montaigne's and Johnson's essays. Conscience is an increasingly frequent topic in Montaigne's *Essays*, as a concordance to his work indicates.[2] It provides the title for two essays in Book II (5 and 19) and is a central topic in many essays. Montaigne's discussions reflect longstanding debates about whether conscience is rational or irrational, a natural and inborn or a culturally acquired capacity, universal in form or variable according to the individual. Montaigne often seems to endorse the Stoic and Christian view of conscience as *a priori* knowledge implanted in essential human nature, yet he also recognizes the relativity of the verdicts of conscience to the contingencies of personal and cultural background.[3]

Montaigne's most important discussions of conscience are the first two essays in Book III. 'Of the Useful and the Honorable' explores conflicts between expediency and morality, or what is now sometimes called the dilemma of dirty hands. This subject deeply concerned Montaigne as a political leader during the terrible religious strife of the late sixteenth century. Montaigne sees the need for political leaders sometimes to sacrifice 'their honor and conscience' for the good of all, yet thinks he could not bring himself to do this:

> Let this part be played by the more vigorous and less fearful citizens, who sacrifice their honor and their conscience, as those ancients sacrificed their life, for the good of their country. We who are weaker, let us take parts that are both easier and less hazardous. The public welfare requires that a man betray and lie and massacre; let us resign this commission to more obedient and suppler people. (600)[4]

Montaigne concludes that one should not 'prostitute one's conscience' (606) even for a great public good, and that 'not all things are permissable for an honorable man in the service of the king, or of the common cause, or of the laws' (609).

In 'Of Repentance' Montaigne appears to reject repentance, and characterizes his conscience as usually serene: 'Let me here excuse what I often say, that I rarely repent and that my conscience is content with itself – not as the conscience of an angel or a horse, but as the conscience of a man' (612). He asserts that a good conscience is a vital source of satisfaction and joy: 'Indeed there is a sort of gratification in doing good which makes us rejoice in ourselves, and a generous pride that accompanies a good conscience . . . . These testimonies of conscience give us pleasure; and this natural rejoicing is a great boon to us, and the only payment that never fails us' (612). Although this apparent rejection of repentance contrasts with many Christian views, including Samuel Johnson's, Montaigne's is not a smug or complacent position that would insulate him from the pains of a guilty conscience. Throughout the *Essays* Montaigne does not shrink from finding errors in all aspects of his being, including the most valued ones. The theme of 'On Repentance' is not that all repentance is wrong, but rather that much professed repentance is mere show or self-deception. When sins are repeated and become part of a person's character, 'I cannot imagine that they can be implanted so long in one and the same heart, without the reason and conscience of their possessor constantly willing and intending it to be so. And the repentance which he claims comes to him at a certain prescribed moment is a little hard for me to imagine and conceive' (617). Since true repentance leads to reform, most assertions of repentance are hypocritical: 'I know of no quality so easy to counterfeit as piety, if conduct and life are not made to conform with it' (617). Montaigne is equally opposed to those forms of self-reproach which are based on contempt for the bodily needs of human creatures. The real burden of this essay, then, is to distinguish a truly repentant conscience from the forms of morbidity, self-pity, and hypocrisy which masquerade as Christian piety. Montaigne rejects these corruptions of conscience, but he does not spare himself constant and vigilant self-examination, and he remains subject to the pains of conscience as well as its approval.

'Of the Useful and the Honorable' and 'Of Repentance' express what is probably the chief theme of Montaigne's and Johnson's explicit references to conscience: the assertion that self-esteem should be based on conscience rather than on the approval of others. 'To found the reward for virtuous action on the approval of others is to choose too uncertain and shaky a foundation' (612). The desire for a good conscience should outweigh not only temptations to do wrong, but competing goods such as glory: 'The shortest way to attain glory would be to do for conscience what we do for glory' (614). Johnson, too, often speaks of a peaceful conscience as its own reward. In many instances he explores how a person feeling the reproach of conscience wrongly turns to some external judgment or standard for solace or assurance.

These essayists' discussions of conscience are inextricably linked to reflections on virtue. Both men share the faith that satisfaction of one's own conscience is the virtuous person's only certain reward. For Johnson conscience is 'the sentinel of virtue' (348).[5] The two authors are at one in their assertions of the centrality of conscience in the virtuous life. This is so for Montaigne because all external moral rules and theories are relative and uncertain, and for Johnson because conscience is the basis of the Christian virtues of self-examination and repentance. In contrast to Montaigne, Johnson encouraged regretful meditation on past failings, provided that this would make future conduct more virtuous: 'Regret is indeed useful and virtuous, and not only allowable but necessary, when it tends to the amendment of life, or to admonition of error which we may be again in danger of committing' (344). At the same time, he is as aware as is Montaigne of the folly of dwelling on a vanished past if this produces no beneficial effect on character: 'A very small part of the moments spent in meditation on the past, produce any reasonable caution or salutary sorrow' (344). Periodical remorse is of value only if it helps a person to guard against complacency and vanity and leads to renewed efforts to correct a vice. As we will see in the last section of this chapter, many of these authors' most acute insights into conscience arise in the course of reflection on the virtues and vices.

Issues of conscience are central in these essayists' many treatments of truth-telling to others and truthfulness with oneself, and the correlative vices, lying and self-deception. Not only his essays on lying (I, 9 and II, 18) but all of Montaigne's work is concerned with questions of conscience arising in speech and writing. Johnson is equally attentive to the ways that communication between persons raises moral issues, as well as to all that is at stake in a person's capacity to admit to himself his own errors. A recurring topic in Johnson's essays is the question of how much truth-telling is permitted between friends, given our conscious wish to please and our unconscious tendency to choose friends with similar values.

In regard to truthfulness, one of Johnson's most surprising and uncharacteristic statements about conscience deserves comment. In Idler 84, a discussion of biography, Johnson reflects on 'those relations . . . in which the writer tells his own story' (347). Johnson asserts that we can confidently expect truth from such a work: 'That which is fully known cannot be falsified but with reluctance of understanding, and alarm of conscience; of understanding, the lover of truth; of conscience, the sentinel of virtue' (348). Although Johnson admits that self-love provides a motive to falsify an autobiography, he is amazingly sanguine about the truthfulness of such accounts, even given the condition of non-publication: 'He that sits down calmly and voluntarily to review his life for the admonition of posterity, or to amuse himself, and leaves this account unpublished, may be commonly presumed to tell truth, since falsehood cannot appease his own mind, and fame will not be heard beneath the tomb' (349). This view of the conscience of an autobiographer contrasts markedly with Johnson's usual awareness of the ways conscience may be corrupted by forms of self-deception rooted in the natural human disinclination to recognize one's own errors and faults.

A number of contrasts can be drawn between Montaigne's and Johnson's ideas about conscience. Already I have contrasted Montaigne's reluctance to repent with Johnson's assertion that repentance and remorse may serve a useful function in the moral life. Johnson tends to stress more the rationality of conscience, and to describe its central role as that of ordering, regulating, or disciplining the passions and appetites: 'He, therefore, that would govern his actions by the laws of virtue, must regulate his thoughts by those of reason' (27). Montaigne sees the indispensable role of reason in the moral life, but he also characterizes it as a source of vanity and presumption. Although both authors were much influenced by Stoic thought, Johnson has a marked ascetic or puritan tendency, while Montaigne, especially in the later essays, reveals an epicurean or hedonistic aspect. Montaigne encourages expression of natural impulses, at least in moderation, rather than repression or rigid control. Johnson sees moral norms as fixed and permanent: 'Right and wrong are immutable; and those, therefore, who teach us to distinguish them, if they all teach us right, must agree with one another' (246). Montaigne has a greater awareness of, and emphasizes more, the variability and diversity of standards of conscience. Their ideas about conscience reflect Johnson's deep Christian faith and Montaigne's ambiguous fideism, topics which cannot be pursued here.[6]

These differences, and the two writers' contrasting positions on specific moral issues, should not obscure our recognition of many shared assumptions about conscience, assumptions reflecting both men's grounding in similar Christian and philosophical traditions of moral thought. References to conscience recur throughout the essays, and cluster around any topic that provokes moral reflection. To discuss only passages in which conscience is mentioned, however, is to miss the larger significance of Montaigne's and Johnson's work for our study of the conscience of the autobiographer. For many essays examine the workings of conscience without actually invoking that term. W. Jackson Bate, in a discussion of Johnson's conception of aesthetic experience, has noted 'how frequently Johnson prefers to use the word "mind" rather than terms that express separate faculties'.[7] The point is equally applicable to Johnson's view of ethical reflection, which encompasses all the powers and capabilities of the mind – including feeling, imagination, memory, and logic – rather than being the function of a single distinct part of human nature. Johnson's practice reflects a wisdom about conscience to which many contemporary theories of conscience aspire, as they criticize views describing conscience in terms of 'faculty psychology', thereby impoverishing its full scope and complexity. It is somewhat artificial to isolate Johnson's and Montaigne's explicit references to conscience, for their understandings of conscience are deeply connected with their ideas about many other aspects of human experience, and with specific ethical concerns.

Above all, we must discern both the common elements and the contrasts in the two men's *practice* of moral reflection in the essay. The deepest originality, interest, and value of the essays of Montaigne and Johnson is not their definitions or theories of conscience, but their dramatizations of conscience at work. I turn, therefore, to the task of interpreting the ways in which the exercise of conscience provides not only the subject matter but the structure and method of their essays.

II NARRATIVES AND GENERALIZATION

In the other chapters of this book, the conscience of the autobiographer is studied as it is articulated when a writer assesses his or her past and present condition. In this chapter, in contrast, I focus on ways in which conscience is expressed obliquely and indirectly in Montaigne's and Johnson's work, since the autobiographical dimension of their essays is often implicit rather than directly expressed. The form of Montaigne's and Johnson's moral essays reflects in several ways the exercise of conscience. For instance, the essayist's interpretation of narratives about other persons often engenders moral self-assessment. Furthermore, the author's conscience is sometimes at work in his attempts to generalize about the human moral condition. What are the connections between conscience, the interpretation of narratives, and moral generalization?

The moral essay is shaped by the writer's attempt to generalize about the human condition without falsifying or oversimplifying the particular experiences of individuals. The climax of the essay, both formally and in terms of its basic moral thesis, is the achievement of the first person plural. The author's right to say 'we' is not assumed but must be earned or proved in the course of the essay. Even when he begins an essay by making an assertion about the human condition, as Johnson so often does, the peculiar genius of the great essayist is his talent for integrating analysis of the idiosyncrasies of individual experience with generalizations about human nature. The interest of the essay does not lie in the isolated generalization, but in the author's ability to formulate the essential shape of the human condition without abstracting from or glossing over the particular contours of a unique individual's life. With all their interest in diversity, Johnson and Montaigne reflect on particular incidents or individual experiences in order to understand the human condition itself. Their practice of the essay shows that convincing generalization about such matters – the ability to say 'we' persuasively – depends upon examining narratives of individual experience. The way they demonstrate their assertions about the common nature of human beings cannot be replaced by an abstract discussion of universal truths.

Montaigne and Johnson earn their right to use the first person plural in different ways. Montaigne tends to move from 'I' to 'we', Johnson from 'he' to 'we'. For Montaigne the starting point of ethical reflection is himself. He is extremely skeptical of philosophical claims to know the whole of any reality, including the human condition. Especially in the first two Books of the *Essays*, Montaigne thoroughly undermines the epistemological presuppositions of his time, for he thinks they lead to wildly exaggerated claims of certainty.[8] He often seems reluctant or modest, therefore, about generalizing from his condition to that of others. Yet by the time he wrote his Third Book, Montaigne had become much more confident about his ability to discern the essential shape of the human condition in his own experience: 'You can tie up all moral philosophy with a common and private life just as well as with a life of richer stuff. Each man bears the entire form of man's estate' (611). By the end of his final essay, 'On Experience', he is quite willing to generalize about the common human lot – for instance, about human beings' surprising tendency to forget their physical nature, although even 'on the loftiest throne in the world we are still sitting on our own rump' (857). Montaigne focuses so intently on his own personal experience not because he is uninterested in explaining human nature, but because he is convinced that his own life is the only source of reliable knowledge. 'When reason fails us, we use experience' (815). By examining the idiosyncrasies of his own character, Montaigne made a self-portrait in which countless readers have recognized themselves; he achieved a kind of universality through his extreme particularism. His right to say 'we' seems earned; the reader feels that Montaigne's account of the human condition can be trusted partly because it is so concerned not to overlook or leave out all the oddities and particularities of

a very specific 'I'. Furthermore, Montaigne's generalizations are
formulated to capture the very inconsistencies and paradoxical
aspects of human experience: 'Truly man is a marvelously vain,
diverse, and undulating object' (5).

   Johnson, in contrast, is not as explicitly autobiographical a writer
as is Montaigne. He moves back and forth between claims about
'our' lot and some particular 'he' or 'she' whom Johnson has
read about or encountered. His shift from reflection on a specific
person's moral fallibility to recognition of this vice or weakness as
a common human problem creates a moral structure which gives
much of Johnson's work its distinctive quality. This moral structure
underlies the form, found in so much of Johnson's work, which W.
Jackson Bate calls 'satire manquée': 'a form in which protest and
satire, ridicule and even anger, are essential ingredients at the start
but then, caught up in a larger context of charity, begin to turn into
something else'.[9] One sees this pattern in *The Vanity of Human
Wishes*, *Rasselas*, and even the *Lives of the English Poets*, but it is
especially clear in his essays. Johnson trains his penetrating moral
judgment on the follies of some particular individual: the legacy
hunter who narrates *Rambler* 73, or the poet Cowley in *Rambler* 6,
or, in *Rambler* 146, the eager young author who expects the world
to acclaim his work. Yet what promises to be a devastating satiric
assault on an individual is diverted when Johnson reflects on the
widespread incidence of the fault or vice in question. Initial mock-
ery of the person softens as Johnson, with characteristic charity,
understanding, and conscientious self-examination, discerns one of
the permanent moral problems inherent in the human condition.
Johnson often concludes with a diagnosis of this problem which,
while not quite an apology for the particular individual, changes
the essay's thrust from barbed satire to meditation on the temptations and weaknesses inherent in the human condition. One of
the characteristic patterns of Johnson's moral thought, then, is his
generalizing about human experience after examining some other
person's actions. His moral assessment of this individual culminates
in a formulation of one of the general errors or mistakes to which
'we' are all liable.

   Three of the key elements in the essay are encompassed in my
argument that the essay attains its end when the author speaks
of 'our' condition: the use of narratives, the attempt to formulate
general principles of conscience, and autobiographical and introspective elements. Johnson's and Montaigne's essays are full of

quotations, anecdotes, stories, and references to the lives of historical and literary figures. Their essays are usually structured around an interpretation of these narratives, and thus resemble literary criticism as much as any other form of discourse. Because of the reliance on narratives, the essay is always a movement *towards* 'we'; its culminating generalization is not simply an abstract statement, but the conclusion of an interpretation of specific narratives. The essay offers an analysis of human moral experience which takes as its point of departure a particular story about some person's actions, but seeks to discern in that narrative a truth broadly applicable to other human lives. The essay's tendency to achieve profound moral and philosophical ends by means of commentary on aesthetic forms produces a characteristic irony about its modest pretensions. Georg Lukács has said that this irony consists in 'the critic always speaking about the ultimate problems of life, but in a tone which implies that he is only discussing pictures and books, only the inessential and pretty ornaments of real life – and even then not their innermost substance but only their beautiful and useless surface'.[10] This characteristic sense of irony about the essayist's modest attempt to simply note personal responses to a story or anecdote is a significant source of Montaigne's and Johnson's appeal.

Probably no form of moral discourse can entirely dispense with narratives describing specific human actions, but the essay is unusual and distinctive both in the centrality it gives to narratives and in the variety of functions which they serve in the total argument. A story may serve as the springboard to a generalization, a concrete example or illustration, a puzzling enigma which generates conflicting interpretations, or a striking situation which shows what practical difference a moral principle or trait really makes in experience. The essay in its most powerful and compelling form does not simply use narratives as a secondary and dispensable vehicle to illustrate general truth. But neither does the moral essay simply comment on a particular narrative and stop at the level of practical literary criticism of a text. The best essays involve a tension and an interplay between a particular situation and a general truth about human life. Such general truths are very often considerations that should guide conscience, insights or principles which should shape a thoughtful person's assessment of actions, motives, and desires.

Johnson's *Rambler* 6 provides a good example of the way the essayist moves from a general truth to a particular story and back again in order to illuminate and test the adequacy of each level of thought. This essay begins with a discussion of the adequacy of 'the Stoical philosophy' and of the extent to which 'we can exempt ourselves from outward influences' (16). Johnson finds 'change of place' to be the principal remedy of those who mistakenly believe that happiness depends only upon external conditions. After considering this issue in general terms, he states in the middle of the essay that 'these reflections arose in my mind upon the remembrance of a passage in Cowley's preface to his poems', a passage in which that poet contemplates retiring to an American plantation to escape the distractions and vexations tormenting him. Johnson sees in this chimerical notion an illustration of a general truth: 'Surely, no stronger instance can be given of a persuasion that content was the inhabitant of particular regions' (18). He then returns to Cowley's concrete situation, mingling general observations on human psychology with specific suggestions on how the harassed poet might better have ensured his privacy. *Rambler* 6 concludes with an annunciation of the general truth which Cowley did not comprehend:

> He never suspected that the cause of his unhappiness was within, that his own passions were not sufficiently regulated, and that he was harassed by his own impatience, which could never be without something to awaken it, would accompany him over the sea, and find its way to his American elysium. He would, upon the tryal, have been soon convinced, that the fountain of content must spring up in the mind; and that he, who has so little knowledge of human nature, as to seek happiness by changing any thing, but his own dispositions, will waste his life in fruitless efforts, and multiply the griefs which he proposed to remove. (20–21)

The idea for this essay was originally formed when Johnson read of Cowley's plan, and Johnson's recounting of the poet's scheme of happiness forms the central narrative in the essay. However, this story is not merely the point of departure for an assertion about a universal truth. It is the pivot of the entire essay, showing why the initial philosophical question posed by the Stoics has any practical significance, and providing a concrete situation against which any general conclusions must be tested. Like Dr. Johnson's stone ('I refute it *thus*'), the specific narrative is unmistakably concrete and real. It represents a practical situation which provides resistance to abstract thinking and must be explained if a theory or generalization is to have any use or to make any significant difference for human life.

A similar tension between particular narratives and generalizations about the human condition can be found in Montaigne's essay 'Of Cruelty'. The author's striving to reconcile a general truth with specific instances creates this work's structure. Montaigne first attempts to define the nature of virtue, beginning with a general distinction between goodness, which is effortless and natural, and virtue, which 'presupposes difficulty and contrast, and . . . cannot be exercised without opposition' (307). Though Montaigne says he is satisfied with this general truth about virtue, he is puzzled by the specific examples of Socrates and Cato the Younger, for whom virtue seems effortless. The essay goes on to consider Stoic principles, additional historical examples, and Montaigne's own self-examination. Montaigne then formulates a hierarchical typology of three kinds of virtue: an easy-going natural goodness, rigidly disciplined Stoical virtue, and finally a supreme form of moral goodness (seen in Socrates) in which virtue is no longer laborious but has become part of one's nature. Montaigne turns finally to the topic of cruelty, which he considers the most terrible of all vices. Again he alternates between discussing general principles and analyzing specific instances. Montaigne's ability to integrate analysis of philosophical principles and distinctions with interpretation of particular narratives gives 'Of Cruelty' its many insights into virtues and vices.

The essay form is rooted in the kind of introspection and self-examination usually associated with autobiography, so that to speak of the essay as 'personal' is almost redundant. Montaigne's *Essays* are clearly a self-portrait, as his address 'To the Reader' makes clear at the outset: 'I want to be seen here in my simple, natural, ordinary fashion, without straining or artifice; for it is myself that I portray . . . . Thus, reader, I am myself the matter of my book' (2). Taken together, Montaigne's essays form a fairly complete presentation of the writer, though the portrait that emerges is focused on the writer's present reality rather than a retrospective view of the past; it is organized thematically rather than chronologically; and the author's descriptions of himself are interspersed with discussions of many other topics. Though clearly rather different from what we think of as classical autobiography as practiced by

Augustine or Rousseau, Montaigne's essays have been interpreted as experiments in non-narrative, thematic autobiography.[11]

One cannot make the case that Johnson's essays express a similarly direct autobiographical intention. Johnson, in fact, went out of his way to prevent people from making comparisons between his moral writings and his own life – for example, by initially keeping the *Rambler* essays anonymous. Why he did this clarifies his somewhat different understanding of the essay. In *Rambler* 14, Johnson argues that 'it may be prudent for a writer, who apprehends that he shall not enforce his own maxims by his domestic character, to conceal his name that he may not injure them' (42). This is not hypocrisy, for a person may be 'sincerely convinced of the advantages of conquering his passions, without having yet obtained the victory' (41). Johnson believed that 'argument is to be invalidated only by argument' (41), and not by reference to the character of the arguer. He was modest about his own moral achievements, without wishing to proclaim publicly his inadequacies, and he wanted his ideas to stand or fall on their own merits. Thus his essays can hardly be called autobiographical in the usual sense.

Nonetheless, the reader often senses in the tone of the essays Johnson's relentless examination of his own conscience and his profound self-knowledge. His awareness of his own participation in the common human problems he analyzes drives Johnson both to generalize about errors to which 'we' are all prone, and to leaven rebuke with compassion. Johnson's struggles with his own complex temperament produce that conflict between satiric judgment and sympathetic compassion which is typical of his response to instances of envy, vanity, or self-deception. The subjects of Johnson's moral essays are the issues that preoccupied his own conscience throughout his life, as Bate's biography richly documents:

> Merely to list the topics of the essays that deal with human weaknesses, temptations, and trials is to list what he spent a lifetime in battling himself. Since he had a capricious and varied nature, the list is long, ranging from the hunger for fame or praise – 'reputation' or 'importance' – to the reading of escapist romances (in which he could lose himself for hours); from the self-defeating folly of anger, when his own heady temper was one of his principal enemies, to the inability of the imagination to remain content with the present moment,

but to leap ahead, if not in hope, at least (as he was constantly doing) in order to anticipate imagined future calamities and steel oneself against them. He could write as well as he did about grief or despair, about remorse and guilt, about boredom, satiety, and the habit of arguing 'for victory,' because he himself was so susceptible to all of them and yet was constantly putting them at arm's length in order to see them for what they were.[12]

When Johnson says 'we' it is often because of the scrupulous activity of his conscience.

The essay form, whether or not it is explicitly autobiographical, achieves its keenest insights when the writer's appraisal of the human condition is based on the kind of moral knowledge which comes only from scrutiny of one's own character. This element of introspection and self-examination takes various forms. As in Johnson's case, it need not entail overt self-portraiture, confession, or apology; conscience may be activated by reflection on the case of another person, and influence one's total assessment of a situation. Although Montaigne indicates how direct self-examination yields verdicts of conscience, he, too, shows conscience at work in assessments of other persons. For instance, in a discussion of excessive literary borrowing and quotation, he asserts that 'to criticize my own faults in others seems to me no more inconsistent than to criticize, as I often do, others' faults in myself. We must denounce them everywhere and leave them no place of refuge' (108). This statement is partially a rejection of the charge of hypocrisy, but it also reflects how assessments of oneself and of others constantly engender and influence each other. In analyzing 'the art of discussion' (III, chapter 8), Montaigne suggests that any condemnation of others must be turned back on the accuser:

Let us always have this saying of Plato in our mouths: 'If I find a thing unsound, is it not because I myself am unsound? Am I not myself at fault? May not my admonition be turned around against me?' . . . I do not mean that no man should criticize another unless he is clean himself, for then no one would criticize; nor indeed that he must be clean of the same sort of fault. But I mean that our judgment, laying upon another the blame which is then in question, should not spare us from judging ourselves. (709–710)

Conscience must be ever vigilant, always prepared to assess whether the errors attributed to others are in fact rooted in one's own character.

These two essayists seem to imply, in fact, that a person may best discover his or her moral character not by brooding on the past or simply staring within oneself, but obliquely, by describing one's total response to other persons, events, or books. In the classic essayists we recognize the introspective and self-referential aspects of their work as essential to their most signal achievements. The essay aspires to a sort of collective moral autobiography: a depiction of the nature of conscience, in both its healthy and its distorted manifestations, often expressed in the first-person plural. Johnson and Montaigne are deeply personal writers for whom the meaning of individual experience is never merely personal.

III   THREE CENTRAL CONCERNS OF THE MORAL ESSAY

In addition to its use of narratives, generalizations about the human condition, and autobiographical elements, the essay has a number of other distinctive characteristics as an exercise of conscience. In this section I discuss the essay's unsystematic approach to ethical reflection, its religious dimensions, and its appeals to prudence. These characteristics shape the essay as a literary genre and as a form of moral discourse.

The essay contrasts strikingly with ethical reflection which aims at a systematic or comprehensive formulation of a method or theory which can be applied to any moral issue. Montaigne's and Johnson's ethical perspectives are deliberately unsystematic and occasional. They focus on the task of elucidating a concrete moral problem or situation rather than on demonstrating an overarching theory or a preconceived method. For the essayist, moral knowledge is philosophically untidy, only probable at best, and rooted in the discrimination and judgment of the thinker's character rather than in a systematic method. Conscience must attend not only to general principles, but to an unpredictable variety of details and circumstances. Montaigne and Johnson believe that systematic and theoretical approaches to morality inevitably simplify the task of ethical reflection. They criticize both idealistic and pessimistic models of human nature for falsifying the complexity of moral experience. The Stoical view of morality was a shaping influence on their outlooks, yet they each found its high estimation of human nature to be misleading and unrealistic. Johnson and Montaigne are committed not to the moral theory of any particular philosophical school, but rather to testing every theory to see whether it is grounded in practical human experience and need.

The titles Montaigne and Johnson gave their works reflect their assumptions about the contrast between the essay and the theory or system. An 'essay' for Montaigne is an exercise and test of judgment, and a form of discourse which emphasizes the process of thought rather than the final product. The roots of this literary term in the verb *essayer* emphasize thought as always on the way and in motion. Montaigne was the first to use the word 'essay' in its modern sense to mean a trying out or test of one's judgment.[13] Montaigne's choice of the term *essais* reflects his sense that attempts to formulate knowledge must somehow reflect the provisionality and uncertainty of all human knowing and the inconsistencies and paradoxes in the diverse things we think we know: 'All in all, I may indeed contradict myself now and then; but truth, as Demades said, I do not contradict. If my mind could gain a firm footing, I would not make essays, I would make decisions; but it is always in apprenticeship and on trial' (611). Montaigne highlights the process of assessment, the 'assaying' of contradictory ideas that sway conscience to quite opposite conclusions, rather than any fixed norms or settled beliefs. The individual titles of his essays are often deceptive in that they only indirectly refer to the real matter he considers. In this ironic way, Montaigne indicates that it would oversimplify matters to summarize or focus in a title the range of considerations relevant to an exercise of judgment.

Johnson, too, by his very choice of titles – the *Rambler*, the *Adventurer*, and the *Idler* – seems to disavow any settled direction or method in his essays. In addition to the disarming and engaging appeal of such titles to eighteenth-century readers of periodical essays, these titles implicitly make a point about his basic approach to moral reflection. Johnson's keen insights into the human condition are expressed in works which call attention to their own fragmentary, digressive, random, and apparently accidental nature.

In a fascinating way, Montaigne and Johnson are morally instructive without being pedantic or didactic. The essay as a form of moral discourse tends towards a descriptive rather than a prescriptive approach to ethics. Even when the author explicitly articulates his moral ideals or standards, he usually does so by describing what he admires or approves. More often, however, the essayist takes an indirect approach to morality by exploring basic problems of human life. Montaigne is explicit about this approach: 'Others form man; I tell of him, and portray a particular one, very ill-formed, whom I should really make very different from what he is if I had to fashion him over again. But now it is done' (610). Johnson is often much more assertive and prescriptive than Montaigne in his normative claims about right and wrong. Even Johnson at his most admonitory and judgmental, however, rarely commands or prescribes; he tries to shape the reader's values in more indirect ways. The essayist persuades rather than preaches.

The essay is a secular genre. While their moral views are consistent with their Christian convictions, it is striking how seldom Montaigne and Johnson appeal to religious considerations. They offer wisdom, not the way to salvation. In Montaigne's many discussions of exemplars of virtue and heroism, the absence of the Christian saints is conspicuous. Even when Johnson refers in a general way to 'religion', he rarely tells his readers what they ought to do or believe as a consequence of their religious commitment. While Johnson's essays reflect his Christian beliefs, they do not appeal to them as warrants for his arguments. The contrast with his sermons shows Johnson's understanding of the essay form as a genre in which religious appeals are inappropriate or may even alienate certain readers.[14] The reasons for the avoidance of religious appeals vary for these two essayists. Montaigne wrote during a time of bitter religious controversy and warfare, and his works reflect his sense of cultural relativism about values, his humane toleration, and his general skepticism about religious thought. Johnson's essays are shaped by considerations of the interests of his prospective audience, which was not seeking in a periodical what could be heard in church. During a period of increasing religious pluralism and secularization or in a time characterized by religious conflicts, an essayist usually appeals to those common values and virtues held by all persons regardless of their religious commitment.

Although the essay is a secular genre, however, it expresses certain vital religious concerns. Johnson and Montaigne are keenly interested in how religious beliefs and practices affect morality, both for better and for worse. In addition, a certain significance can be attributed not only to their explicit discussions of religion as the subject matter of some of their essays, but also to the essay form itself as the natural expression of a certain kind of religious temperament. A distinctive religious concern is expressed in the essay's search for general patterns of human moral experience. The person drawn to the essay tends to differ in two main ways from the individual who pours out his soul in what we customarily think of as the religious autobiography, if we take Augustine's *Confessions* as the classic paradigm and Newman and Malcom X as later practitioners of this genre. First, the essayist's basic way of coming to terms with evil is not confession of personal failings before God and his fellow men, but an attempt to understand the general place of evil in human experience by analyzing the errors and mistakes which are characteristic of the human condition. The essayist seeks perspective on his own shortcomings, not to demonstrate that he is the worst or most 'interesting' of sinners. Yet the essayist's conscience may be as fully engaged in reflection on the sources of moral failure as the confessional autobiographer.

Second, the essayist differs from the writer who makes his or her dramatic conversion experience the focus of a personal narrative. Johnson and Montaigne experience the continuities of life as more fundamental than the disjunctures and ruptures. The essay writer sees even change and 'the inconsistency of our actions' (chapter 1 of Book II of Montaigne's *Essays*) as constants recurring in human experience. He discerns among a wide variety of human lives certain basic patterns, and describes these patterns as a sort of natural law. As religious reflection, the essay does not recount the dramatic story of the salvation of a soul, but attempts to discover in the mundane and common experiences of life certain clues to the design of God's creation and to God's general intentions for humankind. The essay's religious roots are in the wisdom literature of the Biblical books of Proverbs and Ecclesiastes and in the Stoics' philosophical accounts of 'Nature', rather than, as with Augustine and later writers of conversion narratives, in the works of the prophets and the apostle Paul. Rather than utilizing a single narrative plot like the converted and confessing author, the essayist achieves his different purposes by combining a number of shorter narratives with philosophical speculation and moral generalization. He or she searches for a vision of the universality of the human fate rather than trying to demonstrate his particularity. While a religious autobiographer such as Augustine shares certain generalizing interests with the essayist, the conversion narrative gives primary emphasis to recounting a climactic conversion and confessing both sin and praise. Augustine's example has so dominated conceptions of religious autobiography that it has not been recognized that the essay form, too, may express distinctive ultimate concerns.

Many ethical thinkers, especially since Kant, have tried to dissociate morality from questions of self-interest, for they fear that the autonomy and integrity of morality will be compromised if it is made a means to happiness. The sphere of conscience is therefore sharply distinguished from considerations of prudence. The typical essayist, however, is usually concerned to show that it is in a person's own interest to be moral. The essay appeals strongly to the motive of prudence, advising readers as to which attitudes and actions are ultimately conducive to happiness and which are destructive of human well-being. In Montaigne's and Johnson's essays, moral considerations are intermingled with discussion of an incredible variety of practical issues involving medicine, publishing, the choice of a spouse, the pleasure and dangers of solitude, material possessions, fame, friendship, idleness, procrastination, clothes, the conduct of warfare, eating and drinking, education – and the list could be extended indefinitely. In some ethical theories, many of these matters would be considered as personal choices, and an attempt would be made to separate them from purely moral issues by defining ethics as an autonomous field of thought. For Montaigne and Johnson, in contrast, an adequate discussion of any of these topics inevitably mixes points of moral principle with matters of etiquette, social convention, common sense, complications of circumstance, and an individual's own character and desires. The activity of conscience for Montaigne and Johnson is not an exercise of logical deduction, but the discernment of how moral principles and values apply to the messy details of everyday life. Ethical reflection on the practical conduct of life must therefore locate the place of moral principle prudently within the whole texture of human existence. Furthermore, since morality is a matter not only of duties to others, but also of duties to the self, a person's self-interest is not only legitimate but necessary. Both Montaigne and Johnson criticize ethical theories such as Stoicism which demand an impossibly high standard of self-sacrifice, renunciation of the ordinary pleasures of human life, or disdain for prudential self-interest.

Yet although they appeal to prudential motives, Johnson and Montaigne also point out the limitations of prudence in realizing the most valuable goods of human life. Each has a courage and a concern for human relationships that far exceeds the standpoint of a merely prudential moralist. Montaigne's late essays especially reveal a determination to embrace risk and danger, and a joyous acceptance and affirmation of life, that transcends the cautious self-protectiveness of the merely prudent individual. In *Idler* 57, Johnson brilliantly points out the limitations of the lonely character of 'Sophron the prudent'. 'Prudence keeps life safe, but does not often make it happy' (320). Although prudence is an indispensable virtue of the moral life, it is insufficient by itself to achieve certain valuable things, and it has its own dangers. 'Thus Sophron creeps along, neither loved nor hated, neither favored nor opposed; he has never attempted to grow rich for fear of growing poor, and has raised no friends for fear of making enemies' (323). This capacity to criticize the very same concerns – here, prudential ones – that he appeals to in the reader is one of the traits by which we recognize the great essayist. We trust him because he discerns and warns us about the limitations of his own values, inviting us to share a similarly complex and self-critical awareness, and an equally discriminating conscience.

IV   THE VIRTUES OF THE ESSAYIST

Prudence is but one of a number of virtues treated by Johnson and Montaigne. Indeed, the essayist's approach to ethical reflection centers on an attempt to describe and assess the virtues and their corresponding vices. There are several tasks involved in this reflection on virtues and vices which require the exercise of conscience, and which the essay form seems especially well suited to encourage. Thus virtue is at once the subject matter of the essay and integral to the essayist's mode of reflection. In the exercise of conscience, the essay writer demonstrates the virtues he asserts are most essential to a well-lived life.

Before a person can reform or choose proper goals he must recognize his vices and bad habits. Montaigne and Johnson often focus on bad habits that it lies within an individual's power to recognize and correct or control. These two moralists are endlessly fascinated by the self-destructive ways in which people ruin their own lives and distress others. They provide a comprehensive survey of the ways in which unhappiness may grow out of a person's own boredom, envy, indifference, indecision, excessive prudence, or undisciplined imagination. Both writers attribute much of the unhappiness of life to what Johnson calls 'the vain imagination which preys incessantly on life'. While they realize that the imagination is an essential and valuable part of human nature, its constant dissatisfaction with the present is one of the chief sources of misery, and each writer insists on the need to discipline its wayward impulses. *Rambler* 8 is a characteristic statement of this aspect of Johnson's moral outlook. Considering 'how we may govern our thoughts, restrain them from irregular motions, or confine them from boundless dissipation', Johnson concludes that a person who 'would govern his actions by the laws of virtue, must regulate his thoughts by those of reason' (22–3; 27). Montaigne, too, points out a number of ways in which failure to discipline the imagination can become a bad habit. One instance of this weakness Montaigne experienced personally in his constant struggle not to anticipate pain from the kidney-stone ailment which plagued him: 'I shall be in plenty of time when I feel the pain, without prolonging it by the pain of fear. He who fears he will suffer, already suffers from his fear' (840).

A vice attacked frequently by these two writers is vanity, which they see as the primary obstacle to moral self-knowledge. Again and again, Montaigne and Johnson point out the ways in which our self-appraisals exaggerate our real capabilities, talents, and merits. Montaigne consistently attacks ideal conceptions of human nature for deluding us into forgetting our bodily natures. He notes the tendency for grand visions of our destiny to justify the most immoral conduct: 'These are two things that I have always observed to be in singular accord: supercelestial thoughts and subterranean conduct . . . . They want to get out of themselves and escape from the man. That is madness: instead of changing into angels, they change into beasts; instead of raising themselves, they lower themselves. These transcendental humors frighten me, like lofty and inaccessible places' (856). Montaigne punctures vain presumptions through unfavorable comparisons between human beings and the animals which he holds surpass us in every virtue. Johnson's moral essays, written in the decade after 'The Vanity of Human Wishes', carry on that great poem's meditation on the ironic thwarting of human hopes largely because of individuals' own self-deception and illusions. The particular attention they give to forms of intellectual and moral pretension reflects these writers' study of the traditions of wisdom literature dating back to the Greek and Roman skeptics and Ecclesiastes. The anticipated audience for the essay is also a factor in their particular emphasis on exposing intellectual and moral forms of vanity. Montaigne's and Johnson's essays are written for the learned, for intellectuals, for men of power and influence. Their essays were not directed to the uneducated, women, or common laborers, but to the sort of well-read, privileged, and well-meaning male who, through his exercise of authority and sincere efforts to act morally, may harm others or himself.

A key theme in the moral essay is what can be called 'the masks of virtue'. The essayist distinguishes true virtue from all the actions and individuals that resemble it, contrasting the real thing with the false appearance. Insight is thus offered into some of the chief methods by which a person learns to flatter his own moral character and deceive his conscience. For example, in discussing repentance, Montaigne attacks pangs of conscience which come only when the body has grown too tired to enjoy its former pleasures: 'I hate that accidental repentance that age brings . . . . In that I see nothing of conscience; sourness and weakness imprint on us a sluggish and rheumatic virtue' (619). When he analyzes 'the inconsistency of our actions', Montaigne warns against judging a person as virtuous on the basis of a single action; 'Therefore one courageous deed must not be taken to prove a man valiant . . . . To judge a man, we must follow his traces long and carefully' (242–3). To distinguish authentic virtue from its simulacra, judgment must encompass both the outward shape of an action and its motivation: 'A sound intellect will refuse to judge men simply by their outward actions; we must probe the inside and discover what springs set men in motion' (244). This kind of moral knowledge must include the point of view of the person actually involved in the action; hence the value of the inside view of conscience offered by an autobiographical account: 'There is no one but yourself who knows whether you are cowardly and cruel, or loyal and devout' (613). Montaigne points out a number of ironic discrepancies between the evaluations of his character made by others and his own self-knowledge: 'I have sometimes seen my friends call prudence in me what was merely fortune . . . My virtue is a virtue, or should I say an innocence, that is accidental and fortuitous' (311).

Many of Johnson's essays also deal with the masks of virtue. *Ramblers* 28 and 76 focus on the various arts of self-delusion whereby we convince ourselves of our virtue. The first of these essays offers a concise account of these strategies. Johnson, too, emphasizes the need for persistence and constancy; we cannot judge of virtue on the basis of one act. 'One sophism by which men persuade themselves that they have those virtues which they really want, is formed by the substitution of single acts for habits' (64). The insidious wiles of moral vanity constantly create new excuses for our errors: 'Those faults which we cannot conceal from our own notice, are considered, however frequent, not as habitual corruptions, or settled practices, but as casual failures, and single lapses' (65). Praise of virtue is not virtue: 'There are men who always confound the praise of goodness with the practice, and who believe themselves mild and moderate, charitable and faithful, because they have exerted their eloquence in commendation of mildness, fidelity, and other virtues' (65). Johnson points out the convenient self-deception which allows men to rate themselves by their opinions rather than their actions, and the mediocrity tolerated by those who 'regulate their lives, not by the standard of religion, but the measure of other men's virtue' (65). Again and again, Johnson detects ways in which envy, malice, or laziness lurk behind a mask of virtue. His experiences in London's literary circles showed him how frequently a person's insistence on judging others by high standards can express hostility and envy. When persons disparage or censure others, they can relieve their own guilt or animosity under the guise of upholding an ideal of virtue. In their astute analyses of the psychological realities underlying the masks of virtue, Montaigne and Johnson help us to understand some of the moral dangers that can arise in the very process of trying to be moral.

From these two writers' essays one could draw as pessimistic a vision of the human condition as has ever been expressed. And yet one of the intriguing things about Johnson and Montaigne is that their works do not leave most readers feeling hopeless or despairing about life, but quite the contrary. For their recognition of the infinite human capacity for vanity and self-deception is only half of their vision. The other half of their perspective encompasses the limited but significant human capacity to recognize and correct bad habits, that is, conscience's capacity for self-transcendence. Unlike most moralists who have emphasized the self-centeredness and vanity of human beings, such as Hobbes, Swift, Hardy, or the writer of Ecclesiastes, these two thinkers discern not only human egoism, but also certain resources which can help a person to change his ways. They testify not only to human folly but to our limited but crucial capacities for freedom and moral responsibility. Though they occasionally describe the heights of human virtue, their more characteristic remedy for vice is the formation of good habits which lie within the power of most individuals. For instance both writers point out the need for detachment from the cares of the everyday routine: Montaigne speaks of the need for 'husbanding the will' (Book III, chapter 10), while Johnson urges 'retirement and abstraction' to aid the regular practice of self-examination (67). Montaigne warns us not to worry so much about moderation that we cannot enjoy ourselves. Johnson promotes good humor and 'readiness to be pleased' by others. Their emphasis on the vices that plague the human condition, then, is balanced by their interest in both heroic virtues and the more modest character traits that make life more tolerable for all.

Both writers are deeply aware that it is not conscious hypocrisy but self-deception that underlies much human evil. Johnson holds that 'it is generally not so much the desire of men, sunk into depravity, to deceive the world as themselves . . . . The sentence most dreaded is that of reason and conscience, which they would engage on their side at any price but the labors of duty, and the sorrows of repentance' (138). What they make of their penetrating insights into various shapes of self-deception explains one of the most characteristic effects of Johnson's and Montaigne's essays. In spite of what would in many other writers be a cynical view of the human condition's deep-rooted vanity, self-delusion, and inconsistency, countless readers have felt the total impact of Johnson's and Montaigne's essays as a tremendously liberating and enabling power. I think this liberating power comes partly through the essayist's ability, not to instruct us directly as to moral duty, but rather to provide us with certain skills, habits, and psychological insights necessary to become a responsible moral agent. For instance, they share the assumption that contradictory intentions and desires must be recognized before self-discipline and moral freedom can effectively be practiced. This explains why so much of their ethical reflection involves demonstrating habits and skills of self-examination, especially the ability to recognize one's own inconsistency and contradictions. This skill, which seems so basic as to be beneath notice, is in fact essential to a truthful conscience.

In this respect, Montaigne and Johnson proceed as does Herbert Fingarette's ideal psychotherapist, who helps her patient to become a morally responsible agent by enabling him to 'avow his engagements' even when they are contradictory. The role of the therapist can be contrasted with the futile attempt to preach to a patient, since it is the very desire for moral integrity and consistency which sometimes prevents a person from recognizing the full significance of his actions:

> If we turn for a moment from considering the role of therapists to a consideration of the role of moralist, ideologue, or minister, we can see now that insofar as they presume the self-deceiver to be fully a personal agent in the matter at hand, they preach, teach, and argue in vain. The futility of preaching to the neurotic has long been remarked by the psychiatrically oriented. Direct appeals to integrity and moral concern, by evoking the motives of self-deception, strengthen the inclination to it and are self-defeating.[15]

Fingarette's account of the kind of help a therapist can offer the self-deceiver illuminates the way the essayist often approaches ethical reflection:

> He needs someone who can help him, tactfully but persistently, though a detailed consideration of the texture of life. This helper must also offer evident, unswervingly dedicated reliability and dispassionateness, wide relevant knowledge, personal strength and humane tolerance; for the self-deceiver must be helped to go to the limits of his courage, but not provoked beyond the breaking point.[16]

Montaigne and Johnson exercise exactly these skills and these virtues in their shrewd analyses of the human moral condition. They educate the reader's conscience, helping him or her to develop certain of the conditions for moral freedom and responsibility. Their means of doing this is not simply preaching or teaching the importance of moral virtue, but showing how conscience can be corrupted and how it can work truthfully. They train a person to recognize – first in another's life and then in his own – patterns of self-deception, masks of virtue, and evasions of conscience. They nurture the skills involved in detecting inconsistencies in our own behavior, and contradictions between our actions and our principles. Montaigne shows the reader by his own example how to become self-critical and skeptical about one's own rationalizations: 'I learn to mistrust my gait throughout, and I strive to regulate it' (822).

Indeed, it is by their own examples as thinkers rather than because of their beliefs or specific conclusions that Montaigne and Johnson are most instructive about moral virtue and about conscience. Their moral essays are paradigms of this genre because of their practice and mode of procedure, not because of their definitions of virtues or their insistence on specific principles to guide conscience. 'The essay is a judgment, but the essential, the value-determining thing about it is not the verdict (as is the case with the system) but the process of judging.'[17] It is the example of their practice of ethical reflection that shows the reader the meaning of such virtues as truthfulness, honesty, courage, and detachment. Montaigne holds that writing essays decisively shaped his own character: 'I have no more made my book than my book has made me – a book consubstantial with its author' (504). For this consciously autobiographical essayist, truthfulness includes the capacity for ironic detachment from the self, skepticism about one's own best intentions, and the courage to recognize complex and often contradictory motives. In his essays we see Montaigne 'leading the moral life in the very search for it, and . . . following his search, searching too, we likewise come finally to realize that the search *is* the moral life and the way, therefore, the end'.[18]

The same holds true of Johnson's best essays: they demonstrate the meaning of certain virtues as integral to the exercise of conscience. The significance of his essays lies finally in the unique way they show a mind in motion as it strives to do justice to all the complexities of a particular situation in its final assessment. Of course, any convincing moral argument must consider all the relevant considerations. What is peculiarly characteristic about the essays of Montaigne and Johnson, however, is the way that they so unforgettably dramatize the process of moral reflection in terms of interaction between different virtues. Bate describes the essential quality in Johnson's dramatic portrayal of the mind as 'the active interplay of qualities – of compassion and anger, of humor and moral profundity, of range of knowledge and specialized focus, of massive moral honesty and specific technical or psychological acumen'.[19] Johnson's and Montaigne's essays do not simply display different virtues in scattered places; again and again, they show conscience struggling to reconcile and balance diverse human qualities in one complex act of evaluation. What is most essential and valuable about their work is the example set by their own practice as certain virtues interact in the process of ethical reflection.

The essay as an exercise of conscience has been characterized in terms of a number of themes and concerns shared by Montaigne and Samuel Johnson: use of narratives, an interest in generalization, an autobiographical element, appeals to prudence, and skepticism about theories and systematic methods of ethics, along with a focus on the process of ethical reflection. The moral essay makes use of a secular framework of values, and yet by its author's keen interests in both the sources of evil and the commonalities of the human situation it may express the search for universality of a distinctive type of religious sensibility. Above all, an essayist such as Montaigne or Johnson both investigates and demonstrates the meaning of certain crucial virtues. My understanding of the essay as an expression of the autobiographer's conscience can be summarized in two central claims, which I have tried to substantiate using the essays of Montaigne and Johnson. First, the essay can be interpreted as an attempt to generalize about the common human moral condition on the basis of certain narratives which directly or implicitly reveal much about the essayist himself. And second, the essayist practices crucial moral and intellectual virtues, and trains his readers to develop similar skills and habits. The exercise of conscience in the moral essay both instructs us as to the meaning of these virtues and demonstrates their role in ethical reflection. It is their pre-eminence in the practice of such virtues as honesty, courage, and scrupulous self-examination that constitutes Montaigne's and Johnson's most significant influence on later essayists and their enduring contribution to our understanding of conscience.

5
Franklin and the Critics of Individualism

In several recent books by critics of individualism, *The Autobiography of Benjamin Franklin* has served as the primary historical example of individualism's negative aspects. While these critics echo long-standing disputes in scholarship on Franklin, placing the man and his autobiography in the context of the debate about individualism raises new issues. In effect, Franklin is said to lack a social conscience: a genuine appreciation of the interconnectedness of individuals in society and a concern for community. In spite of his benevolent actions, Franklin's way of thinking is held to betray an essentially self-interested and self-serving outlook. Communitarian critics of Franklin's individualism raise significant ethical issues which deserve more careful analysis and scrutiny. Neither Franklin's autobiography, his active social conscience, nor the complexity of the many ideas and tendencies loosely categorized as 'individualism' are adequately interpreted when Franklin's autobiography becomes the epitome of an ideology rejected as morally unscrupulous.

The Autobiography of Benjamin Franklin, I will argue, provides insights into both the conception of society called individualism and the conception of the self called individuality. (Individualism and individuality are distinct but related concepts, as we shall see.) Franklin's critics are mistaken when they discern in his work only individualism's deleterious effects, for his autobiography has surprising relevance as a positive resource for communitarian critics. Analysis of his autobiography – using the terms proposed by communitarian critics – will disclose a rather keen understanding of the need for individual commitment to public social goods, one of the characteristics of a social conscience. In the last section of this chapter Franklin's view of individuality will be seen to enrich our thinking about the relations of self and society, even though later autobiographers' contrasting views of the chief threats to individuality raise significant questions about the viability of Franklin's model of the self. In these ways Franklin's autobiography serves as a resource for thinking about crucial ethical issues raised by discussions of individualism. I must defer interpretation of the autobiography, however, until the terms of the debate about individualism have been explained, and some basic definitions and distinctions have been clarified.

I   THE COMMUNITARIAN CRITICS OF INDIVIDUALISM

Individualism has come to mean so many things in Western culture that no careful thinker can simply affirm or reject it. The usual strategy is to distinguish the 'good' individualism from the bad, asserting that certain aspects of this complex conception have enduring value and can be preserved or reformulated without the negative or destructive tendencies also associated with individualism. Thus, for example, Steven Lukes argues that taking seriously the individualist 'values' of liberty and equality requires us to abandon the 'doctrines' of political individualism and economic individualism.[1] A recent collection of essays on 'reconstructing individualism' assumes that 'the individualist order of the modern Western world has met with challenges that have rendered its beliefs and doctrines problematic', and that the concept of individualism needs to be rethought in light of these criticisms. Reconstruction 'does not imply a return to a lost state but rather an alternative conception of the experience of subjectivity, enriched by the chastening experiences of the last century'.[2]

An ideal of community inevitably underlies criticisms of individualism. Lukes' account of the semantic history of the term shows that in its earliest usage, in early nineteenth-century France, individualism carried a pejorative connotation and was contrasted with an ideal of social unity. De Tocqueville is the best-known exemplar of a tendency to equate individualism with isolation and egoism, and to view it as a threat to some ideal of social solidarity and cohesion, whether the political left's co-operative utopia or the right's norm, the traditional hierarchical order. There is a venerable European intellectual tradition of communitarian critics of individualism. In the United States, however, individualism has usually been celebrated, extolled as the basis of capitalism and liberal democracy. 'Even those who criticized American society, from New England Transcendentalists to the Single Taxers and the Populists, often did so in the name of individualism.'[3] This pattern has changed; American cultural critics now challenge individualism as they articulate communitarian themes.

Both socialist and feminist critics see a connection between individualism as a theory of society and as an underlying view of the self. Marxist and socialist critics attack the social alienation and economic inequalities that accompany individualist societies and, in the Hegelian tradition, argue that the self is necessarily social. Criticisms of individualism are often closely associated with assessments of liberalism, because individualism is seen as the theory of the self which underlies and authorizes the organization of society according to liberal principles. 'On the liberal view, the self is prior to its ends – this assures its capacity to *choose* its ends – and also prior to its roles and dispositions – this assures its independence from social conventions, and hence its separateness of person, its individuality.'[4] Critics of liberalism such as Michael Sandel and Michael Walzer challenge the rights-based tradition of ethical and political thought, appealing instead to the communitarian or republican tradition which makes claims about the good primary in moral thinking. A 'critique of individualism' also runs through much of feminist thought. Feminists argue that a male orientation produces a lopsided concern for autonomy in political and ethical thought, whereas a 'female ethic' and 'maternal thinking' are held to account better for the interdependence of persons and the communal context of thought and action.[5]

The most powerful and provocative of the contemporary communitarian critics is Alasdair MacIntyre. His *After Virtue* examines the modern fragmentation and miscommunication that result from the failure of the 'Enlightenment Project' to justify morality by appealing to some 'moral fiction' – such as rights, utility, or rationality – rather than to a community's traditions and narratives. MacIntyre associates individualism with many of his targets, including emotivism, the bureaucratic mentality, and the calculated role-playing described by Erving Goffman. MacIntyre's influence is pervasive in *Habits of the Heart*, in which Robert Bellah and four co-authors analyze the historical sources and contemporary manifestations of American individualism, which they believe undermines the capacity for commitment to both local communities and the common good.

In many ways Benjamin Franklin seems a paradigmatic example of the individualism challenged by communitarian critics. Marxists have showed how Franklin's ideal of success epitomizes the values of the rising middle class and how his scheme of virtues nicely supports a capitalist economic structure. Franklin's attitudes toward family and friends – for example his rather mercantile assessment of his wife's value to him – provide evidence for the feminist claim that emotional distance and exploitation of others are inherent in the patriarchal outlook. Ever since Max Weber used Franklin as his chief example of how the secularized 'Protestant Ethic' contributed to the development of capitalism, Franklin has been interpreted in terms of utilitarian attitudes.[6] In *Habits of the Heart*, Franklin appears as the fountainhead of 'utilitarian individualism', which is defined in this way:

> A form of individualism that takes as given certain basic human appetites and fears – for Hobbes, the desire for power over others and the fear of sudden violent death at the hands of another – and sees human life as an effort by individuals to maximize their self-interest relative to these given ends. Utilitarian individualism views society as arising from a contract that individuals enter into only in order to advance their self-interest . . . . Utilitarian individualism has an affinity to a basically economic understanding of human existence.[7]

Although they make clear that Franklin's view of self-improvement was linked to social responsibility and public concern, Bellah *et al.* see Franklin's utilitarian influence as contributing to the egoistic individualism that undermines commitment to community. Franklin's understanding of social morality is said to follow from his conception of individual success, and thus to be a utilitarian means towards that end.

> For many of those influenced by Franklin, the focus was so exclusively on individual self-improvement that the larger social context hardly came into view. By the end of the eighteenth century, there would be those who would argue that in a society where each vigorously pursued his own interest, the social good would automatically emerge. That would be utilitarian individualism in pure form. Though Franklin never himself believed that, his image contributed much to this new model of human life.[8]

Franklin's utilitarian individualism left little room for human feeling, pleasure, or intimate relationship with others, and thus indirectly influenced the development of 'expressive individualism' in reaction to the limitations of his vision of life.

Similarly, MacIntyre takes Franklin to task for his individualistic understanding of the virtues. What is at stake is not simply a matter of the particular thirteen virtues which Franklin views as comprising moral perfection, but rather Franklin's understanding of what a virtue is. MacIntyre distinguishes between an 'internal' relationship between virtue and the good – when the end of an activity cannot be specified independently of the means – and Franklin's 'external' understanding of the relationship between means and ends, which reduces virtue to a utilitarian strategy. In contrast to the Aristotelian and Christian traditions, which see virtue as a necessary and intrinsic part of a conception of the good for human nature, Franklin's virtues are essentially means to the end of success in Philadelphia.

Central to MacIntyre's critique is his notion of a 'practice', a concept which also plays a crucial role in the argument of *Habits of the Heart* and in responses to that book.[9] By a practice MacIntyre means 'any coherent and complex form of socially established cooperative human activity through which goods internal to that form of activity are realised in the course of trying to achieve those standards of excellence which are appropriate to, and partially definitive of, that form of activity, with the result that human powers to achieve excellence, and human conceptions of the ends and goods involved, are systematically extended'.[10] Franklin's utilitarian understanding of virtue and his constant calculation of how exercising the virtues will enhance his business career seem to MacIntyre divorced from truly cooperative social endeavor, from practices. For Franklin does not distinguish between goods internal to and goods external to a practice. Nor does he recognize that to realize the internal goods involved in a practice, a virtue must be exercised without regard to consequences, especially the achievement of the external goods which inevitably accompany, but may come to corrupt, any practice. 'The road to success in Philadelphia and the road to heaven may not coincide after all.'[11]

The communitarian critics do not wish to reject entirely the individualism epitomized by Franklin, but to distinguish and assess its many aspects. For example, the authors of *Habits* affirm a first meaning of individualism: 'a belief in the inherent dignity and, indeed, sacredness of the human person'. They criticize, on the other hand, what they call 'ontological individualism': 'a belief that the individual has a primary reality whereas society is a second-order, derived or artificial construct'.[12] The latter form of individualism is contrasted with 'social realism', which holds that society is as real as individuals. While I share the communitarian critics' desire to affirm the dignity and sacredness of the individual *and* the importance of commitment to community, their sketchy alternative to present thinking about these ideas leaves many questions unanswered. Especially troubling is the alternately nostalgic or utopian character of the critiques, which either wistfully lament the loss of the past or propose a future community so tightly unified and harmonious that the traditional liberties and rights of the individual seem unnecessary. This 'terminal wistfulness', argues Jeffrey Stout, is 'a function of everybody's inability to imagine a full-blown alternative to liberal society that would be both achievable by acceptable means and clearly better than what we've got now. No one has trouble *imagining* a way of life that, by his or her lights, would qualify as an improvement upon the current order. But it always turns out to be a way of life in which everybody, or nearly everybody, comes to see the light – that is, comes to see things by *my* lights, by light of *my* conception of the good in all its detail.'[13] As Christopher Lasch puts it, 'The communitarian ideal, as elaborated in the past, has usually been anti-political – either pre-political or post-political.'[14]

Theoretical critiques of individualism need to be supplemented, clarified, and made more specific with detailed accounts of individuals in community. The authors of *Habits* include in their book a number of case studies of persons they interviewed, commenting on how individuals' self-understandings and views of society are related. A few of these cases are said to offer intimations of what the authors would like to see more of in the United States. The use of Franklin as historical paradigm suggests, too, the merits of a more sustained examination of autobiography as an expression of individualism. Autobiography is the genre which, according to many practitioners and scholars, is devoted to presenting a person's distinctive sense of himself or herself as an individual. Franklin's *Autobiography*, I will argue, demonstrates some ethical problems with individualism, but it also suggests positive resources for thinking about the individual in society. Analysis of autobiographical theory and of Franklin's work yields alternative ways of thinking about individualism, both as a theory of the self and as a theory of the actual and ideal forms of society. In this way I hope to make the communitarian critique of individualism more pointed and persuasive by examining a specific resource for a realistically reconstructed individualism.

II INDIVIDUALITY AND AUTOBIOGRAPHY

Theories of autobiography almost always make a connection between this form of writing and conceptions of the individual. The specifically modern conception of the individual is seen as arising in the West at a particular historical moment and as profoundly shaping the development of autobiography. However, scholars of autobiography differ markedly on the sources of the modern concept of the individual. Sometimes Augustine's deeply introspective self-scrutiny is seen as the turning point.[15] In contrast, Karl Weintraub locates the essential preconditions of individuality in the two notions of the self's uniqueness and its historicity, and he sees these ideas fully developed and interpenetrating for the first time only as late as Goethe's *Dichtung und Wahrheit* (written between 1808 and 1831). Weintraub's discussion of writing prior to 1800 makes many normative judgments about 'true' autobiography, and assesses works according to how fully they anticipate his conception of individuality. I will discuss two ideas developed in Weintraub's extensive survey of the historical origins of the concept of the individual as articulated in autobiography. First, Weintraub distinguishes between the concepts of individuality and individualism, explicating two sets of ideas often conflated. Second, Weintraub's interpretation of Benjamin Franklin provides an instructive contrast with the view presented by the communitarian critics of individualism.

Weintraub defines his subject most briefly as 'the belief that, whatever else he is, [a person] is a unique individuality, whose life task is to be true to his very own personality'.[16] The conception of individuality contains a number of distinct elements: a valuation of the unique and specific over the general or universal; an awareness of the self's temporal development or growth; the notion that one has a task or duty to realize some inner potential; and an interest in cultivating a personal style which harmonizes diverse aspects of one's character and background. Following Rousseau's example, devotees of individuality often – though not inevitably – take an adversarial stance towards society, which they perceive as a threat to the self. The ideal of individuality opposes any claim that a person should pattern his life on a normative model, for such patterning would hinder the fulfillment of the unique and unrepeatable form of each person's selfhood. 'The ideal of individuality is marked by the conviction that ultimately no general model can contain the specificity of the true self. The ineffable cannot be defined by the general – *individuum ineffabile est.*'[17] Paradoxically, however, this antipathy to models itself becomes a model, an ideal personality conception which orients autobiographical writing. This understanding of individuality thus entails a sort of 'anti-model model' of the self.

Weintraub's term 'individuality' refers to a personality conception, a form of selfhood that certain persons have sought to attain in their own lives. Individuality is distinct from individualism, which is a theory of society. Individualism holds that social control over the individual should be kept to a minimum so that persons may be as free as possible to define themselves. Weintraub posits an intriguing relationship between individuality and individualism:

> It is entirely thinkable that individualism does not lead to a preoccupation with individuality. If, in a society dedicated to individualism, everyone freely opts for the realization of a common model – that of a truly rational man, for example (as implied perhaps in Kant, Comte, Marx, or Freud) – a society of homogeneous personalities may be sought which denies the value of individuality. The complication lies in the fact that a society of individualities, however, seems to demand the freedoms of a society devoted to individualism.[18]

In other words, the cultivation of individuality may well be possible only in a society granting the freedoms associated with individualism, but individuality will not flourish where everyone in a society models his or her life on the same ideal of selfhood. Individuality (the personality conception) is a possible but not necessary outcome of individualism (the social theory).

We may correlate Weintraub's distinction between individuality and individualism with two distinct intellectual traditions deriving from France and Germany. 'Individualisme' in French thought

tends to be a pejorative reference to the sources of social disso-
lution, however a thinker conceives of those sources. In Germany,
in contrast, the ideal of 'Individualität' expresses the positive values
of the Romantic movement: uniqueness, originality, self-realization,
the consciousness of historical change, and the organic unity of the
individual and his society.[19] It is one of many ironies associated
with the concept of the individual that the central themes of two
distinct intellectual traditions take their name from the same root.
A further irony and cause of confusion is that these two concepts
– one of society and one of the self – may be seen as harmonious,
antithetical, or, as in Weintraub's view, existing in a rather unstable
alliance at certain historical moments. In Anglo-American thought
the concept of individualism has come to encompass elements from
both of these traditions; one must infer from the larger context of
ideas what a writer means by the term. Although the thinkers
discussed in this essay do not mean exactly the same thing when
they refer to individualism, a common theme recurs. Much of the
contemporary debate about individualism represents an attempt to
salvage the ideals of individuality – above all, the importance of
self-development and a sense of the uniqueness of each person –
while rejecting the negative view of society believed to be inherent
in individualism.

Weintraub sees Benjamin Franklin's autobiography as only partially revealing the emergence of full-blown individuality. He, too,
follows Weber's interpretation of Franklin as a secularized version
of the Protestant Ethic. Franklin 'pursued secular ends and had secular motivations', revealing the diminishing authority of the Puritan
ideal of personality.[20] Yet Franklin's intense didactic concern to
present himself as a model for his new nation overrides any interest
in developing aspects of the personality that became important
components of the ideal of individuality. True individuality arose
as a reaction *against* Franklin's model of the self and his view of
society, especially his devotion to orderly method, system, and a
rational relation between ends and means.

> Experience must still fit a script. The cultivation of emotional
> richness, the fulfillment of aesthetic needs, the opportunity for
> spontaneity and irrational urgings was sacrificed for the ben-
> efit of an extraordinarily efficient personality. Indeed, it was
> as a countervailing force to the restrictions imposed by the
> purpose-rational system of science, industrial capitalism, and

utilitarianism which the Puritan personality helped to create, that modern man came in time to invoke the ideal of individuality.[21]

Weintraub's view of Franklin thus converges with that of MacIntyre and Bellah (and is similarly indebted to Weber) in that he views Franklin as a primary exemplar of the growth of the utilitarian mode of thinking that so pervades modern thinking about the self's involvement in society. Weintraub names this outlook 'individualism', while Bellah calls it 'utilitarian individualism' and MacIntyre refers to it as 'bureaucratic individualism'. Moreover, Weintraub speculates that individuality, the view that the self should cultivate emotions, aesthetic experience, spontaneity, and intimate relationships, arose partly in reaction to the constricted self-conception offered by Franklin. This theory parallels MacIntyre's suggestion that the 'character' of the 'aesthete' arises in modern society in response to that of the bureaucratic 'manager' whose rationality efficiently matches all means to ends. Weintraub's view of individuality corresponds, too, with the contention of *Habits* that 'expressive individualism', which 'holds that each person has a unique core of feeling and intuition that should unfold or be expressed if individuality is to be realized', arose partly in opposition to utilitarian individualism.[22]

Weintraub argues another thesis very similar to one advanced by communitarian critics of individualism. His account concludes with a discussion of the autobiographies of Rousseau and Goethe, who present two sharply contrasting visions of the self's relation to society. Rousseau interprets his life as a conflict between a basically good self and the corrupting influence of society. 'In that vision of an unreconcilable confrontation of the individual self and society lay a fundamental dilemma from which our thinking about the notion of individuality has suffered ever since.'[23] The dilemma involves a choice of whether to withdraw from society or to try to reform it by manipulating human circumstances so as to encourage virtue. In either case, Rousseau turns away from a conception of individuality which sees fruitful interplay and mutually beneficial influence between a self and its social world.

In contrast, a socially responsible understanding of individuality is expressed in Goethe's *Dichtung und Wahrheit*: 'A self could not value itself apart from its world; a love of self includes the love of its circumstances. Goethe did not set the self and the world against each other; he did not think well of self-cultivation at the cost of the world. He thus warned against the false cult of self-idolization which threatened commitment to individuality when it became fashionable.'[24] Goethe's vision of individuality warns against ego-centric self-absorbtion and irresponsibility to one's society. For Weintraub, Goethe is a positive example of how the self may be nurtured by active involvement in work and by loving cultivation of particular cultural traditions. In portraying Rousseau and Goethe as two possible outcomes of the ideal of individuality, Weintraub concurs with communitarian critics who wish to salvage certain ideas about the individual even as they warn of ways that aspects of individualism may undermine commitment to the self's communal context.

However, unlike the communitarian critics, Weintraub does not attribute to Franklin the egocentric version of individuality. (In fact, in Weintraub's view, Franklin is not concerned with individuality at all, since he presents himself as a model to be emulated.) While the paradigmatic example of an adversarial stance to society is Rousseau's *Confessions*, Franklin's project of self-perfection is said to lead naturally to an effort to improve society. 'Character is effective in work; effective work inevitably leads to success; and individual success readily translates itself into social benefit. As soon as the individual has made an internal order of himself and his own life, the concentrated energy flows over into the effort to order his wider social world.'[25] The virtues Franklin cultivates first in his own person are transmuted to talents and skills which effectively order Philadelphia and his country.

In sum, Weintraub's study of individuality in autobiography converges with the communitarian critics in seeing Franklin as an important source of the utilitarian outlook which is part of modern individualism, and in lamenting the egoistic disregard for society that often accompanies striving for individuality. However, he diverges in his interpretation of Franklin's stance towards society, viewing Franklin as a cultivator of society rather than a clever entrepreneur whose involvements in society only further self-interested motivations and objectives.

Franklin's *Autobiography* is a central document in these two very different arguments, the communitarians' criticisms of individualism and Weintraub's analysis of the development of individuality. His autobiography raises crucial questions about the relationship between his self-conception and his vision of society, and suggests insights into the links and tensions between the emergence of individualism (a theory of society) and the concept of individuality (a theory of the self). Although these concepts were not fully developed or explicitly named until the nineteenth century, Franklin's autobiography provides crucial evidence about how and why these ideas evolved. Turning directly to his autobiography, I will assess those aspects of individualism and individuality which undermine and those which support commitment to a community.

III   FRANKLIN'S INDIVIDUALISM AND HIS SOCIAL CONSCIENCE

The criticisms of Franklin draw attention to deficiencies or inadequacies in what we commonly refer to as a 'social conscience'. In the analysis which follows, I will focus on an autobiographer's conscience in a somewhat different sense than in much of the rest of this book. Franklin has only a cursory interest in interpreting his moral lapses and their significance. Even though periodic examinations of conscience were the basis of Franklin's 'Project of Arriving at Moral Perfection', he soon abandoned his private discipline of self-examination. His autobiography rarely demonstrates the probing self-scrutiny or relentless discrimination of motives that we find in the works of Augustine, Montaigne, or Mary McCarthy. The autobiography mentions in passing certain 'errata', but records no confession of sin, and very little guilt, shame, or contrition. And yet Franklin's autobiography reveals an intense concern with another of the things we associate with an active conscience: a person's commitment to the public good or the flourishing of his community and, as important as his practical commitments, his very way of conceiving how an individual and his society are related. In this section I inquire as to what Franklin's supposed individualism discloses about his social conscience. The analysis of Franklin's individualism will be organized according to three related issues raised by the theories discussed above: Franklin's understanding of 'practices', his utilitarian outlook, and the basic question of how to characterize his view of the individual's relationship to society.

Even though MacIntyre portrays Franklin as the paradigmatic example of how individualism undermines practices, MacIntyre's valuable concept of a practice illuminates Franklin's involvements in society. The problem in applying the concept of a practice is that the purpose of a person's activity can always be described either in such a way that the goods sought appear to be intrinsic to the activity, or so that they appear as external, and the activity as only a means. How does one know whether the goods sought are primarily internal or external when any practice involves both? The least we should expect is an account that discerns both internal and external goods. Unfortunately, most criticisms of Franklin have left out of account precisely those 'internal goods' that he cared most about. The purpose of Franklin's multifarious activities has frequently been described in terms of a pursuit of external goods such as status or money. He is viewed from a Machiavellian or Nietzschean perspective, as if his activities were only the most efficient means towards the end of power. These interpretations fail to characterize adequately Franklin's endeavors and the reasons why they elicited his commitment. A more sustained examination of his autobiography, however, will disclose his view of the internal goods involved in two of his chief pursuits, philanthropy and science.

A great deal of Franklin's miscellaneous activity is the expression of the practice of philanthropy. Philanthropy, which Franklin more characteristically calls charity, is the organized effort to promote human welfare. There is no need to catalogue the many ways in which Franklin contributed to the welfare of his city and nation. What is crucial is the way he conceived of his activities. This, unfortunately, is not a topic which Franklin develops at length in the *Autobiography*; he is content to chronicle his acts. Yet many of the characteristics of MacIntyre's idea of a practice – a 'socially established cooperative human activity' – would apply to Franklin's continual efforts to create and sustain philanthropic organizations. Franklin constantly sought ways to establish or institutionalize his projects for social betterment, and to enlist the resources of others through such devices as matching grants. He had little false modesty, and took credit for his achievements, but popular acclaim was not the primary goal of his efforts. He contributed generously to other people's projects. The internal goods realized by philanthropy go beyond material improvements in society; such human excellences as discernment, judgment, imagination, and many of Franklin's thirteen virtues – resolution, industry, justice – are cultivated in this field of activity. So, too, does philanthropy involve MacIntyre's ideal of a systematic extension of practitioners' conception of the ends and goods involved in their activities. Franklin's public service was constantly transformed as his experience led him to envisage further ways to contribute to various communities.

Franklin was highly conscious of the need for institutions to sustain the activities he valued, and much of his philanthropic work focused on the founding and funding of organizations. His philanthropic career can be summarized by the institutions he began, most of which were the first in his city or the United States: a self-improvement and mutual-aid club, the Junto; a subscription library; a company to prevent and extinguish fires; a citizen militia; a learned society, the American Philosophical Society; the University of Pennsylvania; the first hospital; a fire-insurance company; and the city departments which paved, lighted, and maintained the streets. Many of these institutions were essentially self-help organizations or hygienic instruments; his goal was always to make possible the social conditions which would allow individuals to work diligently to improve their own lives, exercising the Franklinian virtues. After devoting several pages to an admittedly dull recital of his attention to the city streets, Franklin acknowledges that 'some may think these trifling matters'. But it is by improvements of this nature that the welfare of society is most enhanced. 'Human Felicity is produc'd not so much by great Pieces of good Fortune that seldom happen, as by little Advantages that occur every Day' (108).[26] Franklin's tireless institution-building exemplifies MacIntyre's point that 'the making and sustaining of forms of human community – and therefore of institutions – itself has all the characteristics of a practice'.[27] However, Franklin seems unaware that institutions can corrupt practices through their control of the external goods which are necessary to sustain practices. The *Autobiography* implies that once an institution is founded it will continue to pursue its worthy purposes. Franklin lived before the negative consequences of bureaucracy became apparent, and before systems of charity were understood to perpetuate structures of power.

It has sometimes been held that Franklin's philanthropic career began only after he had made his fortune in business, and that this ordering of priorities reveals a basic problem in his understanding of the relation between self and society. But in fact many of his projects were begun while he was still a relatively unknown printer. Both self-interest and public service characterize all periods of Franklin's life. Indeed, Franklin never tires of asserting the essential connection between individual success and public involvement, for he is convinced of the interdependence of happiness and virtue.

MacIntyre contends that Franklin's utilitarian outlook cannot accommodate the legitimate place of pleasure and enjoyment in a practice.[28] This claim echoes the view of many critics that Franklin is so devoted to efficiency that his ascetic scruples empty life of enjoyment. What, however, are we to make of Franklin's confessions of satisfaction when his philanthropy is publicly recognized? Franklin is not as ascetic as his critics, who apparently credit only those forms of service which are wholly self-sacrificing or without Franklin's evident enjoyment of his endeavors. When Franklin is chosen for several public offices, he admits both his motive of 'doing Good' and his appreciation for the confidence of his community:

> I conceiv'd my becoming a Member would enlarge my Power of doing Good. I would not however insinuate that my Ambition was not flatter'd by all these Promotions. It certainly was. For considering my low Beginning they were great Things to me. And they were still more pleasing, as being so many spontaneous Testimonies of the public's good Opinion, and by me entirely unsolicited. (101)

He takes pride in the compliment made to him that 'there was no such thing as carrying a public-spirited Project through, without my being concern'd in it' (102). It is not that, seeking praise or publicity, Franklin adopts the most efficient means towards that end. What he welcomes is specific: exactly that kind of respect and recognition which attach to a philanthropist and public servant, a form of respect earned through no other activity than the sort of practice in which Franklin engaged. He is candid about his enjoyment of public reputation, but this good is not an external one separable from the nature of his practical commitments. Franklin wants only a certain sort of public reputation. More fundamentally, he seeks the self-esteem of the public servant, an internal good. This form of satisfaction is one of the legitimate rewards of philanthropy, although it is not the sole purpose or point of Franklin's activities. To his detractors, Franklin's admission of his self-esteem and his enjoyment of public esteem appears as smug complacency and haughtiness. Franklin would surely have held that disdain for this form of approval was feigned, and that no honest and reasonable person would pretend indifference to either the external good of reputation or the internal good of that form of self-esteem based on effective public service.

In many ways Franklin's practice of philanthropy overlaps with his practice of science. 'This is the age of experiments' (141), he announces in connection with one of his many investigations of the natural world. He derives from the practice of science not only the satisfaction of seeing the public welfare improved, but a great deal of intellectual pleasure as well. The *Autobiography* displays several instances of boyish excitement as Franklin recounts the details of experiments to determine the best street lantern, or the speed of a ship, or the construction of the most efficient plan for street gutters. His many inventions – including bifocal glasses, the Franklin stove, and the lightning rod – were at once contributions to the practice of philanthropy and to that of science. He refused to take a patent for his stove because of his principle 'that as we enjoy great Advantages from the Inventions of Others, we should be glad of an Opportunity to serve others by any Invention of ours, and this we should do freely and generously' (98).

When a French scientist challenged his theory of electricity, Franklin did not bother to defend himself. His explanation of his reluctance mentions his habitual dislike of 'disputing', his aversion to dogmatic claims of any kind, errors in translation, and the pragmatic test of further experiments:

> On Consideration that my Writings contain'd only a Description of Experiments, which any one might repeat and verify, and if not to be verified could not be defended; or of Observations, offer'd as Conjectures, and not delivered dogmatically, therefore not laying me under any Obligation to defend them; and reflecting that a Dispute between two Persons writing in different Languages might be lengthened greatly by mis-translations, and thence misconceptions of one another's Meaning, much of one of the Abbe's Letters being founded on an Error in the Translation; I concluded to let my Papers shift for themselves; believing it was better to spend what time I could spare from public Business in making new Experiments, than in Disputing about those already made. I therefore never answered M. Nollet. (132)

Franklin's theory of electricity was verified by others, making him the best-known American scientist of his time. We can discern in this passage Franklin's understanding of science as not a duel between competitive rivals or a quest for individual status, but a truly co-operative social activity. Evident, too, is his pursuit of science for intrinsic goods. When these goods are realized the consequences are not simply external rewards but excellences and enjoyments inherent in the practice itself – such as 'the infinite Pleasure I receiv'd in the Success of a similar [experiment] I made soon after with a kite at Philadelphia' (133).

Franklin also thinks of many of his projects of social improvement as 'experiments'. Franklin is a precursor of one ideal of modern social science, the hope that the techniques of research and experiment which work so well in the physical world can be transfered to society and enlisted in the cause of promoting human welfare. Franklin's rhetoric in the third part of his autobiography is shaped by his eighteenth-century understanding of the experimental method, and by his view of how it can be applied to public life. His advice mixes the avuncular wisdom of the elderly man of the world with the empirical observations of the social scientist: 'In the Course of my Observation, these disputing, contradicting and confuting People are generally unfortunate in their Affairs. They get Victory sometimes, but they never get Good Will, which would be of more use to them' (111; see also 14). Franklin passes on to fellow practitioners of social science his experiments with the best ways of raising funds or reaching a compromise between intractable parties. He assumes that his audience shares his public spirit, intellectual curiosity about human nature, and observance of the proper rules and standards governing experiments. His scientific experiments in both the natural and social worlds were conceived of in the ways MacIntyre associates with a practice.

Interpretation of Franklin's activities in terms of his involvement in the practices of philanthropy and experimental science thus places the question of his individualism in a different light. His understanding of the interdependence of self-development and commitment to co-operative endeavor should establish him as a positive resource rather than a foil for the communitarian critics of individualism.

Communitarians argue that Franklin's 'utilitarian' perspective on life undermines the value of tradition and sees communal activity as only a means of satisfying self-interest. Franklin evaluates everything by the standard of usefulness. What does he mean by 'usefulness'? His selective appropriation of only certain aspects of Christianity is a prime example of this mode of assessment. He puts aside his Deist ideas when he sees their consequences in the conduct of his ne'er-do-well companions Collins and Ralph, in Governor Keith's deception of him, and in Franklin's own poor judgment with regard to spending Vernon's money and ignoring his future wife. 'I began to suspect that this Doctrine tho' it might be true, was not very useful' (46). When Franklin formulates his basic religious principles, he adheres only to 'the Essentials of every Religion, and being to be found in all the Religions we had in our Country I respected them all, tho' with different degrees of Respect as I found them more or less mix'd with other Articles which without any Tendency to inspire, promote or confirm Morality, serv'd principally to divide us and make us unfriendly to one another' (65). Franklin judges all religious thought and experience by their moral effects on the life of the community. His standard of 'usefulness' encompasses a wide range of moral considerations bearing on communal existence.

Linking Franklin with utilitarian thinking illuminates his concerns for efficiency and the rational assessment of everything from poetry to the choice of a spouse. It is misleading, however, when the imputation of utilitarianism is taken to imply that underlying all choices are egoism, selfish motivation, and an interest only in what benefits the self. Communitarian critics such as the authors of *Habits of the Heart* often equate utilitarianism with egoism. But utilitarianism, both in its nineteenth-century philosophical origins and in its broader cultural context as the standard of usefulness espoused earlier by Franklin, attempted to transcend egoism and partial interests by considering the good of the whole. Franklin's standard of usefulness has to be understood in the light of the question 'Usefulness for what?' His answer to this question is invariably usefulness for the good of society as a whole, or in other words the common good.

Furthermore, Franklin's 'usefulness' should be interpreted in relation to the eighteenth century virtue of benevolence as well as to utilitarian thinking. Often when Franklin speaks of being useful he is more concerned with doing good than with being efficient. It was inconsistent for Franklin to leave off benevolence from his table of thirteen virtues, for the practice of this virtue underlies much of his action. The table of virtues summarizes only the understanding of 'perfection' that he had as a young man, not his mature view. To understand the latter, we need to look beyond the famous table to the autobiography as a whole, asking not only what Franklin preached but what he actually practiced. It is true, however, that Franklin's useful benevolence seems rather coolly prudent, bereft of either the affective aspects of benevolence emphasized by Shaftesbury or Hume, or the heedless self-sacrifice of Christian charity.

Critics such as MacIntyre focus on Franklin's presentation of his scheme of virtue as the *means* to happiness, and argue that this reduces virtue to one among many possible techniques to be evaluated according to the criterion of utility. Franklin does believe that the practice of virtue leads to happiness. However, virtue is the *only* means to that end, not one among many strategies. Surely it is not the case that all thinking about ends and means is 'utilitarian' in a negative sense. Franklin's discussion of a never-completed book on 'The Art of Virtue' uses the language of means to describe the originality and significance of his approach to morality. In one of his few Biblical allusions, Franklin contrasts his focus on the means to virtue with the empty rhetoric of those who merely preach of goodness in the abstract: 'The Art of Virtue . . . would have shown the *Means and Manner* of obtaining Virtue; which would have distinguish'd it from the mere Exhortation to be good, that does not instruct and indicate the Means; but is like the Apostle's Man of verbal Charity, who only, without showing to the Naked and the Hungry *how* or where they might get Clothes or Victuals, exhorted them to be fed and clothed. *James* II, 15, 16.' (74). For Franklin the rhetoric of means had far different connotations than the negative ones associated with a corruption of utilitarian thinking.

Those who follow Weber's interpretation seem to equate Franklin's utilitarianism with the use of a very limited kind of technical rationality. They fear that Franklin's mode of assessing things involves both overconfidence in human reason and blindness to the worth of all that cannot be quantified or measured. However, Franklin was highly aware of the limits of human rationality, and several times made himself the butt of jokes about his 'reasonableness'. When the aroma of fried fish induces him to abandon vegetarianism, he observes: 'So convenient a thing is it to be a *reasonable Creature*, since it enables one to find or make a Reason for everything one has a mind to do' (28). In describing his deliberations with the English governors of the colonies Franklin comments wryly on how particular interests shape one's view of the rational: 'each Party had its own Ideas of what should be meant by *reasonable*' (144). And he describes how 'something that pretended to be Reason' justified lapses from his scheme of perfection, since 'a benevolent Man should allow a few Faults in himself, to keep his Friends in Countenance' (73). Franklin is quite cheerful and humorous about his inconsistencies and contradictions. He does not lament his lack of conformity to a mechanical or mathematical standard, for he knows that human nature is far more complex and commodious than any rational standard allows. In the century often known as the age of reason, Franklin dramatized the limits of reason.

It is undeniable that his utilitarian criteria lead to some rather warped judgments, such as his approval of 'the amusing oneself with Poetry now and then, so far as to improve one's language, but no farther' (30). Because of his insistent practical interests he can be comically blind to the deeper meaning of events, as when he calculates the number of persons able to hear the voice of evangelist George Whitefield but omits mention of the content of Whitefield's message. An elderly woman leading the devout life of a nun impresses Franklin chiefly as an 'Instance on how small an Income Life and Health may be supported' (38). Granted, the particular focus of his utilitarian mind has its limitations. Yet the very miscellaneous contents of the *Autobiography* testify to Franklin's incredibly broad interests and openness to experience regardless of whether it fits with preconceived ideas of what is rational.

Franklin has always impressed foreign-born observers as the first American pragmatist, and pragmatism is a more apt philosophical tradition than utilitarianism with which to interpret this great experimenter in life. Pragmatism underlies a recurring pattern in the *Autobiography* when Franklin expresses satisfaction or mischievous glee as persons with high-minded principles are forced to compromise. He several times recounts with wry humor how Quaker or Moravian pacifists were persuaded to contribute to the defense of the colonies: 'Common Sense aided by present Danger, will sometimes be too strong for whimsical Opinions' (124). Franklin is greatly amused by the success of a Presbyterian Minister who agreed to dispense the soldiers' rum immediately after prayers (126). In these jocular comments on the compromises of principle with practical necessity can be seen not only his ribald acceptance of the sensual needs of human nature, but a kind of moral satisfaction when the high-minded must mingle with the common lot. He approves of the pragmatic 'stooping' required when idealists are compelled by shared necessities to participate in society. This side of Franklin is sometimes associated with his utilitarian views, and he is said to have no fixed principles but immediate expediency. However, Franklin's pragmatic attitude shows a wisdom about the tensions between high ideals and the moral demands of common social existence. And his satisfaction is not always at the expense of other persons. His pragmatic willingness to settle for less than flawless virtue produces his bemused irony about his own youthful attempt at moral perfection. For instance, he wittily describes how he yielded in his own conflict between vegetarian principles and desire to partake in a feast of fresh fish.

Franklin's critical perspective on the claims of communal authority and tradition, and his assessment of them by the standard of usefulness, express a realism and wisdom about the individual's relation to community. In a sense Franklin simply insists on the need for an independent judgement of conscience, based on consideration of all the interests in a society, rather than conformity to the norms of any one tradition. Too often critics of individualism praise 'commitment to community' as an indisputable good. But whether communal activity is in fact good depends on the nature of the community and the form of commitment required. To determine when a commitment should be made to a community, some form of moral assessment must take place, a judgment according to norms of conscience which, while they are shaped by a community, are also used by the individual to evaluate his community. For Franklin a crucial standard of judgment for conscience is usefulness. Although there are significant dimensions of human life which Franklin does not appreciate, his concern for the good of his whole society, as opposed to private interests, is not only compatible with, but identical to the central concern of the communitarian critics of individualism. Criticism of his utilitarian outlook misses this crucial point.

In addition to the idea of a practice and the challenge to utilitarian thinking, the communitarian critics provide a third concept with which to approach Franklin's thought. They suggest that the individualistic view of persons basically thinks of individuals as being both ontologically and morally more fundamental than communities. Does Franklin hold that conception of the abstract individual associated with the social philosophy of individualism?[29] Or does he view the individual as necessarily a member of a community? I think that Franklin does not conceive of persons as existing prior to their community bonds, nor are their basic interests defined apart from their social commitments. However, Franklin is more aware than most of his critics of the fact that a person belongs to *several* communities, no one of which should completely determine the meaning and purpose of life. He is also highly conscious of the fact that every community – familial, economic, religious, or political –

no matter how local or seemingly homogeneous, is itself composed of diverse elements.

Christopher Lasch suggests that recognizing the constant presence of conflict within any community should affect the way one thinks about the problem of individualism:

> Social solidarity does not rest on shared values or ideological consensus, let alone on an identity of interests; it rests on public conversation . . . . We need to develop a political conception of the community, in place of the organic and sentimental conception that now tends to prevail . . . . By overemphasizing the importance of shared values, defenders of a communitarian politics expose themselves to the familiar charge that community is simply a euphemism for conformity.[30]

Lasch argues that a reformulated communitarian ideal must reconceive politics in terms of the protection not of privacy (as the traditional liberal sees the state's primary role), but of practices (as described by MacIntyre). 'Our formulation of the communitarian ideal . . . conceives of politics not as a way of compelling men to become virtuous but merely as a way of keeping alive the possibility that they may learn virtue by fitting themselves for a congenial practice. It insists, moreover, on the need for a plurality of practices, representative of the full range of human talents and inclinations. No single practice must be allowed to monopolize the definition of virtue.'[31]

Franklin's view of the individual in community shows significant affinities with Lasch's ideas. Franklin is keenly aware of the conflictual nature of any community, and for this reason his is a far more modest vision than the ideals of many communitarians. He is concerned about community, but he understands this idea not as conformity to a single standard, but in terms of the typical liberal notion of a plurality of small communities composed of individuals each pursuing a range of activities that give their lives meaning. Franklin's is an early form of liberalism that does not eschew bonds to others but wishes to preserve a diversity of bonds and a variety of degrees of individual commitment to many kinds of human association. To achieve this form of society, certain institutional arrangements are necessary, and certain ways of thinking about particular communities are entailed. Franklin must assess the claims of each community in terms of his moral standards because he knows that every community has a dangerous tendency to become oppressive – even totalitarian – in its demands on the individual, and to neglect its own responsibilities to other groups. Franklin saw this among quarreling Quakers, Presbyterians, and Baptists in Pennsylvania, in the arbitrary demands of the British Proprietors of the colonies, and in the relations among the thirteen fractious communities forming the United States.

Therefore his picture of individuals in community is one which focuses on encouraging continued conversation and debate rather than uniformity of belief. Repeatedly he stresses cultivation of skills that allow one to avoid personal animosity towards advocates of opposing positions – what I call public virtues in Chapter 6. His conception of community insists on every individual's right and duty to assess most carefully the demands made on him by various groups that claim to provide his life with meaning and that often promise a solidarity dissolving all conflicts. Franklin's attitude to politics is wary and skeptical, but it is profoundly discerning about the actual tensions of life in community. His utilitarian mode of assessing community claims, while not the only or always the best method of resolving moral questions, is based on an understanding of conscience in critical relation to its communal context. Franklin does not take the adversarial stance towards society which critics see as the danger of individualism. Nor does he conceive of individuals as abstract beings existing independently of a social context. He provides a realistic picture of the individual as a member of several communities, each of which places conflicting demands on him. Franklin's account insists on the freedom and moral responsibility of conscience to affirm or resist the influence of these communities, and to consider the good for the largest possible human society.

IV   THREATS TO INDIVIDUALITY

Franklin's *Autobiography* presents a shrewd and sensible understanding of the interdependence of a person's sense of identity and his commitment to several communities. And yet the communitarian critics are right to challenge Franklin as the normative model for emulation. For although Franklin's view of the relationship between the individual and the community remains instructive, we perceive new issues and problems with which he never reckoned. We sense different threats to individuality than he did. I propose that we

can understand some of what is at stake in recent debates about
individualism by comparing Franklin's view with what other autobiographers have perceived as the greatest threat to individuality.

Who is not an individual? In an autobiography the achievement of
individuality is often contrasted with failures which disclose what
the writer perceives as threats to individuality. Franklin's ideal for
the self was of course unattainable for many persons in his own
time whom his society did not accord the status to participate as an
equal, such as African-Americans, women, and Native Americans.
The antithesis of Franklin's ideal of individuality is his horrified
portrayal of Indians drinking and fighting at Carlisle. All social dif-
ferentiations and self-control were obliterated in riotous brawling:
'Their dark-color'd Bodies, half naked, seen only by the gloomy
Light of the Bonfire, running after and beating one another with
Firebrands, accompanied by their horrid Yellings, form'd a Scene the
most resembling our Ideas of Hell that could well be imagin'd' (102).
There are, as well, a number of minor characters in the *Autobiography*
who function as 'cautionary doubles' for Franklin, displaying by
their failures what Franklin perceives as the greatest threats to his
ideal for the self.[32] John Collins and James Ralph exhibit vices that
contrast with Franklin's table of virtues. Collins never repays money
he borrowed from Franklin, becomes a drunkard unable to hold
a job, and finally disappears in Barbados. Ralph, who wastes his
time 'scribbling Verses' of poetry, deserts his wife and child when
he accompanies Franklin to London in 1724. There the two men
become intimately involved through their shared lodging, Deist
views, and financial profligacy. The friends become even more
closely identified when Ralph takes Franklin's name while teaching
in a country school, and each is involved with the same woman,
'Mrs. T.' An 'attempted familiarity' with her on Franklin's part
causes 'a Breach' with Ralph, who refuses to repay Franklin's loans.
This rupture marks a turning point in Franklin's life. In ending his
relationship with Ralph, Franklin abruptly sloughs off the wasteful
and licentious tendencies of his own youth. In so doing he frees
himself from the greatest threats to his own individuality.

The next passages in the *Autobiography* record Franklin's determination to drink only water, in contrast to his beer-guzzling
fellow printers. Through Franklin's example, many of his fellow
Compositors gave up alcohol; those who 'continued sotting with
Beer all day' became debtors to Franklin. 'Thus these poor Devils
keep themselves always under' (36). Nearly all the cautionary

doubles have a drinking problem. Alcohol symbolizes all that most threatens Franklin's model self: sensuality, loss of control, wasteful expense. Temperance is the first of his virtues and the foundation of the others 'as it tends to procure that Coolness and Clearness of Head, which is so necessary where constant Vigilance was to be kept up, and Guard maintained, against the unremitting Attraction of ancient Habits, and the Force of perpetual Temptations' (68). Franklin's worldly asceticism begins at this time, when he rejects the vices associated with alcohol that threaten the achievement of his version of individuality.

The remainder of Part I shows the emergence of a new man who has escaped the temptations that distract and defeat his doubles. On his return from London Franklin formulates a Plan for 'regulating my future conduct in Life' which he 'pretty faithfully adhered to quite thro' to old Age' (40). In Philadelphia he begins his business career as a printer; makes the acquaintance of the 'principal people' and 'ingenious people' in the vicinity; abandons Deism as 'not very useful'; forms the Junto, his club for mutual improvement; corrects his 'erratum' with Deborah Read through a common-law marriage; and proposes his 'first Project of a public Nature, that for a Sub-scription Library' (57). Franklin's success as an austere and prudent capitalist is made possible by the failure of another contrasting 'bad example', Hugh Meredith, whose father established the two young men in the printing business. Meredith's alcoholism finally brings Franklin to dissolve their partnership and take control of the press.

These cautionary doubles reveal what Franklin believes to be the greatest threats to his sense of himself as an individual. They model traits which prevent a man from attaining the form of self-respect and social esteem that Franklin sees as essential to individuality. Some of the older men described in the *Autobiography*, such as the too-credulous Keimer and Governor Keith, whose 'wish to please everybody' (33) produces expectations he cannot satisfy, also contrast with virtues Franklin models in his later public career. Franklin wants his own achievements to be measured against these failures to achieve what he sees as the normative relationship of the individual to his community.

Franklin's understanding of what constitutes and what threatens the individual's sense of identity is a benchmark later American autobiographers used to distinguish their own views. Later writers were far more concerned than was Franklin with cultivating their individuality, their sense of being an utterly unique personality. Franklin's model of the self often epitomized for many autobiographers what most threatened their individuality. His *Autobiography* is to the self-writing of the American individualist what Augustine's *Confessions* is to the writer of a conversion narrative: an unavoidable influence even when modified or rejected. I propose six ways in which later autobiographers have perceived in Franklin's model of the self threats to their own individuality.

1. *Threats to one's distinctive origins.* In his efforts to create institutions and new communities Franklin tends to devalue those characteristics which distinguish individuals. Both in his religious and his political thinking, he takes a least-common denominator approach to the problem of securing co-operation. His personal creed was what he deemed 'the Essentials of every Religion': belief in God, God's Creation and Providence, the immortality of the soul, and 'that the most acceptable Service of God was the doing Good to Man' (65). Franklin respected any religion insofar as he could see in it these principles, but had little use for 'other Articles which without any Tendency to inspire, promote or confirm Morality, serv'd principally to divide us and make us unfriendly to one another' (65). He ceased to attend church when he decided the minister's aim was 'rather to make us Presbyterians than good Citizens' (66). Although Franklin was intensely concerned about human community, it is significant that the communities to which he was most committed were ones he helped create, including his nation. He shows little concern for what Bellah calls 'communities of memory': those human groups which we do not choose but are members of by virtue of geographical location, race, kinship, religion, or some other form of communal destiny.

Communities of memory or origin become essential to the individuality of a host of later American autobiographers. For such writers it is the bland results of the American melting-pot that most threaten their sense of themselves. The struggle to find an authentic identity often resembles the form of a conversion narrative, as the author rejects his former aspiration towards a common standard of 'Americanness' and comes to appreciate his roots in a particular local culture based on race, language, or ethnic background. For example, Malcolm X begins to search for a true self when he rejects the repressive model of identity that white society tries to impose on blacks. Recent works such as Maxine Hong Kingston's *Woman Warrior* and Richard Rodriguez's *Hunger of Memory* explore this theme with a new complexity, as the writer finds she or he cannot wholly reject the white mainstream but must find some sort of uncomfortable balance between identification with a community of origin and assimilation into the broader culture.[33]

In religious autobiographies, too, many writers diverge from Franklin by affirming elements of their tradition regardless of whether or not they can be shared generally with the broader American culture. Or the distinctive aspects of a religious tradition may be presented as valuable partly because of their ability to ground commitment to a broader public conception of the good. In Dorothy Day's *The Long Loneliness* intense commitment to public political issues and concern for justice on the national and international scale are nurtured by participation in the Roman Catholic mass, the veneration of the saints, retreats, and solitary prayer. Many autobiographers, then, have presented their identities and their public commitments as having been shaped far more than were Franklin's by a community of origin and memory.

However, insofar as in composing an autobiography a person reaches out to a broader community and interprets her individuality in public discourse that addresses those outside the community of origin, we may discern a resemblance to Franklin. To tell the story of one's life and one's community in the form of public discourse is to share something of Franklin's desire to be part of a larger and pluralistic community. A writer such as Kingston may feel she has to compromise her Chinese-American tradition in order to interpret it, betraying secrets and risking potential misunderstandings by those in her original community. The controversy provoked by Rodriguez's *Hunger of Memory* shows vividly this conflict of loyalties. Rodriguez has been criticized for entirely dissolving the 'tension between the forces of assimilation and the allegiances of ethnicity and class' by accepting mainstream American culture without hesitation.[34] For many twentieth-century autobiographers, individuality is threatened both by the isolation of being confined to one local community or 'ghetto', and by the loss of distinctiveness through heedless assimilation into mainstream culture.

2. *Attitudes towards economic success.* A second way that later autobiographies diverge from Franklin's understanding of the individual is in their criticisms of his narrowing the self to a prudent business entrepreneur. Though Franklin was a more complicated and many-sided man than his autobiography conveys, this self-representation prunes away a great deal in the interest of defining a

model personality. The focus on his economic career diminishes the importance of a range of Franklin's involvements, both in various relationships such as his family, and in non-economic activities such as his diverse forms of recreation and amusement. D. H. Lawrence's famous satire of Franklin utterly rejects the assumption that any formula for perfection could do justice to the variety in the human race and the potential of every individual: 'The perfectibility of which man? I am many men. Which of them are you going to perfect? I am not a mechanical contrivance.'[35] Lawrence's caustic remarks suggest the nature of Franklin's continuing influence on autobiographical writing. There continues to be a strong tradition of 'success stories' by 'self-made men' (and now women). However, many autobiographers perceive the narrowing of the self to an economic producer as the greatest threat to individuality in American culture. They define their lives instead in terms of the cultivation of human relationships, feelings, religious searching, or aesthetic expression.

Central to such works is often an explicit or implied contrast between the autobiographer and persons who sacrifice their individuality for economic security. Thoreau's sense of self, and of self-worth, is bolstered by his disdain for such profit-maximizers. Henry Adams' individuality contrasts with numerous wealthy entrepreneurs and faceless politicians who lack all that makes life worth living; it contrasts, too, with his friend Clarence King, who, although he managed to get the scientific education Adams lacked, was ruined by the crash of 1893. Malcolm X imagines himself as a successful nonentity in a road not taken: 'I've often thought that if Mr. Ostrowski had encouraged me to become a lawyer, I would today probably be among some city's professional black bourgeoisie, sipping cocktails and palming myself off as a community spokesman for and leader of the suffering black masses, while my primary concern would be to grab a few more crumbs from the groaning board of the two-faced whites with whom they're begging to "integrate."'[36] We may call the 'cautionary double' in these autobiographies a Franklin-figure: a person whose single-minded devotion to economic security, whether successful or a failure, sacrifices the more authentic basis for individuality realized in the autobiographer's own life.

3. *Models of the self.* Lawrence's question, 'the perfectibility of which man?' suggests not only an aversion to the primacy of economic man, but a denial that *any* single model of the self

could be satisfactory for everyone. Any normative prescription for the self whatsoever is perceived as a threat to individuality. The ideal of individuality, as Weintraub explains, is a model of the self which denies the validity of any universal prescription for the individual and instead celebrates unique and unrepeatable human lives. According to this theory of individuality, Franklin's model of the self would threaten autobiographers simply because it postulates a normative model of identity.

However, I would qualify the stark contrast often drawn between Franklin's interest in a model personality and later autobiographers' opposition to models of the self. Individuality is not the only thing with which autobiographers are concerned. To see later writers as devoted only to establishing their utter uniqueness slights the didactic intention of many modern autobiographies, such as Thoreau's account of how nonconformity fosters civil disobedience, Malcolm X's attempt to 'deprogram' his 'brainwashed' black brothers and sisters, or Dorothy Day's vision of a Christian life fully committed to the problems of the world. Of course, in nineteenth- and twentieth-century autobiographies the author usually disavows any intention to pose as a latter-day Franklin, a paradigm of virtue. Individuality is affirmed, and the autobiographer's life is not explicitly presented as a model for emulation in Benjamin Franklin's straightforward way. However, when a writer uses her own life to demonstrate the value of a standard applicable to some group or to all humans, she is following in Franklin's footsteps. An autobiographer may find herself in the inconsistent position of describing how she was threatened by some past demand to conform to a model, while at the same time wanting others to shape their lives by what she has learned.

This is a position in which Franklin never found himself, since he did not believe that models of the self necessarily threaten individual development. Quite the contrary. Franklin acknowledged literary debts to his models of good writing: Bunyan, Addison, Defoe, and Cotton Mather (9). He adapted to his unique ends the Puritan tradition of spiritual autobiography, and he used motifs from a genre describing the rise of a successful apprentice.[37] Though Franklin knew he was one of the most eminent and unique figures of his era, he recognized his indebtedness to models of the self, in the forms of both literary exemplars and persons he respected such as Thomas Denham, whose financial help and fatherly advice to the youthful Franklin provided a model for Franklin's own relations with younger men. Franklin clearly intended his life story to become a model for the formation of other persons' characters. He chose to include within his autobiography letters from Abel James and Benjamin Vaughan which beg him to 'invite all wise men to become like yourself; and other men to become wise' (60). But although Franklin sees himself as both imitating models and being a model for others, he does not expect or desire a society in which everyone imitates his pattern exactly. While Franklin lacks the exuberant enthusiasm for particularity and diversity that characterize the nineteenth-century cultivation of individuality (by Whitman, for instance), he has a tolerance and an appreciation for the pluralism of American life. For Franklin adherence to models does not preclude the individuality of the self.

Does Franklin really lack a concept of individuality? Or is it rather that his understanding of the uniqueness of the self is simply different from the dominant tradition of modern autobiography? Franklin's example suggests an alternative understanding of individuality, one with ancient roots and contemporary relevance. When it is defined in terms of opposition to any model for the self, individuality inevitably leads to that hostility to social commitment challenged by both Weintraub and the communitarian critics of individualism. Insofar as individuality is understood as the 'no-model model' of the self, it is impossible to conceive of a fruitful and nurturing relationship between a person and his culture. But Franklin's autobiography suggests another view of individuality in which the self makes creative use of several traditions, adapting and synthesizing them in a unique way. One aspect of Franklin's contemporary relevance lies in this positive valuation of models. The creative task of striving for individuality need not sever one from the models of self provided by culture. In fact, it now seems amazing that seekers of individuality could ever have supposed that the self creates itself out of nothing, free from the influence of culture. On this point, Franklin seems more credible than many modern autobiographers.

Individuality does not emerge when an autobiographer – or a self – somehow breaks away from culture, but when a person selectively appropriates many cultural influences and integrates them in a personal style. Weintraub's analysis of Goethe shows how individuality can be conceived as fruitful interplay between self and society. Franklin's view of the self has affinities with this socially committed version of individuality, even though Franklin did not make personal uniqueness a matter to cultivate, to strive for, and to treasure to the degree that Goethe did. Franklin's tinkering, trial-and-error, experimental attitude to life is a good metaphor for how the process of self-formation proceeds, both in autobiographical writing and in its larger context, the formation of personal identity. Another metaphor for this process that aptly describes Franklin's self-concept is the theatrical one: the trying on of various masks or the playing of a succession of roles.[38] Franklin's understanding of the necessary role of models in autobiography serves as an instructive example of how the self's uniqueness can be integrated with the norms of culture. Thus Franklin's *Autobiography* is a significant resource in our task of reconceptualizing individuality in socially responsible terms.

4. *Conformity to social conventions.* The modern aversion to models of selfhood is closely related to later autobiographers' perception of another threat to individuality: the roles and conventions of society. Franklin was apparently not much troubled by the problem of discrepancies between the self's public appearance and an underlying reality. One of the most-quoted passages in the *Autobiography* recounts how Franklin carefully cultivated the image of an industrious businessman: 'In order to secure my Credit and Character as a Tradesman, I took care not only to be in *Reality* Industrious and frugal, but to avoid all *Appearances* of the Contrary' (54). This statement is usually taken as evidence that Franklin was a hypocrite. He never seems to worry that fulfilling the expectations of a social role might compromise some aspect of himself. Individuality for Franklin never involves the negative relationship with society's expectations that is part of the modern notion of authenticity.[39] From such an adversarial perspective, conventionality means conformity, and conformity means falseness to and betrayal of the self's individuality. The critical view of conventions and the adversarial stance towards society expressed so powerfully by Rousseau are not asserted until several decades later in American literary history, in the writings of Emerson and Thoreau. For Emerson the supreme virtue of self-reliance is defined as nonconformity:

Society is a joint-stock company, in which the members agree, for the better securing of his bread to each shareholder, to surrender the liberty and culture of the eater. The virtue in most request is conformity. Self-reliance is its aversion. It loves not realities and creators, but names and customs. Whoso would be a man, must be a nonconformist.[40]

Self-reliance was important to Franklin, too, but his path to it, though extremely creative and original, often involved accommodation to the expectations of his social milieu. When he deviated from conventions he did not advertise this fact, nor make it the basis for a claim of virtue.

Later American autobiographers have generally followed Emerson and Thoreau rather than Franklin, and have perceived compliance with convention as a threat to individuality. While there are good reasons for autobiographers' critical stance towards many American conventions, the Emersonian tradition mistakenly severs the connections between self-development and cultivation of one's society. It has not always acknowledged that the isolated self has no more individuality than the conformist. The adversarial stance to society brings new threats to individuality, in the forms of *anomie*, alienation, and disenchantment with social existence itself. While Franklin's social world did not pose the same obstacles to self-development as that of twentieth-century America, his autobiography offers an understanding of the interdependence of self and society which should be a resource for communitarian critics of individualism.

5. *Impersonal power.*   Franklin's view of the self seems remote from more recent conceptions because of another modern threat to individuality. Franklin optimistically assumed an easy harmony of interests in a simpler society and an expanding economy. In his world an individual confronts other individuals, but not impersonal and institutionalized power. Looming threats to individuality were discerned in the nineteenth century in the forms of industrialization, growing bureaucracy, and massive concentrations of power. For Henry Adams, the great scope and power of impersonal forces frustrated the task of self-definition, defeating his searches for meaningful vocation and a comprehensive understanding of his social world. The threats of impersonal power and baffling social complexity present obstacles to individuality which Franklin did not consider. According to some social critics, individuality has no viability under these social conditions, and should be discredited as an outmoded guide to identity. In my view, however, the greater difficulty and precariousness of individuality since Franklin's day makes all the more pressing the need to appropriate, selectively

and critically, the best resources from the cultural tradition of individuality.

6. *The completed self.* Franklin's *Autobiography* is essentially a memoir, a record of public achievements and the character-formation which was their condition. The formation of Franklin's personality is basically completed when he returns from London in 1726; thereafter we see his character's effects on Philadelphia and the world. The form of the second half of the book (parts III and IV) deteriorates into a rambling series of anecdotes, a chronicle of public projects each illustrating a lesson that Franklin formulates in a nutshell. It is significant that we lose interest in Franklin's autobiography just when he becomes wholly identified with his public projects and his commitments to various institutions. For the book then duplicates the official documents of history, describing the actions of a public servant but not revealing any complexity to or hidden aspects of Franklin's character. The autobiography displays little consciousness of a constantly developing sense of individuality, and no interest in how the autobiographical act itself necessitates further reformulations of identity. Franklin records his achievement of individuality as a young man, but the autobiography does not itself represent an act of new discovery. The end-point of self-development does not continually recede as is the case for a writer such as Malcolm X. Franklin's portrayal of a stable and completed self with a firmly established identity differs markedly in this respect from many later autobiographers. For many of the writers who now seem to us most compelling, any fixed identity is experienced as a threat to individuality. Franklin's limited con-sciousness of the self's historicity, then, suggests another respect in which later autobiographers have perceived very different threats to individuality. For writers such as Malcolm X, the self which ceases to change and develop is no longer fully alive. Individuality for many modern autobiographers becomes a lifelong task or process – what Jung calls the individuation process – rather than a permanent achievement.

An appreciation for the historical quality of human existence and for transformations of identity throughout a person's lifetime changes the way that individuality is understood, as Weintraub explains:

> These two different strains – the idea of development and the idea of individuality – eventually merged and interpenetrated

one another . . . . For he who traces a historical development has an implicit interest in the precise moment, the constellation, the specific way in which specific factors interact and result in a new configuration of factors. In the idea of development the idea of individuality found an agency of explanation. For only by telling the story could one account for the continuous differentiation of reality into viable specifications of unique value, a logically undefinable quantity and quality. The two notions interacted, interpenetrated, and in their fusion reinforced one another. The historical way of looking at the world acquired a profound respect for the value of the specified particularity of every historical moment; the specificity of individuality could be made intelligible as a historical phenomenon.[41]

Weintraub sees this fusion of a historicist consciousness and a valuation of the unique individual for the first time in Goethe. Franklin wrote before modern historical consciousness was joined with the romantic sense of individuality. His view of what threatens the self is correspondingly different. He fears not fixity of identity but diffuseness, not rigidity of character but vacillation, not confinement to a specific place in his society, but exile in Barbados. Yet although his understanding of the self now seems to us insufficiently historical, there is much in Franklin's sensibility that speaks to the malaise of modern individualism. His example suggests the need for continuity of character amidst continuing development. The threats to the achievement of individuality he discerned are still with us, along with new ones.

The model of the self Franklin created in his autobiography reveals both benefits and costs, both advantages and dangers, in that tangle of ideas which we call individualism. What the communitarian critics attack – the way he participates in practices, his utilitarian outlook, and his detached assessment of his communities – in fact reflect concerns Franklin shares with his detractors. His critics seem to me misguided because they challenge, not Franklin's limitations, but some of his genuine strengths as a social thinker. Franklin's picture of the individual in society should serve the critics' constructive purpose: calling for the integration of 'individualism and commitment in American life' (as the subtitle of *Habits* puts it), rather than an either/or choice. On the other hand, we have discerned some of Franklin's limitations by comparing his view of the threats to individuality with the concerns articulated by later autobiographers. His virtues – prudent practicality, concern for the common good, curious and versatile intellect, ironic tolerance for roles and appearances, and methodical discipline – contributed to a model of the individual whose limitations inspired the most creative American writers to search for forms of individuality reflecting other dimensions of human existence: the aesthetic, the affective, the organic or biological, the spiritual. Yet his view of the individual can serve as a corrective to the excesses of the 'no-model model' of the self which culminates in the adversarial stance towards society. He demonstrates how the formation of personal identity may proceed hand-in-glove with the development of an active social conscience.

We should neither simply endorse nor reject all aspects of Franklin's individualism or his view of individuality. By distinguishing and assessing some of the aspects of 'individualism' his autobiography epitomizes, we have seen how this book contributes to the current debate about the sources of social commitment, and how it illuminates some contemporary threats to the ideal of individuality.

6

Ressentiment, Public Virtues, and Malcolm X

In this chapter I interpret *The Autobiography of Malcolm X* in terms of the ethical problem of *ressentiment* and the corresponding need for public virtues. The problem of *ressentiment*, or animosity towards human otherness, will be linked to the need for 'public' virtues, those moral qualities affirmed to be normative for the members of every community. I will first explicate the issues at stake in terms of ethical theory, and then turn to Malcolm's autobiography for significant insights into forms of *ressentiment* and into the nature of the public virtues. *The Autobiography of Malcolm X* reveals the workings of conscience as Malcolm struggled to recognize *ressentiment* in his own experience and to practice his conception of the public virtues.

I RESSENTIMENT

The concept of *ressentiment* as I shall use it refers to envy and malice felt towards the persons and values of other traditions. As we shall see, this is a somewhat broader use of the term than Nietzsche's original meaning. *Ressentiment* is a negative reaction to human otherness, whether in the form of religious, racial, sexual, linguistic, or cultural difference. Such attitudes are usually repressed but can erupt in outbreaks of irrational violence. *Ressentiment* is not exactly the same as resentment, which may be morally justified when a person is denied some essential good as a result of the wrongful conduct of others or unjust social institutions.[1] Therefore, in spite of its awkwardness, the term *ressentiment* cannot be replaced by the English word resentment. *Ressentiment* is always a negative moral characteristic – that is, a vice – which leads to continuing rancor and

hostility towards those who are different from oneself, and sometimes to vindictive and purely destructive outbursts of violence.
It is not simply the human tendency to mistrust unfamiliar ways
or persons, but a more complex process involving the projection of
evil, the rationalization of longings for revenge, and the denigration
of the very being of another form of humanity.

The original concept of *ressentiment* is part of Nietzsche's theory
that Christian morality began in a revolt of the weak against the
strong, and in the substitution of ideals of charity and resignation
for the heroic virtues of the aristocratic tradition. *Ressentiment* is an
attitude of negation which arises from the repression of feelings of
hatred, envy, and revenge:

> The slave revolt in morality begins when *ressentiment* itself
> becomes creative and gives birth to values: the *ressentiment*
> of natures that are denied the true reaction, that of deeds,
> and compensate themselves with an imaginary revenge. While
> every noble morality develops from a triumphant affirmation
> of itself, slave morality from the outset says No to what is
> 'outside,' what is 'different,' what is 'not itself'; and this No
> is its creative deed. This inversion of the value-positing eye
> – this need to direct one's view outward instead of back to
> oneself – is of the essence of *ressentiment*: in order to exist, slave
> morality always first needs a hostile external world; it needs,
> physiologically speaking, external stimuli in order to act at all
> – its action is fundamentally reaction.[2]

For Nietzsche, *ressentiment* is the slave's making a virtue of necessity, being humble and kindly only because he is too weak or timid
to do what he would really like to do. This moral facade conceals
impotent hatred and a lust for revenge.[3]

Max Scheler tied the genesis of *ressentiment* to the effect of certain
positions and roles within a social hierarchy. He located its deepest
roots not in Christian values but in bourgeois morality. Scheler
focused on ways in which group identities and social structures
shape the animosities and conflicts among individuals. Two aspects
of his analysis are particularly significant for our study of the role of
ressentiment in autobiography. First, Scheler holds that *ressentiment*
involves envy for something that cannot be attained. It therefore
produces a form of conflict which seems peculiarly motiveless or
purposeless, and which is unrealistic in that it is not directed at an

attainable goal. Envy leads to *ressentiment* 'when the coveted values are such as cannot be acquired and lie in the sphere in which we compare ourselves to others'.[4] The strongest source of *ressentiment* is what Scheler calls 'existential envy, which is directed against the other person's very nature'. Such envy 'whispers continually: "I can forgive everything, but not that you *are* – that you are *what* you are – that I am not what you are – indeed that I am not *you*."' *Ressentiment* involves animosity for the values and innate characteristics of other persons, which are felt as a reproach simply because they are not one's own. This deep-rooted, irrational, and apparently motiveless hatred can develop between the members of different races and traditions, erupting in violence whose only cause seems to be the fact that others are different. Recognition of forms of *ressentiment* in oneself requires scrutiny of one's conception of identity in contrast to others, as well as a scrupulous conscience. This concept will help us define a crucial aspect of the autobiographer's moral struggle.

Scheler's analysis suggests a second reason that *ressentiment* may be a valuable concept in interpreting the conscience of an autobiographer. *Ressentiment* develops partly in reaction to the need for repression of overtly hostile behavior, and yet it culminates in the moral rationalization of negative feelings. Scheler saw priests and religious leaders as especially prone to *ressentiment* because of their need to suppress negative attitudes and to present an appearance of peacefulness and good will. When direct expression of negative feelings is suppressed, a process of rationalization may begin which authorizes one to denigrate the values of another person or group and to long to retaliate against them for real or imagined insults. *Ressentiment* has a moral dimension in that it involves justification of revenge. 'It is of the essence of revenge that it always contains the consciousness of "tit for tat," so that it is never a mere emotional reaction.' The apostate often reveals the power of *ressentiment* as he engages in 'a continuous chain of acts of revenge against his own spiritual past'.[5]

Thus *ressentiment* is a feeling of vindictiveness and malice which is repressed from overt expression but secretly nourished by a sense of injured honor, and which comes to justify itself as a duty. *Ressentiment* occurs when self-discipline comes about because of a feeling of impotence, and it involves rationalization of hostile attitudes. Moral constraints inhibit the expression of negative feelings, and moral rationalization allows a person to nurse his or her ill will and denigrate the values of the persons or traditions envied. The genesis of *ressentiment* is, then, deeply rooted in certain processes of conscience, which may demand the suppression of overt negative behavior and yet rationalize the denigration of the other.

Fredric Jameson has argued that in nineteenth-century fiction *ressentiment* operates as a key 'ideologeme': a class-based worldview that may be projected either as a philosophy or value system or as a form of narrative. An ideologeme shapes the structure of a narrative genre by providing the terms for an 'imaginary resolution of the objective contradictions to which it constitutes an active response'.[6] Jameson's Marxist orientation leads him to see *ressentiment* as fundamentally a phenomenon arising out of antagonisms based on economic class. A novel's depiction of conflicts between other forms of human identity is a 'displacement' of the basic struggle for power between economic classes. For Jameson *ressentiment* is universal and inescapable: those in power as well as those without power tend to denigrate the 'other' because he or she is different from themselves. Not only the weak and impotent feel *ressentiment* (as Nietzsche and Scheler argued), but also the powerful, because of their fear of losing power. Jameson sees the literary representation of *ressentiment* in the powerless as a 'strategy of containment' used by conservative authors such as Conrad and Gissing to discredit certain characters' desire for revolutionary social change. The strategic deployment of *ressentiment* in a literary text – its ascription as the underlying motivation of movements for social change – therefore reflects the author's own *ressentiment*. There seems to be no possibility of transcending a particular position within the class struggle, either for the author, the literary characters, or the reader. This view of the inevitability of *ressentiment* in class conflicts reflects Jameson's basic distrust and rejection of 'ethics': 'Ethical thought projects as permanent features of human "experience," and thus as a kind of "wisdom" about personal life and interpersonal relations, what are in reality the historical and institutional specifics of a determinate type of group solidarity or class cohesion.' For Jameson the very distinction between good and evil serves to discredit other social classes: 'Ethics itself . . . is the ideological vehicle and the legitimation of concrete structures of power and domination.'[7] Ethical reflection is a deception; for him there is only politics and the taking of sides.

I will use the term *ressentiment*, as does Jameson, to speak of a somewhat broader phenomenon than Nietzsche's narrower definition. My focus will be on animosity towards human otherness or difference, a fairly common problem which is not confined to the powerless or slave types whom Nietzsche contrasted with the noble individual. I would extend Nietzsche's insights into how the elements of reactivity, frustrated weakness, and the projection of evil can create deep-rooted suspicion and hostility towards human otherness. Like Jameson, I think *ressentiment* operates between many categories of 'otherness'.[8] *Ressentiment* is an appropriate and helpful term for exploring conflicts between groups defined in terms of racial, national, sexual, political, or religious identities. The concept of *ressentiment* provides a useful point of entry for the critic concerned with the sources of conflict between different groups. It alerts one to attend to the specific 'blind spots', misconceptions, and prejudices that prevent cooperation and mutual respect. To read a narrative as a symbolic mediation between forms of otherness, the critic needs some such general concept for the factors that produce contention and moral conflict. If one essential value of literature is, as Giles Gunn puts it, to present forms of otherness so that we may imagine 'that something else might be the case', literature is equally valuable in showing us why 'something else' is *not* the case for us.[9] That is, literature's moral significance also involves exploring why separate identities and differing values can prevent persons from understanding and appreciating each other, and in exploring why they perceive particular forms of otherness as alien and threatening. Literary narratives may help us to understand why appeals to the deepest loyalties, commitments, and sources of identity, although they resolve some moral quandaries, also create new problems.

However, my understanding of *ressentiment* differs from Jameson's in that I think the moral dynamic of many significant modern works of literature, especially autobiographies and novels, centers on a struggle to transcend *ressentiment*. Certain authors and characters are able to overcome ethnocentric prejudices and animosity. Even when such an act of transcendence is not dramatized explicitly within the text, a literary work may call on the reader to extend his or her moral imagination in this manner. The notion of a false consciousness distorted by *ressentiment* necessarily implies a standard of authentic or true consciousness: the possibility of a more adequate understanding of the 'other', encompassing sympathy, judgment, and respect. Equally at stake is the possibility of a more authentic self, based not on reaction to others but on an unimpeachable, primary sense of self-worth. Interpretation of narratives should therefore not only focus on how *ressentiment* shapes political interests and ideological loyalties, but should also address the self-critical insights an author suggests. The moral significance of such narratives lies in the recognitions and reversals of judgment required of narrators, characters, and readers as they encounter threatening forms of otherness. Read in such a way, literature can be interpreted as a symbolic presentation not only of the conflicts arising because of *ressentiment* between different classes and groups, but also as an exploration of the possibilities for a pluralistic public community that respects diverse forms of otherness. Certain works of literature – such as *The Autobiography of Malcolm X* – enact the kind of insights that must be achieved before particular groups will willingly participate in – or allow 'marginal' others to join – a public. As we shall see, the possibility of moral transcendence of *ressentiment* is a central issue in Malcolm X's autobiography. In Malcolm's work, such transcendence hinges on the ability of conscience to distinguish between *ressentiment* and morally legitimate resentment of injustice.

In summary, a critical focus on *ressentiment* illuminates essential moral conflicts explored in many literary narratives. The struggle to overcome *ressentiment* may be one of the most challenging tasks for the conscience of an autobiographer. And the need to overcome the problem of *ressentiment* may explain and justify an autobiographer's concern with the public virtues.

II PUBLIC VIRTUES

Public virtues are moral qualities affirmed to be normative for any person from any community, not simply for the members of a particular community. I use the term 'public virtues' in this essay not in contrast with private or individual virtues, but in contrast with a particularistic understanding of virtue. The particularist view understands virtue as grounded solely in the interests and values of one group or sect, without regard for the concerns of larger or different groups. Recent work on the role of the virtues in morality has reflected the particularist view of morality and has minimized the importance and even the possibility of public virtues. For Stanley Hauerwas and Alasdair MacIntyre, any specific account of the virtues presupposes and must be displayed in a narrative which represents the structure and the unity of a worth-while human life.[10] Since pluralistic contemporary societies lack both common narratives and any shared notion of the telos of the good life, no understanding of the virtues can be truly public. Hauerwas and MacIntyre criticize the attempt of modern liberalism to found morality on requirements held to be binding on the members of different religious traditions. Such requirements merely guarantee formal correctness of procedure or minimal standards of justice, but do not identify the primary ends individuals should seek. Because of their emphasis on the narrative-dependency of morality, MacIntyre and Hauerwas would probably view a contemporary conception of the public virtues as misguided since we lack the common narrative that would allow us to display the meaning of such virtues. At the most, they would see the public virtues as secondary in morality, enjoining persons only to be tolerant of those from other traditions. This particularist understanding of morality provides no grounds for holding that certain virtues might be morally required of all persons in a pluralistic society.[11]

However skeptical Hauerwas and MacIntyre would be about the possibility of truly public virtues, their emphasis on the importance of the virtues in the moral life is extremely significant. Much ethical thought, both philosophical and theological, has seen the role of the virtues and character as at best a supplement to the foundation of morality in universalizable rules and principles. A conception of the public virtues can therefore be expected to meet criticism both from a position like that of Hauerwas and MacIntyre, who will see in it an impossible attempt to impose universal moral requirements on persons from different traditions, and also from those ethical thinkers who believe that an emphasis on the virtues and character opens up the abyss of moral relativism and does not provide a firm basis for making normative claims. However, I propose that exploring conceptions of the public virtues provides a fruitful way of understanding both common concerns and differences between various religious and cultural traditions. It also explains one way in which the members of a community make normative claims or evaluations of those outside the community. Reflection on the public virtues is a significant intermediate step between understanding the uniqueness of particular moral traditions and the necessary generality and abstractness of attempts to formulate universal ethical norms which can adjudicate disputes between different communities.

Historical communities have usually asserted the need not only for those virtues that find their telos in a direct contribution to the internal life of their community, but also for public virtues.

These virtues are public in the sense that their necessity arises from contact, conflict, and potential strife with the members of other moral communities. Such virtues are affirmed partly because of the perception of the threats that *ressentiment* poses for the ongoing life of the community. Though the public virtues are not sufficient to guide a person's entire life, most moral traditions affirm that certain virtues are absolutely necessary because without them strife with other communities becomes so intense and insoluble as to endanger the community's central tasks. In addition, many traditions assert the value of public virtues because of positive convictions about the dignity, equality, or freedom of persons outside their community. Assertions of the need for public virtues may appeal to three rationales: self-interest in the avoidance of conflict, a disinterested recognition of the rights or the worth of others, or a notion of the common good.

One conception of the public virtues has strong roots in the Christian tradition's understanding of natural law. However, the natural law tradition after Aquinas has usually interpreted common moral requirements as rules in the form of moral prohibitions rather than as desireable characteristics or virtues. A contemporary theory of the public virtues must show that such virtues are not merely a matter of following rules. Neither are public virtues simply a matter of tolerance or indifference to the particularity and differentness of the 'other'. Tolerance is essential, but it is too weak a notion to express the needs for active good will, for genuine appreciation of the otherness of different traditions, and for commitment to a search for common values and concerns. The public virtues involve active striving for the common good and for the well-being of persons from other traditions.

We cannot simply go back to Aquinas for a conception of the public virtues – what he called the natural virtues – even though his thought is one of the richest theoretical resources for reflection on the virtues. We need to explore the differences and conflicts between various understandings of the virtues, without assuming a universally acceptable account of their meaning. Even when different traditions affirm in common the need for a virtue such as justice, they may mean quite different things by the same term. What needs to be sought is not simply a recommendation of a list of virtues, but understanding of what such virtues have meant and might now mean in particular contexts. That conceptions of such virtues differ seems to some ethical thinkers to open up all the problems of moral relativism. But the existence of contrasting views of the public virtues can also be a significant factor in creating the possibility of dialogue between moral traditions. Though different traditions or individuals do not mean exactly the same thing by 'justice' or 'honesty', the shared recognition that certain virtues are essential to any worthwhile human life is sometimes the point of contact necessary for communities to begin to understand each other and to find common needs and values. There are differences but also essential continuities and possible alliances between alternative conceptions of the public virtues.

In exploring understandings of the public virtues, we should draw upon neglected resources in every moral tradition: the narratives of the moral life. Understanding the concrete meaning of a virtue involves seeing how a narrative shows it functioning over a period of time. Every tradition includes narratives which display the meaning of the public virtues by dramatizing confrontations between the members of different moral communities. For instance, a public virtue is presented in Jesus's parable of the good Samaritan, which points to the need to overcome that kind of *ressentiment* and moral insularity that often prevents persons from responding to those outside their own religious tradition. In addition to sacred texts from religious traditions, the attempt to understand the meaning of certain public virtues has been especially important in many modern narratives. Since the seventeenth century one of the central and most insoluble moral issues has been how to maintain peace and ensure co-operation between different groups within the same society. The autobiography and the novel are the primary narratives of this historical period. Many narrative accounts of the moral life explore the problem of *ressentiment* (though they do not rely on this concept to explain the phenomenon), and present the author or certain characters as exemplifying the public virtues necessary to achieve mutual respect and good will in a pluralistic society. Among autobiographies, Benjamin Franklin's work is one of the clearest examples of such an understanding of public virtues, explicating Franklin's famous list of thirteen virtues and what he believed to be the essentials of every religion. Partly because of the problem of *ressentiment* between different groups, the search for public virtues increasingly became the moral center of many of the most significant novels of the nineteenth and twentieth centuries. For example, public virtues underlie the acts of empathy and imagination that enable characters such as Aziz and Mrs. Moore in Forster's *A Passage to*

India to try to understand and respect persons from other traditions, in marked contrast to other characters in that novel.

Analysis of autobiographical narratives can be of crucial significance in exploring the meaning of the public virtues in different traditions, and in showing how the members of different traditions sometimes recognize that they share a common concern with a particular virtue. The critical approach I am suggesting can be illustrated by briefly explaining how the virtue of intellectual justice shapes Newman's *Apologia Pro Vita Sua*. Newman was widely perceived to have emerged as the victor from his controversy with Kingsley in spite of widespread suspicion, open prejudice, and *ressentiment* against Catholics in Britain. He obviously did not have to convert his audience to vindicate his name and his ideas. How could such a polemical debate be resolved despite the lack of religious consensus?

The operation of certain public virtues such as what may be termed 'intellectual justice' makes possible standards by which discourse is judged. Such virtues provide the normative terms to which differing religious positions appeal in their apologetics. In Newman's case the basic aspect of intellectual justice in question was Kingsley's 'charge of Untruthfulness'. Newman welcomed his public's judgment about this matter:

> There are virtues indeed, which the world is not fitted to judge of or to uphold, such as faith, hope, and charity; but it can judge about Truthfulness; it can judge about the natural virtues, and Truthfulness is one of them . . . . Mankind has the right to judge the Truthfulness in a Catholic, as in the case of a Protestant, of an Italian, or of a Chinese.[12]

Truthfulness is an indispensable condition of fairness in evaluating a position with which one disagrees in substance. The *Apologia*, partly through its vivid contrast with Kingsley's vague insinuations about Newman's earlier veracity, provides a classic example of a sustained attempt at intellectual justice in meeting the objections and doubts that could be raised against each stage in the development of Newman's beliefs. Documenting his practice of this virtue requires Newman to show the temporal unfolding of his ideas and his reasons for making them public or not doing so. Thus the ideal of intellectual justice shapes the entire structure of argument in the *Apologia*. Newman's view of intellectual justice requires that certain publicly-valued qualities of mind and character be rendered in his use of language. His writing is a strategy for achieving the norm of intellectual justice invoked at the outset of his autobiography. As much as it is an effort to convince others of the substantive truth of his beliefs, Newman's work is an attempt to vindicate his name by demonstrating and documenting his practice of this public virtue over the course of his career. Analysis of exemplary narrative texts, then, is a significant way of understanding the public virtues.

Of course, that Newman was able to persuade the British public of his veracity hardly guarantees that the public virtues will always resolve or clarify disputes. It clearly is not assured that the members of different traditions will recognize that a public virtue is essential in a particular context and has or has not been practiced. In fact, appeal to the public virtues is sometimes futile or actually divisive. This suggests the need for reflection on the conditions of possibility for a fruitful appeal to the public virtues. The goal is not to formulate rules, but to think about what facilitates or inhibits the exercise of the public virtues, as Hume's 'Of the Standard of Taste' sought to define the qualities that contribute to or interfere with good aesthetic judgment. The factors that make possible or hinder agreement about the meaning and practical implications of a virtue like justice are not only a matter of personal disposition; one must also consider certain cultural factors, such as the metaphors with which persons interpret their lives. In particular, specific conventions and styles of selfhood can inhibit or prevent fruitful discourse between the members of different communities by precluding a positive understanding of the public virtues.

Contemporary appeals to public or common virtues often seem to generate suspicion, mistrust, or animosity towards the very idea of widely-shared moral norms. The deeply-rooted desire for 'authenticity' plays a role in this phenomenon. In *Sincerity and Authenticity*, Lionel Trilling defined the historical evolution of these two idioms for selfhood, tracing the roots of 'authenticity' in works by Rousseau, Hegel, and Conrad, and its function as a normative ideal for contemporary thinkers such as Sartre, Marcuse, and R. D. Laing. 'From Rousseau we learned that what destroys our authenticity is society – our sentiment of being depends upon the opinion of other people.'[13] The ideal of authentic being gradually came to include an intention of 'offensiveness'. 'That this is so suggests that authenticity is implicitly a polemical concept, fulfilling its nature by dealing aggressively with received and habitual opinion.'[14] Since to be authentic means to reject the public conventions and norms of one's society, the ideal of authenticity directly precludes the possibility of agreement about – and often even discussion of – the public virtues.

Authentic selfhood increasingly seems to require opposition to and protest against a status quo. The belief that the self, or an intentional or religious community, can only achieve authentic identity by secession from the imposed constraints of society is no longer limited to a few eccentric intellectuals, that elite group of artists and intellectuals that Trilling called 'the adversary culture'. A basic feature of modern pluralistic societies is the rejection of common moral standards such as ideals of public virtue. Any moral convention claiming public authority is resented as an obstacle to authenticity. A varied assortment of 'authentic' selves and groups all define themselves – sometimes with good reason and sometimes without – against their sense of a repressive and restraining public culture. This situation creates difficulties for the possibility of intelligible public discourse about matters of common concern. Even the 'table manners' to be observed at public discussions – qualities like restraint, decorum, and civility – come to be perceived as conformist, establishmentarian, 'inauthentic'. The notion that authenticity can only be achieved by rebelling against constraining rules and common values is an underlying reason for hostility to the notion of public virtues.

When the desire for authenticity does not produce strident opposition to the very idea of common public virtues, it often results in a quieter but just as fatal indifference or cynicism about their value: they are seen as a matter of merely procedural rules or conventional decorum rather than as active good will or commitment to the common good. This fatalism about public life often results from a particularist understanding of the virtues and the moral life. The authentic virtuous life can only be anti-authoritarian for Alasdair MacIntyre and seems to require withdrawal from the moral issues of public life. MacIntyre is skeptical about the value of any moral qualities that all the members of a pluralistic society can agree upon. His antipathy to the procedural norms and manipulative practices of the 'managers' and 'experts' of modern bureaucracies leads him to emphasize the need for more local forms of morality based on small communities like the Benedictine monasteries. The modern period, in which 'pluralist political rhetoric' only masks insoluble conflicts between competing moral traditions, reminds

MacIntyre of the Dark Ages; he concludes by calling for 'new forms of community within which the moral life could be sustained so that both morality and civility might survive the coming ages of barbarism and darkness'.[15]

The practice of monastic virtues, however, can make only a very indirect contribution to the necessarily public tasks of adjudicating conflicts and devising compromises between the different communities within a pluralistic society. Although MacIntyre laments the Hobbesian struggle for power that results from modern liberal individualism, his own understanding of morality provides no basis for evaluating when public authority is exercised with moral responsibility. As much as the individualist self he criticizes, MacIntyre himself seems to view moral norms broadly applicable in a pluralist society as destructive of the individual's own identity and traditions and thus of his or her authenticity. If it is believed that identity is achieved not through consensus, negotiation, and compromise but through either conflict with authority or withdrawal from public life, the practice of the public virtues can only be seen as an obstacle to the achievement of authenticity. The practice of the public virtues, however, should be understood not as a means of masking or disguising conflict, but as a means of articulating its causes and making disputes less violent and more fruitful. The reason we need such virtues is not to minimize the value of particularist loyalties and commitments, but to ensure their survival by attending to essential problems of social co-operation and reconciliation. To secure effective and widespread consent, any conception of the public virtues must allay the fear that the distinctiveness of separate identities and unique concerns will be sacrificed to a repressive, constraining public authority that only masks the interests of the status quo.

Moral 'styles' such as authenticity are best interpreted and evaluated in a culture's narrative accounts of moral action. A culture's or religious tradition's styles of moral selfhood, which so decisively affect conceptions of the public virtues, are critically accessible as they shape action and character in myth, literature, and autobiography. In literary narratives we can sometimes observe 'the moral life in process of revising itself, perhaps by reducing the emphasis it formerly placed upon one or another of its elements, perhaps by inventing and adding to itself a new element, some mode of conduct or of feeling which hitherto it had not regarded as essential to virtue'.[16] The literary critic, then, may provide valuable insights to the theologian and the philosopher concerned about contemporary society's moral pluralism. For instance, analysis of *ressentiment* may provide significant insights into one of the deepest moral problems confronting religious and cultural traditions that must coexist. The literary critic has a substantial and unique contribution to make to discussions of the nature of morality in a pluralistic society. For when a sense of the meaning and the value of the public virtues is not felt, it cannot be created simply by insisting on its moral necessity. Concern for the public virtues may be encouraged, however, through the long process of diagnosing and understanding the ways ignorance, blind spots, biases, and misunderstanding create *ressentiment* between different groups. Commitment to the public virtues may be nurtured, too, through exploring how certain narrative works help us to imagine a more positive but realistically conceived vision of a truly public common life. In this project, *The Autobiography of Malcolm X* seems to me exemplary.

III   THE EXAMPLE OF MALCOLM X

Malcolm's family was the victim of repeated acts of racism and violence. His father and five of six uncles were to 'die by the white man's hands' (2), and Malcolm held that 'if ever a state social agency destroyed a family, it destroyed ours' (21).[17] Even when white persons tried to act kindly towards him, as when they treated him as their 'mascot', Malcolm perceived deep-rooted condescension based on attitudes of racial superiority. This unconscious racism in even the most well-meaning whites revealed their intensely negative response to the difference and otherness of black persons:

> What I am trying to say is that it just never dawned upon them that I could understand, that I wasn't a pet, but a human being. They didn't give me credit for having the same sensitivity, intellect, and understanding that they would have been ready and willing to recognize in a white boy in my position . . . . Thus they never did really see *me*. (27)

Even when one of the 'so-called "good white people"' sides with blacks, Malcolm claims that 'when the chips are down, you'll find that as fixed in him as his bone structure is his sometimes subconscious conviction that he's better than anybody black' (27). The first turning-point in Malcolm's life comes when his English teacher, Mr. Ostrowski, tells him that in spite of his remarkable mind Malcolm could never be a lawyer and should choose a 'realistic goal for a nigger'. The teacher did not mean his student any personal harm, but his remark brought home to Malcolm the inevitable failure of white persons to recognize the individuality and full humanity of blacks: 'It was just in his nature as an American white man. I was one of his top students, one of the school's top students – but all he could see for me was the kind of future "in your place" that almost all white people see for black people' (36).

Malcolm's career as a hustler in Harlem confirms his conviction that, even when the white man seeks out the culture or the flesh of black persons, he despises them. It is not simply racial prejudice that Malcolm discerns, but *ressentiment*, for white people were deeply attracted towards and envied the very qualities of blacks that they rejected and denigrated. Whites were drawn to the music, dancing, food, and drink of Harlem nightclubs, 'just mad for Negro "atmosphere," . . . Negro *soul*' (93). Under the influence of liquor, whites embraced blacks in a parody of genuine equality: 'A lot of the whites, drunk, would go staggering up to Negroes, the waiters, the owners, or Negroes at tables, wringing their hands, even trying to hug them. "You're just as good as I am – I want you to know that!"' (111–12). Malcolm discerns beneath this facade of camaraderie the underlying contempt with which whites used black people to satisfy their various cravings: 'Harlem was their sin-den, their fleshpot. They stole off among taboo black people, and took off whatever antiseptic, important, dignified masks they wore in their white world' (119). Even a 'hippy' who 'acted more Negro than Negroes' exposes his belief that a white woman should not 'throw herself away with a spade' (94). Malcolm's experience as a pimp strongly influenced his nearly life-long conviction that sexual relations between the races always involved mutual exploitation. His autobiography is full of insights into the ways that whites denigrate the worth of blacks because of their otherness, their difference. Beneath particular incidents of racial animosity, acts of cruelty, and injustice lies the phenomenon of *ressentiment*.

It is not only whites who have this reaction to otherness, however; Malcolm discerns a somewhat different form of animosity in black persons. As Nietzsche and Scheler pointed out, it is especially those in positions of social dependence or inferiority who are likely to feel *ressentiment*. Malcolm believed that the American black person tried to emulate whites because of deep feelings of shame and self-hatred. The symbol of this for Malcolm was his own attempt to 'conk' or straighten his hair:

> This was my first really big step toward self-degradation: when I endured all of that pain, literally burning my flesh to have it look like a white man's hair. I had joined that multitude of Negro men and women in America who are brainwashed into believing that the black people are 'inferior' – and white people 'superior' – that they will even violate and mutilate their God-created bodies to try to look 'pretty' by white standards. (54)

Emulation of the other appears antithetical to the denigration usually associated with *ressentiment*. But in fact *ressentiment* involves both attraction to and repulsion from the other, because of his or her difference from one's own sense of identity. For the dominant white, denial of the humanity of blacks can be expressed overtly, and attraction to blacks is a 'taboo' secret. Condescension and violence are constantly manifested, while envy is usually latent. For an oppressed black person in the 1950's, in contrast, power and status were sought primarily through attempts to appropriate the symbols of whiteness, while hatred of whites was usually repressed. According to Malcolm, even as a black person's envy motivates acts of emulation, hatred – of both the self and whites – festers. In both cases, for whites and for blacks in America, a person reacts with ambivalence to the other, paradoxically both denying the worth of the other and envying just those qualities that make him or her different. In the case of each race, responding to another person solely in terms of his or her membership in a group makes impossible a genuine understanding of his or her individuality and specific actions.

Malcolm was largely freed from the curse of self-hatred when, during his six years in prison, he converted to the Nation of Islam, the so-called 'Black Muslims'. This religion gave Malcolm two things: black pride and a mythology justifying hatred of the white man. Malcolm's faith as a Black Muslim helped him to recover his sense of self-worth, and oriented him towards the message of black pride that he delivered for the rest of his life. It also gave him a demonology: 'The white man is the devil' (159). Malcolm asserts that a black prison convict will find personifying evil in whites to be the best explanation of his experience in American society. 'Among all Negroes the black convict is the most perfectly preconditioned to hear the words, "the white man is the devil"' (183). The Black Muslim doctrine that the white man is the devil provides a religious justification for hatred of another race, a divine authorization for a racial form of *ressentiment*.

In prison, writes Malcolm, 'I made up my mind to devote the rest of my life to telling the white man about himself – or die' (185). Throughout his autobiography, Malcolm probes the reasons why white persons reacted with outrage to his attempts to tell the truth about racism in the United States. The overwhelming public reaction to the growing prominence of the Black Muslims was shock and denunciation of their 'preaching hate of white people' (238). 'Here was one of the white man's most characteristic behavior patterns – where black men are concerned. He loves himself so much that he is startled if he discovers that his victims don't share his vainglorious self-opinion' (238–9). Unlike Europeans, the American white man was 'plagued and obsessed with being "hated." He was so guilty, it was clear to me, of hating Negroes' (240). The theme of the white person's inability to recognize and accept guilt and responsibility for the suffering of blacks is prominent in Malcolm's work. His explanation of this white denial implies the psychological theory of projection; the white man's guilt for past racial violence and his present hatred were attributed to blacks. Malcolm implies that the projection of evil onto other human groups is linked to *ressentiment*, the view of the other as intrinsically evil and 'hateful'. The psychological process and the metaphysical claim about the other reinforce each other. Although Malcolm X never used the term *ressentiment*, he had a profound understanding of how it operated in human experience.

The second major shift in Malcolm X's ideas and allegiances came when, after being 'silenced' by the Black Muslims and hearing rumors of his death having been approved, he went to Mecca and was converted to Islam. As a result of his travels to Arabia and then to Black Africa, Malcolm began to understand how *ressentiment* had characterized his life as a Black Muslim. At the same time, he began to speak of public virtues. The experience of pilgrimage to Mecca gave Malcolm his first experience of a society in which skin color did not produce animosity; 'the effect was as though I had just stepped out of a prison' (321). Unity of belief in Islam allowed the travelers to transcend that form of conflict which had dominated Malcolm's life: 'Packed in the plane were white, black, brown, red, and yellow people, blue eyes and blond hair, and my kinky red hair – all together, brothers! All honoring the same God Allah, all in turn giving equal honor to each other' (323). Items used in communal living symbolize this unity: the rugs on which eating, sleeping, and conversation took place, the shared pot from which all ate, and the outfit of clothing worn by all the pilgrims. In Jedda Malcolm received the hospitality of Dr. Omar Azzam. 'In America, he would have been called a white man, but – it struck me, hard and instantly – from the way he acted, I had no *feeling* of him being a white man.' For the first time in his life Malcolm X experienced from a white person disinterested courtesy and respect; he could find no selfish reason or hidden motive behind Azzam's graciousness. As a result of this experience, Malcolm began to reconsider his view of the white man as the devil:

> That morning was when I first began to reappraise the 'white man.' It was when I first began to perceive that 'white man,' as commonly used, means complexion only secondarily; primarily it described attitudes and actions. In America, 'white man' meant specific attitudes toward the black man, and toward all other non-white men. But in the Muslin world, I had seen that men with white complexions were more genuinely brotherly than anyone else had ever been. (334)

By a 'radical alteration in my whole outlook about "white" men', Malcolm means his learning to judge individuals according to their specific actions, rather than reacting to them in terms of *ressentiment*. There were to be no more devils in Malcolm's world, only human beings.

Malcolm had experienced the qualities that would form his conception of the public virtues: courtesy, kindness, and, above all, respect, the word he uses again and again to describe what is missing in America's racist society. When he returned from his travels he initially thought that the only solution to American racial problems was a common religious faith. 'America needs to understand Islam, because this is the one religion that erases from its society the race problem' (340). For a short time he seems to have believed that American blacks and 'whites of the younger generation' (341) would turn to Islam. But he soon recognized that neither race was going to convert *en masse* to his new religious faith.

Malcolm's ideas were still developing rapidly during the last year of his life; the form of his autobiography was evolving as he continued to work on it; and he created two very different organizations, Muslim Mosque, Inc., and the Organization of Afro-American Unity. For all of these reasons, it is difficult to say conclusively in what direction Malcolm would have moved, and various groups have claimed Malcolm as one of their own. Interpreters must be cautious about the temptation to read their favorite ideas into the final period of this charismatic prophet, projecting their own hopes on his future career. With this caveat in mind, however, I think there is a good deal of evidence in his autobiography that a central aspect of Malcolm's work during the last nine months of his life – from his return to New York in May 1964 to his murder on February 21, 1965 – exemplifies my thesis in this chapter. The part of Malcolm's autobiography devoted to his final months dramatizes his growing consciousness of the need to overcome *ressentiment* and to practice the public virtues.

Again and again, Malcolm X calls for whites to treat blacks with respect: 'Human rights! Respect as *human beings!* That's what America's black masses want. That's the true problem' (272). Respect hardly sounds like a virtue, for it seems so basic a necessity for social existence, so minimal a standard of decency. Yet in so far as in the United States certain humans were not treated with respect, this standard remained for Malcolm both a kind of ideal and the one moral norm that every member of society ought to aspire towards and practice. Amidst his constant denunciations of his society's denial of human rights and respect, Malcolm mentions a few occasions when white persons did treat him with respect. There were a few radio or television hosts, for example, who 'respected my mind – in a way I know they never realized. The way I knew was that often they would invite my opinion on subjects off the race issue . . . . Most whites, even when they credit a Negro with some intelligence, will still feel that all he can talk about is the race issue; most whites never feel that Negroes can contribute anything to other areas of thought' (380).

Malcolm's appeal to white persons is twofold. He asks them first to atone for the specific acts of injustice that have oppressed blacks in America. In addition to these concrete acts of amendment, Malcolm suggests the need for whites to overcome *ressentiment*, to view black persons as fellow human beings rather than despised others. At the end of his life, Malcolm was not sanguine about the prospects for this: 'I want you to just watch and see if I'm not right in what I say: that the white man, in his press, is going to identify me with "hate." He will make use of me dead, as he has made use of me alive, as a convenient symbol of "hatred" – and that will help him to escape facing the truth that all I have been doing is holding up a mirror to reflect, to show, the history of unspeakable crimes that his race has committed against my race' (381). Malcolm often sounded fatalistic about the possibilities of reconciliation in America, expressing bitterness or pointing out the many obstacles to a better society. Yet his realistic recognition of the barriers to mutual respect should not blind us to his deepest goal and hope. Racism is not overcome by denying the existence and the sources of racial conflict. The moral realism of Malcolm's autobiography lies in his disclosing how particular misunderstandings, stereotypes, and insecurities make *ressentiment* so stubbornly deep-rooted. His work shows how tensions and conflicts between groups may limit or thwart the good will of even the most perceptive and well-intentioned person. For example, his insights into the power of the media analyze one of the situational conditions which influence the relations between different groups. Some of Malcolm's comments about Jews and about women reveal, too, that concentration on overcoming one form of *ressentiment* does not necessarily free one from other forms of denigration of the human other.

As important as Malcolm's direct admonitions is his own example as a man who largely overcame *ressentiment* and tried to practice his version of the public virtues. In this respect his autobiography has a moral authority that mere exhortation, preaching, or theorizing lack. His autobiography provides an instructive example of how a person's conscience may recognize *ressentiment* and transcend it, freeing that person to imagine the individuality of others and to practice the public virtues. His autobiography demonstrates this process of self-correction and growth in moral insight.

Malcolm's changed views of white persons did not mean any slackening of his biting denunciations of racism. Malcolm saw the attempt of some blacks to placate or mollify whites and to relent in attacking injustice as a form of 'Uncle Tomming', and he would have criticized such efforts as a false conception of public virtue. The practice of the public virtues does not preclude conflict. Only through direct challenge, Malcolm believed, would whites be forced to confront their own racism. 'Many whites are even actually unaware of their own racism, until they face some test, and then their racism emerges in one form or another' (363). Malcolm X continued to feel deep anger and bitterness about the injustices suffered by African-Americans. Yet this resentment of specific injuries and exploitation is very different from the envious rancor and irrational hostility of *ressentiment*, which denies the value of another form of humanity. The task and the achievement for this autobiographer's conscience lay in distinguishing between *ressentiment* and justified resentment of injustice. After his conversion, Malcolm no longer made blanket condemnations of all white people. 'In the past, yes, I have made sweeping indictments of *all* white people. I never will be guilty of that again – as I know now that some white people *are* capable of being brotherly toward a black man' (362). And although Malcolm continued to *'believe* in anger' (366) as an appropriate response to injustice, he began to realize that anger alone was insufficient to achieve mutual respect among humans: 'I was no less angry than I had been, but at the same time the true brotherhood I had seen in the Holy World had influenced me to recognize that anger can blind human vision' (375).

Malcolm's primary message to African-Americans, as I understand it, was the importance of black pride. A sense of self-worth, of self-esteem, was necessary to replace shame and self-hatred. His message to whites was to recognize the existence of racism and to end it, both on a personal level and in terms of institutional changes. His goals and stragegy for each race depended on an understanding of racial conflict as rooted in *ressentiment*. Besides protesting against specific acts of injustice, Malcolm was trying to interpret racism as a deep-seated structure of attitudes, as a matter of *ressentiment*. 'It isn't the American white *man* who is a racist, but its the American political, economic, and social *atmosphere* that automatically nourishes a racist psychology in the white man' (371). He wanted not only to end the overt forms of exploitation suffered by blacks, but 'to clear the air of the racial mirages, cliches, and lies that this country's very atmosphere has been filled with for four hundred years' (273).

Malcolm's hopes – short of the unity of humans in one faith – rested on his conception of the virtues common to all humanity. For Malcolm X, these public virtues included mutual respect, equal regard, and honor between the members of different human groups. Malcolm X was committed to the particularity of African-American identity, and not to bland commonalities, or to integration if it weakened the sense of black identity. Yet insofar as he spoke and wrote with a white audience in mind (and, increasingly, with an international perspective), Malcolm assumed a shared moral vocabulary and universal ethical standards, and he articulated them not only in terms of basic human rights, but also in the language of virtue. The appeal to public virtues, I believe, depends on the ideal of a common humanity, which for Malcolm X was ultimately based on his religious faith in 'the Oneness of Man under One God' (330). Malcolm's autobiography is a powerful demonstration of how the search for common moral ground and the assertion of a distinctive identity need not be opposed to each other. For practicing the public virtues is always expressed by means of particularist commitments and loyalties.

The Autobiography of Malcolm X deserves its reputation as one of the most penetrating analyses of American racial attitudes and problems. It is also one of the truly great spiritual autobiographies. This is true not only in the obvious sense that it records the journey of a soul undergoing two different conversions to organized religious faiths. Malcolm's work is also a powerful example of how the conscience of the autobiographer demonstrates the act of religious and moral transcendence. Malcolm recognized and came to terms with *ressentiment* by acknowledging it in his own past. Conscience was at work in the painful struggle to admit that this negative but all-too-human phenomenon had been present in his life. The most moving and amazing things about the life of Malcolm X are that he finally did overcome *ressentiment*, learning to judge others according to the specific nature of their actions, and that he tried to practice the public virtues as he conceived of them. Given Malcolm's background, this is an extraordinary achievement, and I interpret it as finally a religious one. It was almost inevitable that Malcolm would come to feel deep hatred and wish for revenge against whites, finally viewing them as personifying evil: 'I think that an objective reader may see how when I heard "The white man is the devil," when I played back what had been my own experiences, it was inevitable that I would respond positively; then the next twelve years of my life were devoted and dedicated to propagating that phrase among the black people' (378). What was not inevitable was that he would transcend *ressentiment*, affirming the necessity for black pride and justified anger but rejecting animosity for the very being of white persons. Self-esteem, he came to understand, need not be based on hatred of the other. And commitment to membership in a particular group need not preclude the search for those common virtues that would make possible a pluralistic society where the differentness of another human being would be felt as a gift rather than a threat. 'True Islam taught me that it takes *all* of the religious, political, economic, psychological, and racial ingredients, or characteristics, to make the Human Family and the Human Society complete' (375).

In this way the example of Malcolm X is a profound example of the working of the conscience of the autobiographer. Surrounded at the end of his life by both black and white persons who could not understand or accept his vision, and still struggling to clarify how his hopes could be implemented in practical terms, Malcolm's appeal to the public virtues was certainly not successful at resolving racial conflicts in the United States. His most lasting influence, however, is surely his autobiography, which demonstrates how Malcolm X overcame racism in his own character and transcended this form of *ressentiment* – to the extent that anyone in America can 'transcend' what Malcolm called the 'atmosphere' we exist in and breathe every moment. His autobiography provides a powerful testimony that conscience may, if all too rarely, move a person to moral and religious self-transcendence. Malcolm recognized a form of *ressentiment* – which he called racist psychology – in himself. He attempted, not always successfully but always honestly and courageously, to practice the public virtues, which he most often characterized in the language of respect for the other. The example of conscience at work in his autobiography is his enduring legacy, an appeal and challenge to his readers to recognize their own suscep-tibility to *ressentiment*, and to imagine and practice the public virtues that enable individuals and communities from diverse backgrounds to communicate, cooperate, and sustain each other in their distinct identities and traditions.

7

Shame in the Autobiographies of Mary McCarthy

Episodes of shame are central events in Mary McCarthy's two autobiographical works, *Memories of a Catholic Girlhood* (1957) and *How I Grew* (1987). McCarthy's narratives deepen our understanding of shame, a painful moral emotion and sanction of conscience that has often puzzled theoretical reflection. The value of her autobiographies for understanding shame lies in three areas. McCarthy's first-person narrative examines sources of shame with much greater specificity and detail than theoretical accounts, with attention to recurring patterns and her long-term development. Second, in her assessment of shame McCarthy distinguishes between genuine moral shame and false shame by clarifying the proper grounds for self-esteem and self-respect. And third, her autobiographies provide insights into the healing process by which shame may be surmounted and self-esteem recovered. In these three ways McCarthy's explorations of shame illuminate the workings of conscience in autobiography.

I THE SOURCES OF SHAME

Shame is the painful feeling a person has when his or her self-respect or self-esteem is damaged. Shame refers to a feeling of embarrassment or humiliation so profound that one experiences the entire self as basically inadequate or bad. Many psychologists distinguish shame from guilt in that, while guilt refers to the consciousness of having committed a wrong act or having transgressed a moral law, shame affects the entire sense of identity.[1]

143

Shame is not easily isolated from other negative feelings about the self, including embarrassment, depression, self-disgust, self-consciousness, humiliation, and self-hatred. Because the self is felt to be so deficient an ashamed person has an overwhelming desire to hide, to disappear, to cover up. Shame is derived etymologically from a word meaning to cover, veil, or hide (old High German *scama*, Anglo-Saxon *scamu*), and it retains this root meaning of being exposed and wishing to hide. Probably everyone learns to feel shame by seeing specific persons' negative reactions; later one can imagine a more generalized spectator's view of the self. What is essential in shame is not consciousness of how one appears to others, but sudden self-recognition: 'Experiences of shame appear to embody the root meaning of the word – to uncover, to expose, to wound. They are experiences of exposure, exposure of peculiarly sensitive, intimate, vulnerable aspects of the self. The exposure may be to others but, whether others are or are not involved, it is always . . . exposure to one's own eyes.'[2] Shame arises from the perceived discrepancy or incongruity between an individual's positive ideals or aspirations and her consciousness of failure, shortcoming, or inadequacy.

In her autobiographies McCarthy explores a number of incidents when she experienced shame before others, most often because they saw through her pretenses or role-playing. As an orphan shuttled between various relatives and schools, McCarthy lacked a stable context in which to understand herself. Her development may be plotted by the different groups in terms of which she sought to define herself. Recurring in McCarthy's autobiographical and fictional work are her interest in a person's distinctly different character in various social situations, and her probing examination of whether or not a coherent identity underlies various roles. Her comment on her first volume of short stories applies equally to her autobiographies: 'It is a case of lost identity. The author and the reader together accompany the heroine back over her life's identity.'[3] Experimenting with various identities by role-playing makes McCarthy vulnerable to shame, for she recognizes that her roles do not correspond to her deepest sense of herself. During her adolescent and college years McCarthy experiences mortifying shame when others see through her poses of worldly wisdom. When she initially meets her first husband she desires intensely to appear sophisticated, but realizes that her dress and manner of talking seem only weirdly precocious. 'It was the pits, as people say now, a fierce humiliation of all my pretenses' (*H.I.*, 178).[4] Her habit of playing the role of a more experienced woman produces a number of embarrassing incidents when others recognize that her assumed part does not accurately express the 'real' Mary.

What is most crucial in shame is not one's appearance to an audience or the judgment of other people, but one's own consciousness of degradation. Thus shame may occur in spite of others' approval. McCarthy is ashamed when, even though her role-playing succeeds, she becomes conscious of having deceived others. In this way lying in some of its subtler forms becomes a central moral issue in McCarthy's work. She repeatedly experiences both guilt and shame for lying, an act which is for her one of the worst of the vices. Her account of her first significant moral experience discloses what she holds to be the pattern of all subsequent dilemmas: 'I have battled, usually without avail, against a temptation to do something which only I knew was bad, being swept on by a need to preserve outward appearances and to live up to other people's expectations of me' (*M.G.*, 20–1). When at eight years of age McCarthy takes her first communion in what she believes is a state of sin, she feels keenly her moral inadequacy. No one else knows of her condition; she alone recognizes her failure to act according to her ideal. She suffers guilt for lying, an action she knows transgresses a moral law, and also experiences shame because of her inability to live up to her image of herself as an honest and truthful person.

A related pattern which recurs in McCarthy's life is shame about doing the right deed for the wrong motive. The motif of lying accompanies her description of her first confession, when a Catholic priest, satisfied with her proper conduct, shows little interest in her 'impure thoughts'. Again and again, discrepancies between McCarthy's actions and her intentions or motivations leave her with a sense of hypocrisy and dishonesty, about which she feels ashamed. The pattern can be seen in 'My Confession', an autobiographical essay of 1953, which describes how she briefly became involved in Marxist political activities during the 1930s without a genuine sense of moral justice: 'I see no reason to disavow my actions, which were perfectly all right, but my motives give me a little embarrassment, and just because I cannot disavow them: that fevered, contentious, trivial show-off in the May Day parade is still recognizably me.'[5] The deepest motivation for her involvements was a fascination with the varieties of Communists and fellow-travelers, which reflected a lasting temptation in her life: 'I was allowing myself to be influenced by the Party in the field where I was most open to suasion – the field of social snobbery . . . . It is only now that I see the social component in my attitude.'[6] More significant than any guilt for not having revealed her motives to others is McCarthy's shame for having failed to integrate her conduct and her inner dispositions. What is at stake for her is not just deceiving others, but a matter of integrity or wholeness, which is, as we will see, the crucial value threatened in experiences of shame.

Self-esteem can be lost not only through one's own failure, but because of the 'shaming' actions of others. One of shame's peculiar characteristics is that a person is susceptible to it because of the way others treat her. During her early life McCarthy was the victim of a number of destructive instances of shaming behavior, especially on the part of her 'Dickensian' Uncle Myers. When McCarthy wins a city prize for creative writing, her punitive and vindictive guardian beats her with a razor strap 'to teach me a lesson, he said, lest I become stuck-up' (*M.G.*, 63). Myers' unpredictable punishments, often administered 'as preventive medicine', produce self-doubt and isolation in his niece, and a policy of concealment and lying that lasts for years. Erik Erikson's insight illuminates McCarthy's childhood response to shaming:

> Too much shaming does not lead to genuine propriety but to a secret determination to try to get away with things, unseen – if, indeed, it does not result in defiant shamelessness . . . . There is a limit to a child's and an adult's endurance in the face of demands to consider himself, his body, and his wishes as evil and dirty, and to his belief in the infallibility of those who pass such judgment.[7]

In the deepest experiences of shame the wish to hide oneself from others becomes an instinctive survival tactic, an attempt to prevent their making judgments about one's worth.

'As a child, I had no self-consciousness; my seriousness prevented me from seeing that other people might be laughing at me. Now I had to learn this' (*M.G.*, 126). The origin of self-consciousness in shaming behavior is the subject of 'Names', in which two classmates give Mary the nickname 'Cye' but never explain this term's meaning. The name 'represented some aspect of myself that the world could see and I couldn't', and it 'solidified my sense of *wrongness*' (*M.G.*, 135). This incident occurs just at the time when

McCarthy is in a false position with the Mother Superior, feeling that she has to 'pretend to have become a woman' because of the nuns' misunderstanding of a few spots of blood on her sheet. In 'Names' the experience of shame is so powerful because it is associated with the exposure of sexuality, usually the first aspect of the self that a child learns must be covered up, hidden from others. McCarthy feels that a false personality has been thrust on her against her own volition, and is deeply ashamed of her inability to assert her real identity:

> The basest pretense I was driven to was the acceptance of the nickname . . . . To all those girls, I had become 'Cye McCarthy.' That was who I was . . . . I loathed myself when I said it, and yet I succumbed to the name totally, making myself over into a sort of hearty to go with it – the kind of girl I hated. 'Cye' was my new patron saint. This false personality stuck to me, like the name. (*M.G.*, 136)

Here, as in the incidents of her first communion and her pretending to have recovered her lost faith in 'C'est Le Premier Pas Qui Coute', McCarthy feels ashamed when she finds herself reluctantly conforming to what she thinks other people expect of her. Shame has to do with our identity, with how we are known by others, and this involves many things over which we have only limited control, such as names and nicknames. The trauma of this event for McCarthy is the constant public exposure of an identity that others can see but that remains hidden from herself. The incident recounted in 'Names' dramatizes the involuntary, uncontrollable nature of shame, the way it seems to befall one like fate. Yet at the same time shame involves the feeling of responsibility; McCarthy chastises herself because she thinks she ought to be able to change the situation by asserting what she feels to be her genuine identity.

Recent theories of psychotherapy explore ways in which shame originates and is perpetuated in families. Fossum and Mason define three elements in the 'shame-bound family system': shame-inducing events such as child abuse, attempted suicide, or alcoholism; 'the inherited generational shame passed on to family members . . . when the shaming events and the feelings they involved were denied'; and the maintained shame which individual family members keep alive in their psychic lives.[8] This pattern corresponds closely to McCarthy's relationship to her Preston grandparents. In

'Ask Me No Questions' McCarthy probes her confused feelings growing up in the Preston household, where she spent her high school years. 'There was something strange, abnormal, about my bringing-up; only now that my grandmother is dead am I prepared to face this fact' (*M.G.*, 195). Delving into the silences and secrets surrounding her grandmother, McCarthy must overcome strong internal resistance to revealing the sources of her family's shame: 'Starting to tell that story now, to publish it, so to speak, abroad, I feel a distinct uneasiness, as though her shade were interposing to forbid me. If I believed in the afterlife, I would hold my peace . . . . She would never forgive me for what I am about to do, and if there is an afterlife, it is God who will have to listen to my explanations' (*M.G.*, 198). McCarthy reconstructs her discovery of three traumatic events that shaped the life of Augusta Morganstern Preston and her family. The nature of the first event was suggested by her grandmother's denial of her Jewish background, an aversion to discussing this subject probably caused by an early encounter with anti-Semitism. 'What the first offense was, I do not know, but I imagine it had something to do with her Jewish pride and sensitiveness; some injury was dealt her early in her marriage, and it may have been a very small thing – a chance word, even – that caused her to draw back into an august silence on this topic, a silence that lasted until her death' (*M.G.*, 239).

McCarthy was struck by her grandmother's isolation and lack of interest in family or friends. For a long time she saw this as Augusta's angry response to the death of her beloved daughter, Mary's mother Tess, in the 1918 influenza epidemic. 'And that is how I see my grandmother, bearing her loss like an affront, stubborn and angry, refusing to speak not only to individual persons but to life itself, which had wounded her by taking her daughter away' (*M.G.*, 239). However, at the climax of 'Tell Me No Secrets', Mary realizes that her grandmother's withdrawal from life dated not from Tess's death, but from an earlier traumatic event, an unsuccessful face-lifting operation in 1916. Augusta was left with minor scars, and spent hours every day in the bathroom making up her face. 'The bathroom figured to me as the center of everything in the Preston family from which I was excluded . . . . The strongest memory that comes back to me is of shut doors and silence' (*M.G.*, 228–9). Augusta must have been ashamed of her loss of physical beauty, and perhaps of its becoming known that she was vain enough to submit to this operation. McCarthy conjectures that this disaster was probably the most crushing tragedy for her grandmother, and that it explains the puzzling rituals of McCarthy's childhood home:

> My grandmother's withdrawal from society must have dated, really, from this period, and not from the time of my mother's death, which came as the crowning blow. That was why we were so peculiar, so unsocial, so, I would add, slightly inhuman; we were all devoting ourselves, literally, to the cult of a relic, which was my grandmother's body, laved and freshened every day in the big bathroom, and then paraded before the public in the downtown stores. (*M.G.* 241)

McCarthy's sustained examination of her grandmother's secret past is illuminated when we see it as an exploration of the dynamics of shame within her family. The bungled face-lifting – not Tess's death – becomes the clue to Augusta's strange behavior: her refusal to be photographed, her daily ritual in the bathroom, the retreat from society into aloof isolation and uncomfortable reticence, her grand shopping tours in which she 'defied these people, her suitors, to please her' (*M.G.*, 219). Her shame for what she must have seen as her disfigured face explains all of these puzzling routines.[9] Many of McCarthy's adolescent feelings of awkwardness and embarrassment were acquired in this atmosphere of silence and secrecy. In common with many children in shame-bound families, Mary blames herself for the Prestons' lack of connection or intimacy with other people: 'I blamed this on myself, thinking there was something wrong with me, like a petticoat showing, that other people could see and I couldn't' (*M.G.*, 235). Just as with her nickname 'Cye', she feels a confused sense of shame but cannot trace its origin.

Her mother's mother functions as a sort of alter ego for McCarthy in her own struggle with shame.[10] Augusta Preston is lonely, proud, and, at least about her appearance, 'at once vain and self-critical' (*M.G.*, 219). Both women are orphans who attempt to hide their need to be loved. In *Memories*, Mary often reflects – both as adolescent protagonist and as narrating autobiographer – about the similarities and differences between her own character and the dominant female relative in her girlhood.[11] McCarthy's discovery of sexuality during her adolescent years, involving a good deal of embarrassment and shame, is punctuated by several moments when she intuits her grandmother's 'mature sensuality'. Seeing her eating apricots,

McCarthy feels as though she has 'witnessed what Freud calls the primal scene' (*M.G.*, 225). Twice McCarthy catches 'a disturbing glimpse of her thighs' (*M.G.*, 226, 242), the second time when her grandmother has a hysterical fit after learning of her sister Rosie's death. In a highly charged scene the exposure of sexuality is associated with the one occasion on which Augusta reveals a deep emotion, raw grief:

> She was writhing on the bed; the cook and I could barely get hold of her. My uncle appeared in the doorway, and my first thought (and I think the cook's also) was to get that nightgown down. The spectacle was indecent, and yet of a strange boudoir beauty that contrasted in an eerie way with that awful noise she was making, more like a howl than a scream and bearing no resemblance to sorrow. (*M.G.*, 242)

Sexuality and uncontrollable emotion are both so revelatory of one's vulnerability that their open display may induce the wish to hide. Because of her close identification with her grandmother, Mary is both horrified and fascinated when Augusta's privacy is violated and secrets – sexuality and unrestrained emotion – are revealed.

This final story in *Memories of a Catholic Girlhood* is not, as might first appear, a digression from or an appendix to McCarthy's autobiography. Probing the enigmas underlying each chapter, McCarthy felt that 'the sense of a mystery back of the story I had already told traced itself more and more to the figure of my grandmother' (*M.G.*, 193). Though its terminal position in the book violates the chronological order of the other sketches, it is a most appropriate ending, for its focus on shame illumines the meaning of *Memories* as a whole. The chapter's title indicates the central place of her grandmother's story in McCarthy's own self-understanding. Unlike the woman whose 'august' bearing seemed to warn others to 'Ask Me No Questions', McCarthy determines to uncover and confess the secret sources of her own shame. Recognizing the destructive effects of her grandmother's failure to face shame gives McCarthy incentive to explore and reveal the sources of shame in her own life. Her grandmother's story is in this way a fitting culmination to McCarthy's autobiography, clarifying the way in which the book as a whole is a 'confession' of shame.

'I was born as a mind during 1925', begins *How I Grew*, focusing McCarthy's second autobiography on what influenced her as a writer and an intellectual. Friendships play a more important role in her mental development than family or academic education. 'You can date the evolving life of a mind, like the age of a tree, by the rings of friendship formed by the expanding central trunk' (*H.I.*, 27–8). In her involvements with successive friends and in her assessment of their influences, experiences of shame play a crucial role. During her year at Garfield High School in Seattle, McCarthy appears on stage to recite a silly comic monologue by Stephen Leacock, 'Alice and her Dog'. She receives wild applause but is suddenly deeply ashamed. She won the approval of a group of students from Mercer Island at the price of her self-respect:

> I became aware that I had let them take me over too quickly. Those friendly millstones were pulling me down to their level. And that dawning suspicion, I now conjecture, was what has made me efface the success of Alice and her dog from my memory: I was ashamed of it then and there, stricken *in media res*. I must have wished to drop through a trap door. (*H.I.*, 51–2)

McCarthy speculates that her first intellectual friend, 'Ted', may have been in the audience, and that – whether she was there or not – her intense shame arose when she suddenly viewed herself from Ted's perspective:

> Ted could have been in the audience, and what would she have thought? Being far more a loving soul than a critical spirit, she might have tried to see the best in Stephen Leacock. The critical spirit was me. Borrowing her eyes, I would have looked on myself far more harshly than it was in her nature to do. (*H.I.*, 54)

McCarthy needs to 'borrow the eyes' of her friend in order to recognize and judge her action. As a result of this experience, McCarthy distances herself from the Mercer Island group and becomes more seriously involved in reading, theater, and intellectual pursuits. The incident on stage marks the transition between two sets of friends and the values they represent. It is typical of her experiences of shame that she feels disgraced not when an audience rejects her, but in spite of its approval. Her shame indicates her rejection and hatred of 'the side of myself that wanted the mindless applause' of an uncritical audience. Once again she is ashamed of a misrepresentation and betrayal of herself.

An intriguing confession in *How I Grew* is McCarthy's avowal of shame for a failure to commit suicide. Even though she had no reason to wish to die, she continues – writing at the age of 73 – to feel shame for 'cowardice' about this incident:

> I felt sadly ashamed of my cowardice. I *ought* to have taken the iodine, having made such a parade of it. There was no excuse. Lack of nerve had stopped me – nothing else. Though a few hours ago I had had no particular reason for ending my days, now I had one, in discovering myself to be such a craven. I went to bed. It was my first encounter with self-knowledge – a very bleak sensation. And, though I cannot truthfully say today that I think a better person would have gone ahead and killed herself, I still feel something of that shame. (*H.I.*, 110)

If the better course was not to kill herself, why should she feel shame for not going through with self-destruction? Why, if she acted rightly, should she be ashamed? 'It was all theatricals, which I was putting on for my own benefit' (*H.I.*, 108). She imagined herself being found, wearing a certain yellow dress, in the yard of a man with whom she was infatuated. 'My main motive for that theatrical suicide was to have an occasion to wear the yellow dress. I see it hanging in my clothes closet – a perfect symbol of deluded expectations' (*H. I.*, 109). This incident still evokes shame because it reminds her of how she could play a role with little or no commitment. The experience revealed a failure of integrity or wholeness about her character, a lack of unity between conviction and action. She is ashamed of the lack of self-knowledge that produced flirtation with suicide followed by 'cowardice'. It is a strange double bind and a puzzling dilemma when a person feels shame even though her conscience would condemn her for acting in a way that would avoid the shame. Yet sometimes a person places herself in such a position that no course of action is entirely free of shame.

In *How I Grew* McCarthy recounts several incidents when she experienced intense shame following sexual intimacy and exposure to a man in whom she had only passing interest. 'A true girl of my generation, bent on taking the last trace of sin out of sex' (*H.I.*, 156), she threw herself into a number of brief liaisons she later regretted. Having romanticized her first seducer, McCarthy was horrified to realize how cold and casual was Forrest's attitude: 'To fuck was to do *it* straight, with no love, the way men did with prostitutes . . . . The message had come through clear and strong' (*H.I.*, 77). She learns that Forrest and his friends describe to each other in detail their encounters with girlfriends, and she wonders how she will be discussed. On another occasion, her remorse focuses on particular actions: 'Some of the things he did in bed made me cringe with shame to think of afterwards' (*H.I.*, 156). In this case shame was felt not so much for what she actively did, but for what she passively submitted to or allowed to be done to her. Shame brings a loss of self-respect, which may occur either when one actively violates one's ideals or when one passively tolerates others' actions that are experienced as degrading. Shame is a sign – 'a deep-lying instinct, part of my interior warning system' – that she has revealed too much vulnerability or trusted the wrong person. McCarthy's treatment of sexuality in her fiction reflects this perspective. Though some critics have held that her novels reflect a kind of puritanism or distaste for sexuality itself, what is more central to McCarthy's vision is her understanding of the self-betrayal, indicated by their shame and disgust, that her heroines experience when they sleep with men whom they do not really love.

In three ways shame is an important element in McCarthy's unhappy relationship with her first husband, Harold Johnsrud. We must wonder why McCarthy was drawn to a man who abused her psychologically. During the summer of 1932 she returned to 'the streams of abuse he subjected me to – sarcasm, irony, denunciation' (*H.I.*, 250):

> He *made* me cry every day, for there was a kind of deliberateness in it, or so it appeared. And almost the worst was my total mystification. What made him so hateful I never found out, and this left me with a sense of being hopelessly stupid, which I fear John liked. (*H.I.*, 249)

McCarthy's mystification as to why anyone would so persistently and cruelly shame her repeats her puzzlement about her guardians' behavior. Her involvement with Johnsrud seems comprehensible partly in terms of her habituation to the shaming behavior she experienced during much of her childhood. She became used to this destructive pattern of relationships during that period of ill-treatment, which may have influenced for some years her expectations of any close relationship.

Second, McCarthy stays with Johnsrud to prove to her friends
at Vassar that she was not just his temporary partner. When one
friend assures her, 'You're just another feather in the Johnsrud
cap', McCarthy bristles: 'My pride was at stake' (H.I., 251). Fearing
that if 'ditched' by John she would feel shamed by her friends, she
steels herself to persist in a hopeless relationship. Third, McCarthy
mentions how impressed she was that Johnsrud had nearly killed
himself in a car accident that was probably an attempted suicide.
In fact, 'if there was a single factor that decided me to go on and
marry him, it was probably that' (H.I., 257). An odd reason to marry!
However, given McCarthy's shame for her own 'cowardice' about
suicide, her admiration and awe for this '*colossally* unhappy' man
become more understandable. For Johnsrud was a person much like
her idealized image of herself, a Byronic figure of heroic suffering.
Acting was his profession – and apparently theatrical gestures were
his typical mode of interaction with McCarthy – but he was a person
who to the youthful Mary represented a kind of authenticity and
commitment, backing up dramatic gestures with readiness to take
the consequences and an apparent indifference to the opinions of
others. Shame about her own deficiencies and lack of self-confidence
– epitomized in the failed 'suicide attempt' – seem to have been
strong forces in her attraction to this destructive man.

McCarthy is one-quarter Jewish. The references to Jewishness and
anti-Semitism scattered through both of her volumes of autobiography are often linked to shame. Her encounters with both Jews
and anti-Semites continually re-activate a sense of shame probably
related to her grandmother Preston's secrecy about this aspect of
her past. At Vassar, when a group of McCarthy's friends tease a
girl with a rumor that she is Jewish, Elly acknowledges that indeed
she is. 'It was a terrible moment; there was no way we could take
those hee-haws back' (H.I., 215). As a consequence of this blunder,
each member of the group of girls remains friends with Elly: 'Out
of shame, we were forced to stay friends with her' (H.I., 216). The
painful memory destroys the group's unity, however: 'Elly's being
Jewish was the cause of our break-up. Our mass refusal to believe
that she was Jewish made us look like a bunch of anti-Semites;
the common memory of that was an embarrassment' (H.I., 217).
Whether or not the anti-Semitism was only an appearance or in
fact the case, the group had to dissolve because its identity was
linked to a trait its members recognized as a vice and were ashamed
of. Again we witness the dynamics of shame playing a crucial

role in fostering and in ending McCarthy's friendships and group memberships.

McCarthy goes on to examine her own anti-Semitism, asking why she never mentioned to Elly her own Jewish grandmother. Her analysis demonstrates the way that in trying to avoid one form of shame a person can become trapped in an even more painful and degrading form of it. She also shows how, because the admission of shame is a confession of weakness or inadequacy, a person may become trapped in the misery of shame about shame. As a young woman at Vassar, McCarthy appears to have been ashamed of both her Jewishness and of being an anti-Semite. When another friend visiting Seattle planned to see Mary's grandmother, McCarthy was tortured for months by uncertainty about how Jewish Augusta Preston looked. Yet she was deeply ashamed of this anxiety: 'I was too much ashamed of these worries to confide them in any-one . . . . My fears were the more shameful in that Frani, as I knew, was free of prejudices' (*H.I.*, 219). Frani would surely wonder why her friend had never shared this important part of her history, and correctly infer a degree of shame about being Jewish. Yet McCarthy claims that she was not really anti-Semitic; she was only ashamed that she would appear so to Frani:

> It would be useless to plead that the subject had never happened to come up, that if I had been asked, I would have told, which was true: I would not have gone so far as to deny Augusta Preston, or, rather, her Jewishness, outright, like Peter in the Garden, whom I could never forget – 'I know not the man.' Still, that did not make me better, only less bad than some famously craven apostle. (*H.I.*, 219)

That McCarthy never found out what Frani discerned about Augusta Preston seems to her a just punishment for 'that old sin of mine (a variety of false witness)'. McCarthy's false position with Frani involves a half-conscious denial by silence of identity, an effort to mask this original shame leading to even greater shame, and the suffering of isolation and estrangement from others.[12]

The sources of shame in McCarthy's life have been traced to a variety of situations and causes. Her autobiographical work is not only a chronology of painful incidents, however, and a search for origins. McCarthy's work involves an assessment of shame that suggests how confronting this experience can play a crucial role in the growth of a person's conscience.

II   THE ASSESSMENT OF SHAME

Shame is an affective response to certain events, a spontaneous, uncontrollable, and often unpredictable feeling. As is the case with benevolence or anger or other feelings, this natural reaction may be judged and found to be either morally justifiable or not. After considered reflection a person may or may not be able to approve a response of shame in a given situation. Philosophers usually distinguish in this way between natural shame and moral shame, the latter being explained by moral concepts. From an ethical point of view what is crucial is not the nuances of shame as a sensation or feeling, but its meaning as a moral judgment, and the reasons why conscience may justify or criticize a reaction of shame in a particular situation. It is the assessment by conscience which determines whether a person can fully endorse a feeling of shame, or whether an occasion of this emotion conflicts with her most self-conscious and deliberate commitments.

Shame is puzzling in that it seems at once a good and a bad thing. Shame has often been seen as a desirable trait, as almost a form of virtue. The Greek term's double meaning connotes not only shame but respect or reverence. Philosophers including Plato, Spinoza, and Scheler have asserted that it is sometimes better to feel shame than not to feel it.[13] And yet, paradoxically, it is a painful emotion which it is supposed to be bad to feel, for it implies dishonor and disgrace. Shame, like some other negative experiences in life, is not unqualifiedly good, but it can serve a good purpose. As a response to certain of one's deeds it may be comparatively better to feel shame than not to feel it. For a reaction of shame to one's behavior indicates a commitment to the standards that one has failed to achieve. Shame may be a transitional moment in moral development, when a person affirming a value is unable to realize it in his or her own life. That shame is elicited by failure to embody an ideal in action reveals both seriousness of moral commitment and vulnerability until the new ideal is firmly rooted in character. A person who is 'shameless' seems to lack ideals of conduct and character for himself; no act or motive is viewed as unfitting or inappropriate. For this reason having a sense of shame seems to be necessary in a morally serious life. Shamelessness implies a lack of serious self-assessment, a refusal to take anything to heart, an avoidance of one of the most painful but necessary penalties of conscience.

A person's assessment of his shame is a most revealing index of his conscience, disclosing the standards and the ideals of character which shape self-evaluation. Autobiography is invaluable in understanding shame, for it offers the opportunity for a writer not only to expose failures, but to assess their overall significance, and thus to reflect on the proper grounds of self-esteem. Such an understanding of autobiography is evident in Augustine's *Confessions*, as may be seen in his reflections on the pear-stealing episode, the death of his unnamed friend in Book IV, and his experience of 'sober shame' and powerlessness just before his conversion in the garden. Donald Capps sees Augustine's confrontation with shame in these 'parabolic events' as the means by which Augustine opens himself to trusting God:

> While Adam sought to hide his shame from God, Augustine dares to reveal his shame through his *Confessions* because he knows that, through such self-disclosure, God will appear to him. The problem with concealing one's shame is not that one thereby hides from God, but that one hides God from oneself. By forcing himself to confront his shame, Augustine opens himself to the presence of God.[14]

In a highly significant passage, Augustine links his examination of conscience, his confession of shame (not guilt), and his 'choosing' God:

> O Lord, the depths of man's conscience lie bare before your eyes. Could anything of mine remain hidden from you, even if I refused to confess it? I should only be shielding my eyes from seeing you, not hiding myself from you. But now that I have the evidence of my own misery to prove to me how displeasing I am to myself, you are my light and my joy. It is you whom I love and desire, so that I am ashamed of myself and cast myself aside and choose you instead, and I please neither you nor myself except in you.[15]

An autobiographer reflecting on the sources of shame in the past may discern continuity or discontinuity between his present sense of values and that of an earlier self. Either he may continue to feel ashamed of what once caused shame; or he may no longer feel ashamed of what once caused intense feelings of humiliation; or he may detect in a past action reasons to feel ashamed which he did not recognize at the time of the action. Thus in assessing his experiences of shame an autobiographer may both reflect on how his conscience and his deepest values have evolved, and exercise his conscience in the very process of writing.

Not every autobiographer undertakes such an examination of shame to probe fundamental convictions and beliefs. A writer may not wish to exhibit publicly his mistakes and inadequacies. Furthermore, the examination of professed failure may be an elaborate means of self-justification or an evasion of the real sources of shame. One suspects this to be the case in *The Education of Henry Adams*. Adams repeatedly confesses his failure to get a useful education, to acquire political power, and to comprehend his world. Yet he omits completely the twenty years of his life during which his wife committed suicide and his extensive historical works failed to be appreciated. It has been argued that Adams constructed a 'myth of failure' which hides the real sources of his feelings of inadequacy – and the sources of his shame.[16] Autobiography does not require but only offers an opportunity for exploring the sources of shame, and for assessing the significance of shame. What an honest and accurate assessment of shame means is what I wish to understand, taking McCarthy's work as a highly instructive case.

McCarthy's autobiographies are vitally concerned with appraising the moral lapses in her life. Planning *How I Grew*, she wrote to her publisher: 'In the garden, reflecting on the autobiography, I thought of a grisly title: *Excuse Me For Living*. That gives a hint of what I have, at least partly, in mind: a catalogue of my sins, both of commission and omission.'[17] For McCarthy confession of sins entails conscientious examination of the incidents which produced shame. Her autobiographies seem to me unusually honest and discerning not only in disclosing, but in assessing her experiences of shame. An instance in *How I Grew* is McCarthy's analysis of her shame for reciting 'Alice and her Dog'. McCarthy is struck by the fact that her earlier self, 'the heroine of the occasion, has become unrecognizable to me, so that I cannot account for her feelings and behavior' (*H.I.*, 48). Wondering about the cause of her failure of memory, she finally decides that the answer lies in her rejection of the 'claque' of which she was a part. 'Evidently the self that felt the attraction of Garfield's mob scene has been sloughed like a snake's skin.' Shame struck her when she realized how much she had lowered herself in her own estimation to win the approval of the contingent of students from Mercer Island. McCarthy affirms that her reaction of shame was not irrational but justified: 'If some psychoanalyst is moved to tell me "You felt imperiled by success," I do not deny it: I *was* imperiled by success and at the age of thirteen apparently had the good sense to know it' (*H.I.*, 52). Her emerging intellectual standards condemned the 'mindless applause' she won, and she was properly ashamed of the part of herself that would do anything for approval. This incident dramatizes the central struggle in her life between the courting of approval and a need for individuality and autonomy. Because of her growing sense of herself as a distinct individual, she rejected the 'claque', the 'Mercer Island entity', whose members are no longer distinct in her mind but 'have stuck together in a lump, like candy in a coat pocket, like their fatal watchword – "Let's stick together, kids"' (*H.I.*, 50).

Interpreting this incident, McCarthy analyzes the significance of two phenomena associated with shame: amnesia and identification with others. Shameful memories are so painful that a person often blocks them from conscious recall. McCarthy's amnesia is interestingly partial; it is her feelings and intentions before she was ashamed that she cannot remember. Although she says she has 'no recollection of my emotions', her reconstruction of the incident is one of the most vivid in the book. In McCarthy's case protective amnesia was only partly successful, blocking out her memory of herself before the traumatic event but not the intense moment of shame itself, when elements in a more enduring identity suddenly crystallized. McCarthy interprets her memory's denial of an earlier self in the light of a Biblical passage with great significance for her: '"I know not the man," St. Peter said, denying Jesus, and I can say with greater truthfulness, of that thirteen-year-old pennant-waver, "I don't know that child." In what I am about to relate the disassociation is almost complete, resulting in big patches of amnesia' (*H.I.*, 48). When McCarthy referred to Peter's denial in the context of her own disavowal of Jewish identity, the allusion suggested McCarthy's cowardice and self-betrayal (*H.I.*, 219). In connection with the 'Alice' recital, in contrast, the passage suggests not self-castigation or remorse for lying, but McCarthy's attempt to deliberately choose a new identity by rejecting a despised earlier self.

The account of this incident in the context of her dissociation from the Mercer Island group and her growing involvement with Ted (who was in the audience in spirit if not in body) shows how shame is often based on identification with the perspectives of other persons and communities. A person's choice of an 'audience' reflects a choice of values. The emotion of shame suddenly erupts as McCarthy views herself through the critical eyes of her intellectual friend. The consequent disaffiliation with the Mercer Island group marks this incident as the climax and turning point of a lengthy and complex process of transition between different groups of friends and the values they represent for her: 'Having lowered myself to the limit of degradation (thank God no member of my family was there), then mercifully dropped into an oubliette, in mind, if not in body, I began to "space" my meetings with the Mercer Island crowd' (*H.I.*, 52). This experience continues to be a painful but significant memory for McCarthy, for it both reminds her of a recurring temptation to compromise her integrity and discloses standards of self-respect that she still holds. The account shows how experiences of shame can shape conscience and moral character, and how an autobiographer's assessment of shame reveals enduring commitments.

In assessing her shame an autobiographer reveals much about her understanding of virtue, the moral traits she holds to be part of the good life. Shame is the negative side of an ethic of virtue. If morality is not just a matter of following moral rules, but also an attempt to live an honorable life, a 'good life', essential negative moral judgments will take the form of shame. Reactions of shame will indicate which virtues a person includes in his conception of the good life. For 'someone is liable to moral shame when he prizes as excellences of his person those virtues that his plan of life requires and is framed to encourage'.[18] The failure to measure up to one's personal standard of virtue will result in a loss of self-esteem, or shame. McCarthy's work clarifies the interdependence of these moral concepts – shame, self-esteem, and virtue – in the workings of conscience.

McCarthy feels ashamed when she cannot achieve her ideal of moral excellence or goodness, as well as when she falls short of her notions of grace and beauty. Her attempt to integrate her various ideals in one life gradually focuses on the idea of being an intellectual. A central concern of *How I Grew* is McCarthy's assessment of the various elements which influenced her evolving conception of an intellectual. This identity entails for her a notion of honor, a concept often linked to shame.[19] The particular kind of honor she associates with being an intellectual brings with it certain moral obligations and a very marked pride. Her own failures to measure up to her high standards bring shame; the failures of other intellectuals elicit McCarthy's scorn, contempt, or scathing rebuke.

The ideals of virtue that determine when a person will feel shame are derived from communities to which she belongs or aspires. The community of intellectuals to which McCarthy aspired was a hypothetical fellowship composed of influential teachers, friends who shared her interests, and authors she admired. Part of the appeal of being an intellectual for her is freedom from some of the institutional constraints and mores of a typical face-to-face community. McCarthy rejects a community's right to shame an individual, criticizing the ways in which small communities coerce conformity in their members. In her treatment of friendships at Vassar College, for instance, McCarthy pronounces a harsh judgment on people who allow their mental horizons to be bounded by a safe little society of peers. 'I was depressed by the clannishness of their behavior, typical, I now know, of society people, who are great stickers-together' (*H.I.*, 266).

McCarthy's alliances with and breaks from particular groups are often determined by her negative assessment of the shaming practices associated with those groups. For example, in 'My Confession', McCarthy suggests that mechanisms of shame distorted the political and moral judgments of liberals and Communists during the 1930's. Her position as an anti-Communist came about, she admits, 'by accident and almost unwillingly' because of her insistence on maintaining her independence when her signature was used in a letter by a 'Committee for the Defense of Leon Trotsky'. Although she disliked having her name used without her permission, she disliked even more the pressures that were placed on her to withdraw her name. She thus found herself more or less politically committed to one party because of her efforts to avoid the coercive tactics of another group. This sort of awkward backing-into a group with which she has only partial agreement occurs several times in McCarthy's life. She insists on choosing deliberately her affiliations and commitments, rather than being subject to shaming practices. However, her relationships to particular groups are frequently shaped by her negative reactions to the pressures they place on her. McCarthy is strongly influenced in this way by her view of shaming behavior as a wholly destructive force interfering with a person's search for a distinctive identity and with the individual's conscience.

We have seen how McCarthy feels shame when she fails to live up to her expectations of herself. In reviewing her early life she decides that sometimes those expectations were appropriate and at other times they were misplaced. Thus she distinguishes between genuine moral shame and false shame. Instances of suffering from false shame were based on confused, uncertain, or mistaken values. McCarthy is particularly insightful about the ways that for her intellectual values became associated with wealth, social prestige, Eastern schools, and knowing the right people. All of these things brought her closer to her deepest concerns but were finally distractions. She discerns how commitment to ideals of truth and beauty was misdirected towards class snobbery: 'Did nobody ever worry about the effect on a girl from the Northwest of exposure to the contagious disease of snobbery and the New York Social Register? . . . Social ambition occurred too classically in literature to be regarded as greatly harmful, lying so very close, as it did, to the passion for excellence, beauty, fine ornament, and to the gift of worship. What English major was – or ought to be – free from the vice?' (*H.I.*, 234). Confusion about values produced instances of embarrassment and false shame that, in retrospect, indicate commitment to the wrong standards. Judgments about false shame thus depend on a distinction between genuine or enduring values and mistaken or temporary loyalties.

McCarthy's assessments of shame are shaped by her sense of integrity and self-respect. Integrity refers to the wholeness of the self, and thus to a person's ability to acknowledge her deeds as truly her own. A person with integrity 'owns' all her deeds, and judges them according to a consistent standard. The lack of integrity means a person ignores or tolerates certain acts or motives which are inconsistent with her ideal of herself. She does not feel shame when she should. As Gabrielle Taylor explains, the connection between shame and integrity is self-respect: 'If integrity is the identity of the person in terms of her commitments then self-respect protects this identity by protecting the relevant values: the person who has self-respect will not tolerate certain types of behavior on her own part, nor certain types of treatment offered her by others.'[20] Shame will be felt about a loss of self-respect, a loss which may take either an active or a passive form. One may be ashamed of one's own actions, as was McCarthy after reciting 'Alice and her Dog', or shame may be elicited when a person tolerates a situation which injures self-respect, as when McCarthy submits to subtle sexual exploitation. Shame serves a vital moral function in protecting her integrity and self-respect, warning her of a failure to be or do what she expects of herself. In this way the experience of shame reveals the role of conscience in monitoring the consistency, continuity, and wholeness – the integrity – of personal identity.

The moral significance of autobiography's first-person perspective is evident in the assessment of shame. Moral guilt is understood with reference to impersonal laws and standards. Interpreting shame, however, requires understanding personal standards of honor and integrity which may seem irrational or arbitrary to the impartial observer or disinterested spectator of much ethical theory. Why should Augustine make so much of taking a few pears, or McCarthy be so concerned with reciting a silly lyric? The significance of these incidents lies not in the objective wrong done to others, or in the violation of a universal norm, but in what they symbolize about integrity and self-respect to the conscience of an autobiographer. Episodes of shame are often precipitated by the violation of an image of the self which can not be universalized, generalized, or even stated in terms of a rule or law. These self-images, metaphors of an ideal self, shape a person's conscience in elusive but profound ways, the import of which can best be understood as they are articulated in an autobiographer's assessment of shame.

III CONSCIENCE, SHAME, AND SELF-ESTEEM

To what extent can shame be transcended, or coped with in a constructive way? On this issue the psychological studies of shame differ markedly. For some writers it is the idea that shame is total and irreparable that distinguishes it from guilt.[21] For others, shame has a much more positive role in a person's development, spurring growth and clarifying values. Lynd says shame offers a 'clue to identity': 'Experiences of shame if confronted full in the face may throw an unexpected light on who one is and point the way toward who one may become. Fully faced, shame may become not primarily something to be covered, but a positive experience of revelation.'[22] In my view, shame does not necessarily lead to any predictable outcome. All depends on how a person responds to the experience. McCarthy's work demonstrates both strategies of avoidance and some of the ways in which facing and assessing one's shame can help a person overcome it, contributing to a coherent sense of identity and a clearer knowledge of one's deepest values.

How I Grew reveals several ways in which McCarthy's earliest efforts at writing were rooted in experiences of shame, and may be interpreted as attempts to overcome shame. McCarthy speculates that satiric writing helped her to defend herself from one of the most destructive consequences of manipulative shaming behavior: self-pity.

> I had the choice of forgiving those incredible relatives of mine or pitying myself on their account. Laughter is the great antidote for self-pity, maybe a specific for the malady. Yet probably it does tend to dry one's feelings out a little, as if by exposing them to a vigorous wind. So that something must be subtracted from the compensation I seem to have received for injuries sustained. There is no dampness in my emotions, and some moisture, I think, is needed to produce the deeper, the tragic, notes. (*H.I.*, 17)

In these sentences McCarthy reflects on how her background may have affected her literary vision. The passage suggests that her response to a traumatic and shame-filled childhood influenced certain qualities of her vision as a person and as a writer, making tragedy an unlikely vehicle for that vision. I think McCarthy's response to shaming – her toughness and 'dry' contempt for weakness and dishonesty in any form – may have diminished her sympathetic understanding of others' errors, and predisposed her towards the mode of satire.

This passage shows, too, that a victim of shaming behavior can recognize the injustice of the 'system' that fosters this practice and attack it, effectively displacing negative criticism from the self to others. Although she asserts that she does not feel vindictive towards her guardians, her satiric portrayal of them in *Memories* involves not only exposing injustice, but also an element of revenge. The disapproval and aggression formerly directed at herself were directed outwards at the source of the shaming behavior.

McCarthy's first attempts at fiction-writing were satiric attacks on the vice of self-deception, with 'reality being represented by fat; both heroines have a grave figure problem' (*H.I.*, 97). What she hates about her heroines is not 'fat or shortness of stature, however displeasing when combined; but moral traits – triteness and self-deception' (*H.I.*, 101). McCarthy wonders about the source of her passionate hatred of self-deception, and about the reasons why her treatment of this vice now seems to her so ferocious, so vehement. She speculates that her desire to be a writer, first expressed in stories attacking the vice of self-deception, may be related to shame about her Jewishness and latent anti-Semitism: 'It almost looks as if my impulse to write had had some relation to a juvenile anti-Semitic bias, to an anger which had to be directed against the Jewish quarter of me that I half-tried to disavow – a project all the more tempting in that "it" did not show' (*H.I.*, 102). Dismissing this possibility, however, she confesses to uncertainty as to 'what made me so sensitive at the age of fourteen to the perils of self-deception'. Strangely, McCarthy does not consider that her literary concern with self-deception grew out of her own moral struggles. She seems to assume that her conscience was always alert to and prevented the phenomenon of self-deception:

> In all honesty, I don't recall lying to myself, ever, though I do recall trying to. On the other hand, if I *had* lied, would I know? How, unless someone else caught me? And who could that be? Unless there is in each of us a *someone else* watching – what used to be called our conscience. I believe that there is: I *know* that other person. (*H. I.*, 104)

Although she is surely right that she is not a 'dyed-in-the-wool hypocrite', the claim that she never caught herself in self-deception is puzzling. In her autobiographies she exposes many instances of a tendency to lie to herself as well as to others when, playing a role or courting approval, she justified self-interested actions with rather specious reasoning. McCarthy's fervent hatred of self-deception, which 'remains, in my book, a major sin or vice' (*H.I.*, 104), seems in fact to be rooted in one source of shame in her life. Transferring the vice she dimly perceived in herself to a fictional character whom she satirized was one of the ways she came to terms with this source of shame. This process is psychologically similar to the 'strategy of transfer' whereby a person copes with shame by blaming someone else or making another feel shame.[23] To locate the source of McCarthy's hatred of self-deception in her early experience in no way undermines the authenticity or worth of her mature commitment to this value. My point is rather that writing was one of the means by which an inchoate sense of what is truly important in life, which when violated precipitated shame, was articulated, clarified, and consciously appropriated as part of McCarthy's identity.

Writing offered McCarthy a means of dealing with shame through the analysis of moral psychology as subject matter. Writing also established a new focus for achievement. When McCarthy explains how her writing style and concerns developed, she often belittles her earliest efforts ('the tritest and trashiest of all my study-hall narratives'). Her remarks on her writing suggest that individuals come to terms with shame by changing the sources of self-esteem, especially through commitments to their work. In adolescence the focus of shame is partially displaced from one's given nature to achievements, so that a person is no longer as susceptible to being ashamed of appearance or background, but more vulnerable to shame about the quality of one's efforts or performance in some chosen field. Since shame is experienced as a lack of control, one response is to try to master a particular field of competence. If a person's self-esteem could be made to rest exclusively on her accomplishments, she might even believe that it was completely within her control.

Unfortunately, the notion that a person can be invulnerable to shame is an illusion. Indeed, it is one of shame's most puzzling characteristics that I am subject to it because of factors beyond my control. This is so because my identity is inextricably bound up with others, and their adversity and shame affect me. King Lear's demand for a public profession of love makes unavoidable for Cordelia not only shame for her father but shame about her position as a daughter asked for a fine, but finally self-interested, profession of love.[24] Similarly, in *The Brothers Karamazov* Dostoevsky explores the way in which each of the brothers deals with his shame for Fyodor – who is himself a most profound study of attempted shamelessness as a strategy for avoiding shame. We are always vulnerable to shame because of our relationships with other persons and our commitments to institutions and communities. McCarthy provides a minor example of this form of shame in explaining her response to her boarding school's loss of identity. The Annie Wright Seminary gave up its distinctive practices to imitate Eastern schools. 'It is the story of a loss of regional identity, and I doubt that anyone else feels the shame of it as keenly as I do . . . . Weep with me, Reader . . . for what *was*, ineluctably, and on whose like no "Annie" will ever look' (*H.I.*, 172). Presumably this plea to 'weep with me' is largely facetious, but the passage contains a note of seriousness and reveals a truth about one's susceptibility to shame as a member of a group. When a person loses a job because of large-scale economic changes, or his child experiences failure, or his nation bullies a weaker country, or a parent is an alcoholic, he may feel a form of shame which is especially painful because it seems so remotely related to his sense of individual responsibility, and inflicted on him by external circumstances.

There are some forms of shame, then, which seem unavoidable, ineluctable. And, if conscience is alert, we are and should always remain vulnerable to shame brought about by our failures to measure up to our own standards. However, shame need not be seen as inevitably destructive. It is possible to come to terms with a great deal of shame – if not the spontaneous feeling at least the maintained sense of worthlessness and failure – through judging that a particular incident of shame should not weigh heavily in self-assessment. 'The influence of shame is counteracted by estimating any weakness (assumed to be insurmountable) at its actual importance, that is, by the development of an accurate sense of values.'[25] In assessing shame, a person may reflect on the proper sources of self-esteem, and revise his views of this matter. For Augustine, the self's worth does not rest on its possessions, affiliations, or achievements, but on its status as a created being in relationship to God. It is the conviction that his final worth is not undermined by shameful actions that allows him to confess his sins and to find in God's love solace and support for moral renewal. The belief that God's love is the only firm basis for self-esteem allows Augustine to criticize sources of false shame, which are as various as the innumerable idols which displace God as the standard of value.

Although McCarthy does not share Augustine's theological perspective, she, too, discriminates among various experiences of shame according to whether or not she can still affirm the values she violated. McCarthy deals with many experiences of shame by attributing them to a faulty assessment of the importance of the quality in which she felt deficient. Being ashamed of her clothes or her home in the Northwest, for example, cannot be justified as a legitimate reason for self-castigation. The discernment of false shame is often a crucial transition point in moral development. The original experience of shame is transcended – in any case the pain of its memory is diminished – when new values make clear the proper standards for self-assessment. One cannot continue to feel shame for the lack of that which no longer appears so important.

Is it ever wrong to overcome one's shame? McCarthy describes how she learned to overcome shame and guilt (which she does not distinguish in this passage) by repeatedly reliving in her mind sexual experiences which disturbed her:

> When you have committed an action that you cannot bear to think about, that causes you to writhe in retrospect, do not seek to evade the memory: *make* yourself relive it, confront it repeatedly over and over, till finally, you will discover, through sheer repetition it loses its power to pain you . . . . It works, but I am not sure that it is a good thing. Perhaps I did something to my immortal soul . . . . As I forced revolting memories to surge up before my closed eyes, almost burning the closed lids with fiery self-disgust, did I kill a moral nerve? To flinch from such memories, simply suppress them, might have been healthier. Is it right to overcome self-disgust? (*H.I.*, 156)

McCarthy used this method only to overcome sexual inhibitions, but suggests that it might also be used to overcome repugnance about such vices as cowardice or cruelty. She wonders whether it was stupid to try deliberately to diminish her sense of shame, overcoming a reaction which was 'a deep-lying instinct, part of my interior warning system, hence necessary to my animal safety'. Her guarantee that this method works is not entirely convincing. This passage would not have its power without her continuing repulsion from what was felt as – and still seems to her – a degrading form of sex. Her advice really describes a form of shamelessness, the attempt to overcome shame by 'killing a moral nerve'. McCarthy tried this method again, 'getting myself in training for my adult "career of crime."' Shamelessness means brazenly defying one's understanding of the conditions of self-respect, deliberately hardening oneself against reproach from any source, especially one's conscience.

This sort of rebellious defiance is an element in McCarthy's ambivalent attitude towards those who represent moral authority: her grandfather Preston; her favorite teacher, Miss Gowrie, with her 'Presbyterian conscience'; and even the character of Caesar, whose writing – 'just, laconic, severe, magnanimous, detached'

– she reluctantly grew to admire (*M.G.*, 154). Again and again she professes innocent surprise when others react negatively to her iconoclasm and defiance of expectations. McCarthy's story 'The Figures in the Clock' is a discerning analysis of the conflict within her own nature between a need to violate expectations, rules, and conventional norms, and a deep attraction to the persons and symbols representing fixed standards of conscience. Both sides of her ambivalence spring from childhood experiences of shame: 'The injustices my brothers and I had suffered in our childhood had made me a rebel against authority, but they had also prepared me to fall in love with justice' (*M.G.*, 167). She provides a most valuable study of the shameless individual, whose rebellion against certain norms often masks a stern conscience and a longing to live by those very ideals.

Psychotherapists tell us that we must face our shame to avoid its destructive power. From the therapeutic perspective, sharing one's shame with another person and feeling his or her support can help free a person from the condition of isolation and estrangement that constitutes much of the curse of shame.[26] Such a supportive relationship with another person, either inside or outside the framework of therapy, does not figure in McCarthy's written work as an important resource for dealing with shame. Hers is not the way of receiving solace from others, but the way of solitary reflection on one's life. The goal, however, is much the same: overcoming shame's destructive effects and recovering self-esteem through insight into one's deepest values. Writing an autobiography may in several ways contribute to the overcoming of shame. Insofar as a writer exposes his failures to public gaze, the very writing of autobiography seems to indicate that shame has been transcended – or else that he is shameless. Writing about the past may be therapeutic if repetition dulls the ache of a painful memory (McCarthy's 'sure-fire guilt-eradicator'). Continued reflection on one's past may lead to viewing the self as almost another person, since one becomes distanced from the shameful self in the process of objectifying it in words. Or autobiography may help in overcoming shame because the search for the origins of shame leads one to realize that feelings of inadequacy and worthlessness had causes which have changed or could be altered. 'In the act of searching . . . a person takes on the definition of shame as "acquired" rather than "inherent." This is contradictory to the whole shame experience, because shame is felt as fundamental to one's whole identity. In effect, a person can hardly look for how he or she *learned* to feel ashamed and *feel* ashamed at the same time.'[27] This therapeutic and healing insight may be realized, I think, through the writing process as well as through the 'talking cure' of psychotherapy. Incidents of shame may contribute to the learning process necessary for a person to realize his real commitments, deepest values, lasting standards. The interpretation of shame may be a necessary and beneficial aspect of the education of conscience.

Yet feelings of shame do not die easily. An autobiographer both distances herself from and identifies with the past self. At least a trace of shame returns in the admission that one was capable of this action or that timid submission. The constant tension between shame and self-esteem produces autobiography's inner dialectic of self-criticism and self-justification. It is the opportunity autobiography offers for confronting and assessing the sources of shame, and for recovering self-esteem, that explains the value of this literary form and activity for many minorities, women, and others who have been 'shamed' by society.

Shame and self-esteem are interdependent in the actual workings of a healthy conscience. For self-esteem, at least insofar as it is based on self-respect and integrity, demands that one acknowledge all that one has done, including the failures and foolishness. And shame, when it is honestly admitted and courageously confronted, testifies by its very nature to a person's commitment to those moral standards on which self-esteem is based. In excessive amounts shame can destroy a person's sense of the worthwhileness of life. But on the right occasion – one that can be justified by moral self-appraisal – shame indicates a person's genuine commitment to a value. Shame has no positive role if it merely demoralizes or leaves one despondent. And there is surely no reason why guilt or shame should be deliberately cultivated! Self-loathing by itself indicates no direction for future efforts. If in recalling the past, however, we are moved to a clearer consciousness of our enduring commitments, and if we can take corrective instruction that may help us in the future, shame may serve an essential function in the development of character:

> Shame and regret are literally helpless, for they are concentrated upon what we can do nothing about, on the past . . . . But if we *go on* from such feelings to weigh and measure, chart and explore – if, that is, they can instigate us to consideration of the

future – then guilt and remorse will be replaced by a purpose, a resolution, one test of whose efficiency is precisely the degree to which the penalty of conscience has been surmounted. Shame, then, is seen as a *price* we may have to pay for our weaknesses and the attempt to cope with them; and morbidity, or the tendency to linger in self-reproach, is the evidence of the failure of that attempt, of the inability to act.[28]

If my reflections on the past are accurate I cannot forget whatever has made me ashamed. And morally appraising the past exposes me to shame again, in the present moment. Yet shame need not be wholly destructive. The proper attitude to incidents of shame is neither forgetfulness nor tormented regret for what cannot be changed, but – as we see in the autobiographies of Augustine and McCarthy – accurate judgment about the significance of the event as an indication of character. This sort of assessment of shame does not completely dispel regret, or even remorse, but it should help to overcome the most destructive effects of shame. For in the very act of facing shame the self is seen to be not *altogether* worthless. While in the depths of shame a person feels totally worthless, recovery from shame depends on putting the experience in perspective, realizing that the failure pertains to only one capacity and occurred in a particular context. Recovery depends, too, on recognizing that there are other sources of self-esteem, including the ability to acknowledge the truth about oneself. The capacity to admit and reflect on one's errors, to confront them with courage and interpret their significance, shows honesty and integrity. These capacities should be, for a thoughtful and conscientious person, a source of self-respect and self-esteem. A truthful conscience is not only necessary to face shame, then, but should help a person overcome shame by serving as one source of self-esteem.

In the sense that the precipitating deed cannot be undone, there is no reparation for shame. Yet a kind of transcendence of shame – a refusal to be destroyed by it – may arise out of a person's honest admission of failure to live up to her expectations. New grounds for self-respect may emerge in admitting the truth, however bitter. Joan Didion writes of learning this when, to her great disappointment, she was not elected to Phi Beta Kappa. She recalls 'with embarrassing clarity the flavor of those particular ashes', and in retrospect sees the incident as a matter of misplaced self-respect – what I have called false shame. Real self-respect, she discovered, 'has nothing to do with the approval of others' or reputation. It means making a 'separate peace, a private reconciliation' with one's mistakes and failures:

> People with self-respect have the courage of their mistakes. They know the price of things . . . . People with self-respect exhibit a certain toughness, a kind of moral nerve; they display what was once called *character* . . . . Character – the willingness to accept responsibility for one's own life – is the source from which self-respect springs.[29]

Didion, like McCarthy, holds that shame which derives from a failure to live up to others' expectations is wrong, a kind of weak conformity. Shame based on failure to achieve self-chosen ideals, in contrast, is authentic, valid, and necessary. It reflects the sort of self-respect that frees a person from compulsive conformity to the expectations of others. Such self-respect gives the sense of intrinsic worth without which all our striving and our relationships to others are a vain attempt to be convinced that life is worth living. In short, essential elements in self-respect are the courage to admit mistakes and failure, and to feel shame as a sanction of conscience.

This view of character and self-respect is at work in McCarthy's autobiographies.[30] She attempts to acknowledge the shame in her life without minimizing it or indulging in self-pity, rationalization, or other strategies of avoidance. She earns a kind of moral victory as well as a vindication of self-respect though the honest admission and assessment of the sources of shame in her life. It is as if McCarthy is still convinced – perhaps more so than she realizes – of her original belief that self-knowledge must be painful to be true: 'Is reality, or truth, always so uncomfortable? That is not my opinion now (truth produces elation, surely, because of its closeness to beauty), but I evidently thought so when I was fourteen, for what was I doing but rubbing my heroines' noses in it, furiously, as though to wake them up?' (*H.I.*, 101).

How I Grew ends with just such an act of painfully earned self-knowledge, and the last lines of this autobiography crystallize what is most distinctive and valuable in McCarthy's reckoning with shame. On her wedding night she recognizes her mistake in marrying her first husband, Harold Johnsrud:

As we climbed into the big bed, I knew, too late, that I had *done the wrong thing*. To marry a man without loving him, which was what I had just done, not really perceiving it, was a wicked action, I saw. Stiff with remorse and terror, I lay under the thin blanket through a good part of the night; as far as I could tell from what seemed a measureless distance, my untroubled mate was sleeping. (*H.I.*, 267)

McCarthy was ashamed on her wedding night, and, writing half a century later, still assesses as 'wicked' her failure to have known her own heart and mind. She made a terrible mistake, betraying and inflicting suffering on both herself and Johnsrud, though she was apparently the main victim of their marriage. Paradoxically, this moment of crushing defeat – the recognition of an almost suicidal blindness in herself – represents a victory of lucidity and truthfulness, which is contrasted with her husband's oblivious slumber. McCarthy does not lie to herself even when tempted to pretend that the primary responsibility for her suffering rests outside herself. In McCarthy's ability to confront and assess her shame we discern the workings of a truthful conscience, and one of the most essential conditions for a proper sense of self-esteem.

8
Conclusion

Autobiography is not simply a description of how conscience operated in the past, but a searching assessment of the writer's character in both the past and the present. Thus the writing of autobiography reflects and represents an act of conscience. This thesis has been demonstrated and elaborated through the analysis of a number of autobiographies, especially the works of Montaigne and Samuel Johnson, Benjamin Franklin, Malcolm X, and Mary McCarthy. The moral concerns and the characters of even this select group of autobiographers are so various that one hesitates to make generalizations about the role of conscience in writing about the self. I have been primarily interested in understanding the diverse ways in which individual writers have been influenced by concerns of conscience – for instance, how McCarthy comes to terms with her shame about anti-Semitism, how Franklin reconciles his own self-interest with the welfare of others, or how Malcolm X criticizes racial forms of *ressentiment* in both his society and his own earlier attitudes. The specific issues and concerns that preoccupy each autobiographer depend on many variable factors in his or her situation and do not set the agenda for every autobiographer. Therefore the sort of conclusions I can offer here are more modest than the grand theories proposed by some critics of autobiography. I will summarize some central themes running through this book's chapters and state what I see as the broader significance of my approach to autobiography.

The relationship between the narrator of an autobiography and the past self who is this work's protagonist requires a process of interpretation and evaluation that inevitably involves conscience, or moral self-assessment. Such acts of conscience may take many forms. An author may confess her sins, offer an apology in defense of her actions, present extenuating or excusing conditions, or examine the significance of deeper motivations behind commendable or culpable actions. She may reject or revise a former moral standard or come to appreciate it in a new way. Conscience is both one of the motivating sources of a person's desire to write an autobiography and a primary influence on an autobiographer's self-critical reflections on the writing process. Chapter 2 explored how conscience can sponsor the writing of autobiography, serving as an incentive to truthful writing about the self, and how conscience monitors the autobiographical act, advising, warning, and supervising the writing according to the author's moral standards. Chapter 3 addressed from this perspective the relationship between character assessment and characterization, and later chapters explored in detail specific issues of conscience faced by particular writers.

Autobiographies reveal in especially vivid and complex form the ordinary workings of conscience. For instance, we can discern in these texts crucial relationships between narrative construction and theoretical reflection. The operation of conscience necessarily involves the construction of an autobiographical narrative. Moral self-assessment requires the creation of a story whose elements – such as plot, character, setting, tone, and narrative style – reveal much about a person's moral imagination and conscience. In autobiography, as in any sustained ethical reflection, these narrative elements are integrated with non-narrative moral discourse such as generalizations about principles, abstract formulation of ideals, lists of virtues, religious justifications of the standards of conscience, and theoretical accounts of moral beliefs. The narrative and non-narrative elements – which I will simply call principles – are not merely juxtaposed or co-ordinated, but constantly engender, complicate, and enrich each other. I examined this dynamic explicitly in the essays of Montaigne and Johnson, and a similar process structures the work of autobiographers from Augustine to Mary McCarthy. An autobiographer usually formulates principles, stating the moral significance of personal experience in a general way which may apply to others. Principles, such as Franklin's table of virtues, Malcolm's ideas about public virtue, or the values underlying McCarthy's view of proper shame – generate new narratives, as the author explains how the principles came to be seen as crucial, motivated new undertakings, or were revised in light of experience. Conscience involves not only the application of moral standards to one's personal story, but also narratives about how those moral standards were adopted, as well as reflection on their applicability to the stories of other individuals. The ways conscience integrates narrative and non-narrative elements is a neglected topic

in ethical theory that calls for further study and the insights of
autobiography.

In discussing Montaigne's and Johnson's ideas about conscience,
I held that it is somewhat misleading to separate their explicit
references to this term from their many other discussions of moral
reflection. All the writers studied may illuminate conscience when
they speak of 'mind' or 'heart' or when they demonstate some
aspect of moral assessment. Defined as moral self-assessment, conscience is an act or function of a person's entire being; it is not a
distinct faculty of the psyche, but encompasses feeling, memory,
imagination, logic, and will. In operation conscience involves active
interplay between all of the mind's powers and capacities. Therefore
conscience should not be isolated from these other human capacities. Nor can conscience be separated from many other moral
concepts, for it is inextricably related to ideals of character and
virtue, feelings of guilt and shame, conceptions of the individual's
relationship to society, and religious loyalties. Even as this book's
chapters focused on diverse topics and the concerns of different
autobiographers, we did not stray from the theme of conscience.

Throughout this book I have traced autobiographers' concern
with truthfulness. In Chapter 2 truthfulness was contrasted with
self-deception and presented as both an incentive for writing
autobiography and a crucial issue for conscience. Autobiography
is not only a matter of persuading readers of the credibility of
one's account; it involves a struggle to know one's own deepest
motives and desires. The difficulties of such self-knowledge are
an explicit subject of reflection in Montaigne's and Johnson's
essays. Malcolm X explores the nature of truthfulness in his
criticisms of racist 'brainwashing' and his analysis of his blind
devotion to Elijah Muhammed. Similarly, Mary McCarthy often
presents self-deception as a decisive factor in the situations which
precipitated shame in her life. Even Franklin, who is much less
interested in psychological complexity than the other writers
studied, notes at several points how rationalization hides the real
motives of action, as when he yielded to the temptation of a feast
of fish despite his vegetarian principles. To a skeptical critic, an
autobiographer's concern with truthfulness may seem only a matter
of adopting the proper rhetoric to establish his credibility before
an audience, only a matter of flourishing certain tropes to win the
reader's approval. It is indeed important to examine the various
meanings and rhetorics of truthfulness for different writers. My

approach here, however, has focused primarily on autobiography as a struggle for self-knowledge, as a writer responds to the challenges of understanding, depicting, and assessing oneself.

One of the ambiguities in the autobiographer's work arises from his awareness of his dependence on the conventions of autobiographical writing. Conventions, literary tropes, and fictional techniques are all necessary elements in any public presentation of one's story. As we have seen in the cases of many of these writers, self-consciousness about the literary conditions of autobiography may create scruples about the truthfulness of one's narrative. This theme was central in my account of truthfulness in Chapter 2 and my analysis of character and characterization in Chapter 3. Similar scruples may be seen in Malcolm's concern about his image in the popular media – and in his autobiography – as 'the angriest Negro', in McCarthy's awareness of how she shapes her reconstruction of events to 'make a good story', and even in Franklin's observations on his public *persona*. Franklin is not as troubled by this issue as are the other writers and always justifies skillful control of his public image. However, he does not lack scruples about this matter, as some critics have argued; because his conscience approves his actions he offers an apologia for his conduct. In each of these autobiographies, then, conscientious scruples prompt reflections on the theme of appearance and reality, as well as complex strategies demonstrating the writer's awareness of the necessary but ambiguous role of conventions in self-representation.

These autobiographers all recognize that the self is socially constructed. Similarly, they demonstrate that conscience is not a perennial given, but shaped by a person's particular context and influences. While each writer sees the capacity for moral self-assessment as a general human characteristic, I think each would agree that the way any particular individual's conscience operates is decisively influenced by his culture's beliefs and institutions. A modern 'sociology of knowledge' or critical theory is not required to recognize that conscience is socially constructed; this is a basic assumption of all the writers I have examined. Indeed, we have seen that a principle task of the autobiographer is analyzing the sources of conscience, and assessing whether or not various influences on one's moral development should now be affirmed or challenged. This analysis and evaluation of the sources of one's conscience is itself an act of conscience, and one way in which the autobiographical act offers the possibility for further development of the capacity for moral self-assessment, as well as for self-transcendence and regenerated commitment to one's ideals.

Autobiography represents a distinctive form of moral discourse in that it emphasizes personal moral standards that may not apply to others. I argued in Chapter 7 that part of the value of autobiography's first-person perspective is that it shows the place of standards of honor and integrity that may not be universalized or even generalized. Augustine's theft of pears, Malcolm's 'conking' his hair, and McCarthy's recital of a silly lyric cause these authors deep shame because they symbolize violations of self-respect. It would be difficult if not impossible to translate all of an autobiographer's concerns of conscience into impersonal laws or norms. At the same time, however, autobiography may involve not only a search for more authentic personal standards, but also an exercise of conscience that the author views as exemplary for others. The autobiographers I have discussed strive for the universal in ethical reflection at the same time that they particularize individual experience. What I said of Montaigne and Johnson holds as well for Augustine and Franklin, for McCarthy and Malcolm X: they are deeply personal writers for whom the meaning of their own experience is never merely personal. Therefore the two essayists attempt to generalize about the human condition, and to formulate principles of conscience that hold for every person. Franklin presents himself quite explicitly as a model of the virtues he wants his nation to adopt and practice. Malcolm X shows his concern for the broader significance of his moral experience not only in many didactic remarks about the reality of racism and *ressentiment* in the United States, but in his growing interest in and struggle to practice the public virtues which should be normative for everyone. Even McCarthy, who seems least interested in formulating moral standards applicable to other persons, tries to achieve in her writing a form of conscientiousness according to the same standards to which she holds others. The satirical thrust of so much of her writing, whether directed at herself or others, presupposes certain standards of truthfulness, sexual fidelity, and intellectual integrity that she believes are not simply subjective preferences, but rooted in objective reality. Common or public moral principles are as much a concern of these autobiographers as is the search for those insights and crises of conscience which give an individual a sense of uniquely personal identity.

In contrast to the way in which many literary critics approach autobiography, I see a good deal of continuity between writing a book about oneself and ordinary reflection on past and present experience. The functions of conscience in a person's private reflections and in his production of a public document such as an autobiography involve significant analogies as well as crucial differences. In opposition to the currently fashionable ideas that autobiographical narratives only refer to themselves or other texts, and that their ambiguity defers meaning endlessly, I submit that autobiographies illuminate many aspects of moral experience, especially the ways we reflect on and articulate understandings of the past, our personal and communal identities, and the development of our deepest convictions. Although this book focused on the role of conscience in writers rather than readers and critics of autobiography, I think that what first-person writing reveals about conscience has, potentially, deep personal significance for readers. Those who may never write an autobiography could learn much in regard to self-deception from Augustine's *Confessions*; they can be instructed by McCarthy about the need to face the sources of shame in one's life; and with Franklin they may reflect upon how an individual's relationship to a community is best understood. The act of reading an autobiography may itself engender conscientious self-assessment, as you compare your own experience to that of the autobiographer.

Throughout this book I have tried to practice my conception of ethical criticism. I have focused on and emphasized one dimension of my response to autobiography: the moral assessment of the writer's character as it shapes his or her work. Inevitably and necessarily, critics interpret and evaluate autobiographies partly according to their own moral standards and ideals of self-knowledge and self-representation. This is true even of those critics who wish to deconstruct traditional notions of the self and of writing, for they assess authors, among other things, according to whether they accept or are critical of the concepts in question. I have attempted to be self-conscious and self-critical about how ethical concerns have shaped my own readings of autobiographies. I tried to understand and describe accurately some of the central interests of Montaigne and Johnson, Franklin, Malcolm X, and McCarthy, but I also interpreted and evaluated these works in terms of their value for elucidating my own moral concerns. I argued for their significance in practicing certain virtues, heeding certain scruples, or adhering to certain ideals that I believe are crucially important in human experience. Thus I have tried to demonstrate the centrality of ethical concerns not only in the writing of autobiography, but in interpretation and criticism of it.

I explored the religious dimensions of conscience in two ways. First, we have seen how these autobiographers were decisively influenced by the Christian tradition, even as they all stand in critical relation to it. Of the five main authors discussed, Samuel Johnson is the most deeply committed to Christian faith, but his essays adopt a secular stance, referring in a very general way to 'religion' or 'belief' rather than invoking specific Christian doctrines. Montaigne and Franklin were each quite critical of certain Christian beliefs and practices in their time, and concerns of conscience led them to reject some of these. Yet they were decisively influenced by Christian conceptions of the self, conscience, and the written text of a life. Even though Malcolm X and McCarthy rejected Christian faith, their self-conceptions were deeply affected by Christianity, as is immediately evident, for instance, in the title *Memories of a Catholic Girlhood* and in Malcolm's ambivalent comparison of his own conversion to that of the apostle Paul. The example of Augustine has been a crucial touchstone in most of this book's chapters. Rather than summarizing the specific influences on and beliefs of each writer, I will simply conclude that Christian norms for moral reflection and for writing about the self cannot be evaded or ignored by a conscientious autobiographer in Western culture. Whether one adheres to them, rejects them, or reinterprets their relevence in a new way, Christian norms and traditions become an inescapable issue of conscience for a self-critical autobiographer.

I have also presented the autobiographical act as involving a second kind of religious dimension. As a writer examines sources of identity and fundamental convictions, she may revise her beliefs about what is ultimately worth commitment and belief. Autobiography thus offers the potential for self-transcendence through a reorientation of value and through a transformation of one's ultimate concerns. To speak of this process as religious will not satisfy those who would limit 'religion' to believers in God. However, I discern in each of the works studied the expression of an ultimate concern, Paul Tillich's definition of religious faith. An ultimate concern means a conviction about what is ultimately true and good, and a commitment to act in accord with such belief. Conscience is deeply bound up with ultimate convictions and commitments, for a person's ultimate concerns ground and justify the principles according to which he assesses himself.

In this larger sense of religion as ultimate concern, it is an essentially religious conviction and motivation that underlies many of these autobiographers' examinations of conscience. We can see distinctive religious concerns in the essayists' reflections on the sources of moral failure and in their search for the common patterns of human experience. Franklin's most fundamental beliefs motivate his attempt to describe an exemplary life that reconciles individual self-interest and the welfare of others. An ultimate and explicitly theological concern is expressed by Malcolm's formulation and practice of the public virtues, which are required of all humans by Allah and justifiable to non-Muslims on other grounds. In her assessment of experiences of shame, McCarthy distinguishes between false shame and the authentic moral shame which indicates a falling away from her highest ideals and standards. I argued in Chapter 7 that this endeavor depends on her discernment of those values which justifiably deserve lasting commitment, in contrast to mistaken or temporary values. In all of these autobiographies, the writer tries to ground personal identity in a conception of moral truth and goodness, and to judge their character according to their ultimate convictions.

In a different context, T. S. Eliot wrote:

> It is not enough to understand what we ought to be, unless we know what we are; and we do not understand what we are, unless we know what we ought to be. The two forms of self-consciousness, knowing what we are and what we ought to be, must go together.[1]

Although Eliot was speaking of the necessity of a religious criticism of literature, his remark applies even more aptly to the role of conscience in autobiography. The two forms of self-consciousness – of what we are and of what we ought to be – 'must go together'. Conscience integrates these two necessary components of identity, synthesizing a person's construction of past and present experience with her commitment to moral and religious values. The autobiographies I have examined, in which each writer reinterprets ultimate concerns and revises ethical commitments, offer articulate, compelling, and instructive examples of how the process of moral self-assessment may reflect religious understanding, transformation, and reorientation.

Thus our understanding of the nature of autobiography, our view of the possibilities of ethical criticism, and our conception of conscience as ethical and religious reflection may all be enriched by study of the conscience of the autobiographer.

Notes

CHAPTER 1: INTRODUCTION

1. For criticisms of deconstruction see Frederick Crews, *Skeptical Engagements* (New York: Oxford University Press, 1986); John Searle, 'The World Turned Upside Down', *The New York Review of Books* (27 October 1983) pp. 73–9; and John Ellis, *Against Deconstruction* (Princeton, N.J.: Princeton University Press, 1989). For a more appreciative assessment, see three works by Christopher Norris: *Deconstruction: Theory and Practice* (London and New York: Methuen, 1982); *The Contest of Faculties: Philosophy and Theory after Deconstruction* (London and New York: Methuen, 1985); and *Deconstruction and the Interests of Theory* (Norman, OK and London: University of Oklahoma Press, 1989).

CHAPTER 2: CONSCIENCE AND TRUTHFULNESS

1. See Elizabeth Bruss, *Autobiographical Acts: The Changing Situation of a Literary Genre* (Baltimore: Johns Hopkins University Press, 1976).
2. Ronald Preston, extending Aquinas' definition of conscience as 'the mind of man making moral judgments', in *The Westminster Dictionary of Christian Ethics*, ed. James F. Childress and John MacQuarrie (Philadelphia: The Westminster Press, 1986) p. 116. In contrast to this broad definition, some views of conscience restrict the term exclusively to negative judgments about action, and some views see conscience referring always to past actions. The range of theological, psychological, and philosophical issues surrounding conscience may be seen in J. Donnelly and L. Lyons, eds, *Conscience* (New York: Alba House, 1973); C. E. Nelson, ed., *Conscience: Theological and Psychological Perspectives* (New York: Newman Press, 1973); Eric Mount, Jr., *Conscience and Responsibility* (Richmond, Virginia: John Knox Press, 1969); and Michel Despland, 'Conscience', *The Encyclopedia of Religion* (New York: Macmillan, 1987) vol. 4, 45–52.
3. Paul John Eakin, *Fictions in Autobiography: Studies in the Art of Self-Invention* (Princeton, N.J.: Princeton University Press, 1985) pp. 213, 218, 219.
4. Ibid., p. 226.
5. Jean-Jacques Rousseau, *Confessions*, trans. J. M. Cohen (New York: Penguin, 1953) p. 17.
6. Saul Friedländer, *When Memory Comes* (New York: Avon, 1978) p. 114.

7. M. K. Gandhi, *An Autobiography: The Story of My Experiments with Truth* (Boston: Beacon Press, 1957) pp. xv, 8.
8. Augustine, *Confessions*, trans. R. S. Pine-Coffin (New York: Penguin, 1961) p. 207 (Book X, ch. 2).
9. Karl Weintraub, *The Value of the Individual: Self and Circumstance in Autobiography* (Chicago: The University of Chicago Press, 1978) pp. 39–40.
10. Mary McCarthy, *Memories of a Catholic Girlhood* (New York: Harcourt Brace Jovanovich, 1957) pp. 20–21.
11. Rousseau, *Confessions*, p. 30.
12. Edmund Gosse, *Father and Son* (New York: Norton, 1963) p. 35.
13. Ibid., p. 250.
14. Augustine, *Confessions*, p. 43 (II, 1).
15. Ibid., p. 245 (X, 37).
16. Ibid., pp. 247–8 (X, 38).
17. J. H. Newman, *Apologia Pro Vita Sua*, edited by David De Laura (New York: Norton, 1968) p. 13.
18. C. S. Lewis, *Surprised by Joy* (New York: Harcourt Brace Jovanovich, 1955) pp. 232–3.
19. See Frederick Kirchhoff, 'Travel as Anti-Autobiography: William Morris' *Icelandic Journals*' in George P. Landow, ed., *Approaches to Victorian Autobiography* (Athens, Ohio: Ohio University Press, 1979) pp. 292–310.
20. Among many recent studies of self-deception, three articles which link the phenomenon to autobiography are Stanley Hauerwas, 'Self-Deception and Autobiography: Reflections on Speer's *Inside the Third Reich*' in Hauerwas's *Truthfulness and Tragedy: Further Investigations into Christian Ethics* (Notre Dame, IN: University of Notre Dame Press, 1977) pp. 82–98; and Anthony Palmer and T. S. Champlin's essays in 'Self-Deception: A Problem about Autobiography', *Proceedings of the Aristotelian Society*, supplementary volume 53 (1979) 61–94.
21. Rousseau, *Confessions*, p. 88.
22. See Kenneth E. Kirk's *Conscience and Its Problems* (London: Longman's, Green & Co., 1927) chapters 5–7, for an interesting Anglican approach to moral casuistry. Other traditional moral categories could be used as a framework for interpreting the conscience of the autobiographer, for example the erroneous, the doubtful, or the perplexed conscience.
23. Krister Stendahl, 'The Apostle Paul and the Introspective Conscience of the West', in *The Writings of St. Paul*, ed. Wayne Meeks (New York: Norton, 1972) p. 433.
24. For a theoretical statement of this view see Dietrich Bonhoeffer, *Ethics* (New York: Macmillan, 1955) especially pp. 224–54, where the responsible acceptance of guilt characteristic of 'deputyship' is contrasted with the good conscience which refuses to sacrifice its integrity. For the autobiographical context of Bonhoeffer's ideas, see *Letters and Papers from Prison* (New York: Macmillan, 1953), for example pp. 17–18: 'The man with a conscience . . . . starts lying

to his conscience as a means of avoiding despair. If a man relies exclusively on his conscience he fails to see how a bad conscience is sometimes more wholesome and strong than a deluded one.'

25. *Joy*, pp. vii, 198.
26. Phyllis Grosskurth, 'Where was Rousseau?' in Landow, ed., *Approaches to Victorian Autobiography*, p. 37.
27. Howard Helsinger, 'Credence and Credibility: The Concern for Honesty in Victorian Autobiography', in Landow, ed., *Approaches to Victorian Autobiography*, p. 56.
28. Avrom Fleishman, *Figures of Autobiography: The Language of Self-Writing* (Berkeley: University of California Press, 1983) p. 54. Here Fleishman draws on the work of Pierre Courcelle.
29. Ibid., p. 50.
30. This is the theme of Roy Pascal's groundbreaking study, *Design and Truth in Autobiography* (Cambridge: Harvard University Press, 1960).
31. Since I completed this manuscript, Timothy Dow Adams published *Telling Lies in Modern American Autobiography* (Chapel Hill, N.C.: The University of North Carolina Press, 1990). Adams shares my view that truthfulness in autobiography can be achieved in many ways, even through lying: 'My standard is not literal accuracy but personal authenticity. For me, narrative truth and personal myth are more telling than literal fidelity; the autobiographer's reasons for telling lies are more important than absolute accuracy' (pp. x–xi). I would emphasize far more, however, the crucial roles of conscience in defining what counts as lying, in shaping the autobiographer's confession or implication of a need to lie, and in the justification for lying in the pursuit of 'personal authenticity' (Adams) or what I call essential truthfulness.
32. In *The Company We Keep: An Ethics of Fiction* (Berkeley: University of California Press, 1988) Wayne Booth interprets the ethical criticism of fiction as our assessment of the quality of the life we lead during the hours of reading. Although we read autobiographies somewhat differently than we read novels, Booth's account illuminates the ways that, in both kinds of narrative, we are constantly assessing the character of the maker of the story.
33. David Little, 'Duties of Station vs. Duties of Conscience: Are there Two Moralities?' in Donald Jones, ed., *Private and Public Ethics: Tensions Between Conscience and Institutional Responsibility* (New York and Toronto: The Edwin Mellen Press, n.d.) pp. 142–3.
34. McCarthy, *Memories*, pp. 4–5.
35. Ibid., pp. 97, 124, 164–5.
36. Ibid., pp. 83.
37. *The Autobiography of Malcolm X*, with the assistance of Alex Haley (New York: Ballantine Books, 1964) pp. 415–16.
38. Augustine, *Confessions*, pp. 210–211 (Book X, ch. 4–5).
39. Rousseau, *Confessions*, p. 262.
40. Jean Starobinski, *Jean-Jacques Rousseau: Transparency and Obstruction*, trans. Arthur Goldhammer (Chicago: The University of Chicago

Press, 1988) p. 198.
41.   Ibid., p. 200.
42.   James Childress, 'Appeals to Conscience', *Ethics* 89 (1979) p. 319:
       'Although a person's appeal to his conscience usually involves an
       appeal to moral standards, conscience is not itself the standard.
       It is the mode of consciousness resulting from the application of
       standards to his conduct. For example, the retrospective bad con-
       science emerges after the moral judgment about the act. Even in the
       prospective bad conscience, a matter of the imagination, conscience
       still comes after the judgment of rightness and wrongness.'

CHAPTER 3:   CHARACTER AND CHARACTERIZATION

1.   In this chapter I will often refer to religious autobiography, although
      many of my points apply more broadly and generally to other auto-
      biographies. Defining religious autobiography and distinguishing it
      from 'non-religious' autobiography is a difficult task, complicated
      by the many and diverse uses of the term 'spiritual autobiography'.
      Although the issues raised by the relationship between character
      and characterization are not unique to religious autobiography, I
      stress their significance for current discussions in religious studies
      and 'narrative theology'.
2.   Sallie McFague, *Speaking in Parables* (Philadelphia: Fortress Press,
      1975); Michael Novak, *Ascent of the Mountain, Flight of the Dove*
      (New York: Harper and Row, 1971); James W. McClendon, *Biog-
      raphy as Theology* (Nashville: Abingdon Press, 1974); Janet Varner
      Gunn, *Autobiography: Towards a Poetics of Experience* (Philadelphia:
      University of Pennsylvania Press, 1982); John S. Dunne, *A Search
      for God in Time and Memory* (New York: Macmillan and Company,
      1967); Stanley Hauerwas, with David Burrell, 'Self-Deception and
      Autobiography: Reflections on Speer's *Inside the Third Reich*', in
      Hauerwas's *Truthfulness and Tragedy* (Notre Dame: University of
      Notre Dame Press, 1977); George Stroup, *The Promise of Narrative
      Theology: Recovering the Gospel in the Church* (Atlanta: John Knox
      Press, 1981); Michael Goldberg, *Theology and Narrative: A Critical
      Introduction* (Nashville: Abingdon Press, 1982).
3.   Stephen Crites, 'The Narrative Quality of Experience', *Journal of the
      American Academy of Religion* 39 (1971) 291–311.
4.   For example, see Stroup, *Promise*, p. 131: 'Personal identity is the
      interpretation of personal history by means of the exercise of
      memory. As we have seen, personal identity takes the form of a nar-
      rative because of its intrinsically historical nature. Precisely because
      "the formal quality of experience through time", as Crites argues,
      "is inherently narrative", personal identity as an interpretation of
      human experience takes the narrative form of autobiography.'
5.   See, for instance, Jerome H. Buckley, *The Turning Key: Autobiography
      and the Subjective Impulse Since 1800* (Cambridge, Mass.: Harvard

University Press, 1984). Similarly, James M. Cox, in *Recovering Literature's Lost Ground: Essays in American Autobiography* (Baton Rouge: Louisiana State University Press, 1989) p. 34, expresses dismay about 'the ease with which literary critics assure themselves that "mere" fact has little to do with the art of autobiography'. This assumption, Cox asserts, has led to a contraction of the definition of literature, so that great memoirs such as those by Jefferson and Grant are neglected.

6. James Olney, 'Autobiography and the Cultural Moment: A Thematic, Historical, and Bibliographical Introduction', in *Autobiography: Essays Theoretical and Critical*, ed. James Olney (Princeton: Princeton University Press, 1980) p. 21.
7. Ibid., p. 23.
8. Louis Renza, 'The Veto of the Imagination: A Theory of Autobiography', in Olney, ed., *Autobiography*, p. 286.
9. Michael Sprinker, 'Fictions of the Self: The End of Autobiography', in Olney, ed., *Autobiography*, p. 342.
10. Barrett J. Mandel, 'Full of Life Now', in Olney, ed., *Autobiography*, p. 50.
11. Jean Starobinski, 'The Style of Autobiography', in Olney, ed., *Autobiography*, p. 75.
12. James Olney, 'Some Versions of Memory/Some Versions of *Bios*: The Ontology of Autobiography', in Olney, ed., *Autobiography*, p. 239.
13. Christine Downing, 'Revisioning Autobiography: The Bequest of Freud and Jung', *Soundings* 60 (1977) 210–228.
14. An exception to the general lack of attention to characterization in religious studies is James Laney, 'Characterization and Moral Judgments', *The Journal of Religion* 55 (1975) 405–14, which explains the significance of the activity of characterization in moral judgment, although Laney does not discuss autobiography. Wesley Kort's *Moral Fiber: Character and Belief in Recent American Fiction* (Philadelphia: Fortress Press, 1982) investigates some ways in which fictional characters are shaped by novelists' cultural and religious beliefs about human nature. Although there are significant analogies between character assessment in fiction and in autobiography, an author's assessment and characterization of his own character raise the distinctive questions addressed in this chapter.
15. Paul Ricœur, 'Narrative Time', *Critical Inquiry* 7 (1980) 178.
16. Frank Kermode, *The Genesis of Secrecy: On the Interpretation of Narrative* (Cambridge, Mass.: Harvard University Press, 1979) p. 77: 'Character does generate narrative, just as narrative generates character. The primitive "ado" must, insofar as it is a series of actions, have agents, and these agents, insofar as ado or fable acquires extension, must transcend their original type and function, must cease to be merely Hero, Opponent, and so on, and acquire idiosyncracies, have proper names. The more elaborate the story grows – the more remote from its schematic base – the more these agents will deviate from type and come to look like "characters." The immediate motive may be realism or something else; whatever

it is, the text of the story is spangled with signs that may be read as part of the evidence from which we habitually construct character.'

17.   Elizabeth Bruss, *Autobiographical Acts: The Changing Situation of a Literary Genre* (Baltimore: Johns Hopkins University Press, 1976) p. 10: 'There is no intrinsically autobiographical form. But there are limited generalizations to be made about the dimensions of action which are common to these autobiographies, and which seem to form the core of our notion of the functions an autobiographical text must perform.'

18.   Olney, 'Autobiography and the Cultural Moment', p. 25.

19.   Quotations in parentheses refer to Malcolm X, with Alex Haley, *The Autobiography of Malcolm X* (New York: Ballantine Books, 1965).

20.   Paul John Eakin, 'Malcolm X and the Limits of Autobiography', in Olney, ed., *Autobiography*, p. 182.

21.   Robertson Davies, *Fifth Business* (Harmondsworth, England: Penguin Books, 1970); *The Manticore* (Harmondsworth, England: Penguin Books, 1972); and *World of Wonders* (Harmondsworth, England: Penguin Books, 1975).

22.   Davies, *Manticore*, p. 251.

23.   Davies, *Fifth*, pp. 261, 261, 262.

24.   Davies, *Manticore*, p. 231.

25.   Davies, *World*, p. 135.

26.   Davies, *World*, pp. 142–3.

27.   Davies, *World*, p. 137.

28.   Davies, *Manticore*, p. 94.

CHAPTER 4:   CONSCIENCE IN THE ESSAYS OF MONTAIGNE AND JOHNSON

1.   Virginia Woolf, 'The Modern Essay', in *The Common Reader* (New York: Harcourt, Brace and World, 1925) p. 216.

2.   *Concordance des Essais de Montaigne*, ed. Roy Leake (Geneva: Librairie Droz, 1981) vol. I, pp. 265–6 cites 124 usages of 'conscience.'

3.   Jerome Schwartz, in '"La Conscience d'un homme": Reflections on the Problem of Conscience in the *Essais*', in *O Un Amy! Essays on Montaigne in Honor of Donald M. Frame*, ed. Raymond C. LaCharite (Lexington, Kentucky: French Forum, 1977) pp. 242–76, surveys Montaigne's use of the term conscience, and sees his conflicting statements on the nature of conscience as characteristic of Montaigne's eclecticism.

4.   Quotations from Montaigne are taken from *The Complete Essays of Montaigne*, translated by Donald M. Frame (Stanford, CA: Stanford University Press, 1965).

5.   Quotations by Johnson are taken from *Essays from the 'Rambler', 'Adventurer', and 'Idler'*, edited by W. J. Bate (New Haven: Yale University Press, 1968). This readily accessible and handy edition has been used rather than the complete Yale Edition, which collects

all of Johnson's essays in Volumes II to V.

6. The subject of Montaigne's religious views and their relationship with his ethical thought has received extensive treatment. I have been most helped by Donald Frame's *Montaigne's Discovery of Man: The Humanization of a Humanist* (New York: Columbia University Press, 1955) and especially R. A. Sayce's *The Essays of Montaigne: A Critical Exploration* (London: Weidenfeld and Nicolson, 1972) which has influenced much of my discussion of Montaigne.

7. W. Jackson Bate, *The Achievement of Samuel Johnson* (Chicago: The University of Chicago Press, 1955) p. 208.

8. On Montaigne's skepticism, see Richard H. Popkin, *The History of Skepticism from Erasmus to Descartes* (New York: Harper, 1968).

9. W. Jackson Bate, *Samuel Johnson* (New York: Harcourt Brace Jovanovich, 1975) p. 295. See also pp. 493–6 for further explanation of 'satire manquée', a term which unfortunately gives the misleading impression that Johnson tried to write in another genre but failed.

10. Georg Lukács, 'On the Nature and Form of the Essay', in *Soul and Form*, translated by Anna Bostock (first published 1911; Cambridge, Mass.: The MIT Press, 1974) p. 9.

11. Among works on Montaigne as an autobiographer, I have been most helped by James Olney, *Metaphors of Self: The Meaning of Autobiography*, chapter two, (Princeton: Princeton University Press, 1972); Karl Joachim Weintraub, *The Value of the Individual: Self and Circumstance in Autobiography*, chapter eight, (Chicago: The University of Chicago Press, 1978); and Jean Starobinski, *Montaigne in Motion*, trans. Arthur Goldhammer (Chicago: The University of Chicago Press, 1985).

12. Bate, *Johnson*, pp. 312–13.

13. On Montaigne's use of the term 'essay', see Sayce, *Essays of Montaigne*, pp. 19–21.

14. Paul K. Alkon compares Johnson's moral essays and his sermons in *Samuel Johnson and Moral Discipline*, chapter six (Evanston, IL: Northwestern University Press, 1967). Alkon's fourth chapter, 'Freedom and Voluntary Delusion', is an excellent study of Johnson's analysis of self-deception, a topic closely connected with ideas about conscience.

15. Herbert Fingarette, *Self-Deception* (New York: Humanities Press, 1969) p. 143.

16. Ibid., p. 143.

17. Lukacs, 'The Essay', p. 18.

18. Olney, *Metaphors*, p. 53.

19. Bate, *Johnson*, pp. 297–8.

CHAPTER 5:   FRANKLIN AND THE CRITICS OF INDIVIDUALISM

1. Steven Lukes, *Individualism* (Oxford: Blackwell, 1973).

2. Thomas Heller, Morton Sosna, and David E. Wellbery, eds,

Reconstructing Individualism: Autonomy, Individuality, and the Self in Western Thought (Stanford, CA: Stanford University Press, 1986) pp. 1, 2.

3. Lukes, p. 28.
4. Michael Sandel, 'Introduction', in Michael Sandel, ed., *Liberalism and its Critics* (New York: New York University Press, 1984) p. 9.
5. The phrases in quotation marks refer to the last three chapters of Jean Grimshaw's *Philosophy and Feminist Thinking* (Minneapolis: University of Minnesota Press, 1986) a sympathetic though critical analysis of these themes in feminist thought.
6. 'Now, all Franklin's moral attitudes are coloured with utilitarianism. Honesty is useful, because it assures credit; so are punctuality, industry, frugality, and that is the reason they are virtues . . . . Those virtues, like all others, are only in so far virtues as they are actually useful to the individual, and the surrogate of mere appearance is always sufficient when it accomplishes the end in view. It is a conclusion which is inevitable for strict utilitarianism.' Max Weber, from *The Protestant Ethic and the Spirit of Capitalism,* in the Norton Critical Edition of *The Autobiography of Benjamin Franklin,* edited by J. A. Leo Lemay and P. M. Zall (New York: Norton, 1986) p. 283.
7. Robert Bellah, Richard Madsen, William Sullivan, Ann Swidler, and Steven M. Tipton, *Habits of the Heart: Individualism and Commitment in American Life* (Berkeley: University of California Press, 1985) p. 336.
8. Bellah, *Habits,* p. 33.
9. See Jeffrey Stout, 'Liberal Society and the Languages of Morals'; Christopher Lasch, 'The Communitarian Critique of Liberalism'; and Robert Bellah, 'A Response: The Idea of Practices in *Habits*'; all in *Soundings* 69, no. 1–2 (1986) a symposium on *Habits of The Heart.*
10. MacIntyre, *After Virtue* (Notre Dame, IN: Univeristy of Notre Dame Press, 1981) p. 175.
11. Ibid., p. 185.
12. Bellah, *Habits,* p. 334.
13. Stout, pp. 44–45.
14. Lasch, p. 71.
15. See John Freccero, 'Autobiography and Narrative', in *Reconstructing Individualism.*
16. Karl Joachim Weintraub, *The Value of the Individual: Self and Circumstance in Autobiography* (Chicago: The University of Chicago Press, 1978) p. xi.
17. Weintraub, p. xvi.
18. Ibid., p. xvii.
19. See Lukes, *Individualism,* chapter two.
20. Weintraub, p. 252.
21. Ibid., pp. 259–60.
22. Bellah, *Habits,* p. 334.
23. Weintraub, *Value,* p. 325.
24. Ibid., p. 336.
25. Ibid., p. 257.

26. All quotations from Franklin's *Autobiography* are taken from the Norton Critical Edition edited by J. A. Leo Lemay and P. M. Zall (New York: Norton, 1986).
27. MacIntyre, p. 181.
28. Ibid., p. 184.
29. Lukes, *Individualism*, p. 73, describes the notion of the abstract individual as follows: 'According to this conception, individuals are pictured abstractly as given, with given interests, wants, purposes, needs, etc.; while society and the state are pictured as sets of actual or possible social arrangements which respond more or less adequately to those individuals' requirements.'
30. Lasch, 'The Communitarian Critique', p. 67.
31. Lasch, p. 72.
32. My discussion of 'cautionary doubles' draws on Michael T. Gilmore's 'Franklin and the Shaping of American Ideology', in Brian M. Barbour, ed., *Benjamin Franklin: A Collection of Critical Essays* (Englewood Cliffs, N.J.: Prentice-Hall, Inc., 1979) pp. 105–124.
33. Maxine Hong Kingston, *The Woman Warrior: Memoirs of a Childhood Among Ghosts* (New York: Random House, 1975); Richard Rodriguez, *Hunger of Memory* (New York: Bantam, 1982).
34. Raymund A. Paredes, 'Autobiography and Ethnic Politics: Richard Rodriguez's *Hunger of Memory*', *A/B: Auto/Biography Studies* 3 (1987) 21.
35. D. H. Lawrence, from *Studies in Classic American Literature*, in the Norton edition of *Benjamin Franklin's Autobiography*, p. 289.
36. *The Autobiography of Malcolm X* (New York, Ballantine Books, 1964) p. 38.
37. See Daniel B. Shea, Jr., *Spiritual Autobiography in Early America* (Princeton: Princeton University Press, 1968).
38. Although I think he exaggerates Franklin's ironic detachment from his various roles, the distinct personae who narrate the parts of Franklin's autobiography are well traced by Robert Sayre in *The Examined Self: Benjamin Franklin, Henry Adams, Henry James* (Princeton, N.J.: Princeton University Press, 1964).
39. On the notion of authenticity see Lionel Trilling, *Sincerity and Authenticity* (Cambridge: Harvard University Press, 1971) from whom I have also drawn the phrase 'the adversarial stance towards society'.
40. Ralph Waldo Emerson, 'Self-Reliance', in *Ralph Waldo Emerson: Essays and Lectures* (New York: The Library of America, 1983) p. 261.
41. Weintraub, p. 333.

CHAPTER 6: *RESSENTIMENT*, PUBLIC VIRTUES, AND MALCOLM X

1. Because it is always a negative characteristic, *ressentiment* is more like envy than it is like resentment. According to John Rawls, *A Theory of Justice* (Cambridge, Mass.: Harvard University Press, 1971) p. 533:

'Envy is not a moral feeling. No moral principle need be cited in its explanation. It is sufficient to say that the better situation of others catches our attention. We are downcast by their good fortune and no longer value as highly what we have; and this sense of hurt and loss arouses our rancor and hostility. Thus one must be careful not to conflate envy and resentment. For resentment is a moral feeling. If we resent our having less than others, it must be because we think that their being better off is the result of unjust institutions, or wrongful conduct on their part. Those who express resentment must be prepared to show why certain institutions are unjust or how others have injured then.' However, while *ressentiment*, like envy, is 'not a moral feeling' that can ever be justified, it becomes entangled in a self-deceptive process of moral rationalization.

2. Friedrich Nietzsche, *On the Genealogy of Morals*, in *Basic Writings of Nietzsche*, ed. and trans. Walter Kaufmann (New York: Modern Library, 1966) pp. 472–3.
3. For an analysis of Nietzsche's conception of *ressentiment*, see Walter Kaufmann, *Nietzsche: Philosopher, Psychologist, Antichrist*, fourth edn (Princeton: Princeton University Press, 1974) pp. 371–378.
4. Max Scheler, *Ressentiment*, ed. with an introduction by Lewis A. Coser; translated by William W. Holdheim (New York: Schocken Books, 1961) p. 52.
5. Scheler, p. 46.
6. Fredric Jameson, *The Political Unconscious: Narrative as a Socially Symbolic Act* (Ithaca, N.Y.: Cornell University Press, 1981) p. 118.
7. Ibid., p. 114.
8. Although he usually translates any conflict into the terms of the Marxist class struggle, Jameson recognizes, in his discussion of Nietzsche, the broader dimensions of the phenomenon whereby 'otherness' in many forms may be equated with evil: 'The concept of good and evil is a positional one that coincides with categories of Otherness. Evil thus, as Nietzsche taught us, continues to characterize whatever is radically different from me, whatever by virtue of precisely that difference seems to constitute a real and urgent threat to my own existence. So from the earliest times, the stranger from another tribe, the "barbarian" who speaks an incomprehensible language and follows "outlandish" customs, but also the woman, whose biological difference stimulates fantasies of castration and devoration, or in our own time, the avenger of accumulated resentments from some oppressed class or race, or else that alien being, Jew or Communist, behind whose apparently human features a malignant and preternatural intelligence is thought to lurk: these are some of the archetypal figures of the Other, about whom the essential point to be made is not so much that he is feared because he is evil; rather he is evil because he is Other, alien, different, strange, unclean, and unfamiliar' (p. 115).
9. See Giles Gunn, *The Interpretation of Otherness: Literature, Religion, and the American Imagination* (New York: Oxford University Press, 1979) p. 83.

10. See Alasdair MacIntyre, *After Virtue: A Study in Moral Theory* (Notre Dame, IN: University of Notre Dame Press, 1981); and Stanley Hauerwas, *A Community of Character: Toward a Constructive Christian Social Ethic* (Notre Dame, IN: University of Notre Dame Press, 1981).

11. For a fuller discussion of MacIntyre's and Hauerwas's approach to ethics see John Barbour, 'The Virtues in a Pluralistic Context', *The Journal of Religion* 63 (1983) 175–82.

12. John Henry Newman, *Apologia Pro Vita Sua*, edited by David DeLaura (New York: Norton, 1968) p. 8.

13. Lionel Trilling, *Sincerity and Authenticity* (Cambridge, Mass.: Harvard University Press, 1971) p. 93.

14. Ibid., p. 94.

15. MacIntyre, *After Virtue*, p. 244.

16. Trilling, *Sincerity*, p. 1.

17. Quotations in parentheses refer to Malcolm X, *The Autobiography of Malcolm X*, with the assistance of Alex Haley (New York: Ballantine Books, 1964).

CHAPTER 7:   SHAME IN THE AUTOBIOGRAPHIES
OF MARY McCARTHY

1. See Gerhart Piers and Milton Singer, *Guilt and Shame* (Springfield, IL: Charles Thomas, 1953) p. 11: 'Whereas guilt is generated whenever a boundary . . . is touched or transgressed, shame occurs when a goal . . . is not being reached. It thus indicates a real "shortcoming." Guilt anxiety accompanies transgression; shame, failure.'

2. Helen Merrell Lynd, *On Shame and the Search for Identity* (New York: Harcourt, Brace, and Co., 1958) pp. 27–28.

3. McCarthy's forward to the first edition of *The Company She Keeps* (1942) quoted in Doris Grumbach, *The Company She Kept* (New York: Coward-McCann, Inc., 1967) p. 92.

4. *H. I.* refers to *How I Grew* (New York: Harcourt Brace Jovanovich, 1987) and *M. G.* refers to *Memories of a Catholic Girlhood* (New York: Harcourt Brace Jovanovich, 1957). All quotations refer to these editions and are cited within parentheses in the text.

5. 'My Confession' in McCarthy's *On the Contrary* (New York: Farrar, Straus, and Cudahy, 1961) p. 84.

6. Ibid., p. 88.

7. Erik Erikson, 'Autonomy v. Shame and Doubt' (from *Childhood and Society*) in Herbert Morris, ed., *Guilt and Shame* (Belmont, CA.: Wadsworth Publishing Co., 1971) p. 156.

8. Merle Fossum and Marilyn Mason, *Facing Shame: Families in Recovery* (New York: Norton, 1986) p. 39.

9. In a letter to me written 24 June 1989, responding to an earlier draft of this chapter, Mary McCarthy elaborates on both the physical and the psychological consequences of her grandmother's operation: [You

speak of my grandmother's] '"disfigured face": that's a bit too strong; probably I've given a misleading impression. If one hadn't known about her operation, one wouldn't have noticed any scarring on her face or neck. In fact the slight scars were in front of her ears (or of one ear; I forget) and originally I was told that they were the result of a mastoid operation. There was nothing disfigured about her face itself. Of course, having been a beauty, she must have *thought* she was disfigured.'

10. Paul John Eakin, in *Fictions in Autobiography: Studies in the Art of Self-Invention* (Princeton: Princeton University Press, 1985), has also interpreted McCarthy's grandmother as an alter-ego. However, Eakin focuses on the common bereavement at Tess' death: 'The grandmother would function as a surrogate for Mary herself. She would be a Mary who consciously experienced the loss of Tess, a Mary who loved the mother and who was genuinely bereaved by her death, as opposed to the six-year-old girl for whom the event of loss was wrapped in a blackout of sickness and repression . . . . To this extent the biographical facts about the grandmother would operate as an autobiographical fiction designed to recover the missing event of McCarthy's own life story' (pp. 53–4). Augusta plays a crucial role both in this regard and also, in my interpretation, as a vehicle for McCarthy to explore the dynamics of shame.

11. In the letter of 24 June 1989 cited in a previous note, McCarthy writes: 'Compared to my grandmother I certainly wasn't lonely, though I didn't have all the friends I wanted, and I wouldn't say that "self-critical" applied to my grandmother. Then: "both women are orphans." I'm not sure how old my grandmother was when she lost her parents, but she didn't grow up an orphan. She must have been in her teens when they died.'

12. In her letter to me McCarthy writes: 'I don't believe I was an anti-Semite, though from time to time, like most people, I fear, I had brief attacks of anti-Semitic attitudes.' McCarthy's silence about her Jewish background corresponds exactly to Augusta's 'not discussing' her identity. In correspondence, McCarthy defends her grandmother in similar terms as she describes her own ambiguous silence in *How I Grew*: 'You speak of my grandmother's "denial of her Jewish background." This doesn't seem quite right to me. She didn't discuss it, but she didn't deny it. How could she, with her two sisters and her brother all in Seattle?'

13. For a good historical overview of how philosophers have interpreted shame, see Nathan Rotenstreich, 'On Shame', *Review of Metaphysics* 19 (1965) 55–86.

14. Donald Capps, 'The Parabolic Event in Religious Autobiography', *The Princeton Seminary Bulletin* 4 (n.s.) (1983) 34.

15. Augustine, *Confessions*, translated by R. S. Pine-Coffin (Harmondsworth, England: Penguin, 1961) p. 207 (Book X, ch. 2).

16. See William Dusinberre, *Henry Adams: The Myth of Failure* (Charlottesville: University Press of Virginia, 1980).

17. McCarthy's letter to William Jovanovich, August 16, 1979, quoted

in Carol Gelderman, *Mary McCarthy: A Life* (New York: St. Martin's Press, 1988) p. 347.

18. John Rawls, *A Theory of Justice* (Cambridge, MA: Harvard University Press, 1971) p. 444. See also p. 484: 'In general, guilt, resentment and indignation involve the concept of right, whereas shame, contempt, and derision appeal to the concept of goodness.'

19. See J. G. Peristiany, ed., *Honour and Shame: The Values of a Mediterranean Society* (Chicago: The University of Chicago Press, 1966). See also Peter Berger, 'On the Obsolescence of the Concept of Honor', in *Vice and Virtue in Everyday Life*, Christina Hoff Sommers, ed. (New York: Harcourt Brace Jovanovich, 1985) pp. 415–26.

20. Gabrielle Taylor, *Pride, Shame, and Guilt* (Oxford: Oxford University Press, 1985) p. 131.

21. For example, see Fossum and Mason, *Facing Shame*, pp. 5–6: 'While guilt is a painful feeling of regret and responsibility for one's actions, shame is a painful feeling about oneself as a person. The possibility for repair seems foreclosed to the shameful person because shame is a matter of identity, not a behavioral infraction. There is nothing to be learned from it and no growth is opened by the experience because it only confirms one's negative feelings about oneself.'

22. Lynd, *On Shame and the Search for Identity*, p. 20.

23. See Gershen Kaufman, *Shame: The Power of Caring* (Cambridge, MA: Schenkman Books, Inc., 1980) chapter 3: 'Defending Strategies Against Shame.'

24. For an analysis of Cordelia's shame see Stanley Cavell, 'The Avoidance of Love: A Reading of *King Lear*' in *Must We Mean What We Say?* (Cambridge: Cambridge University Press, 1976). Cavell also interprets Gloucester's shamelessness as an attempt to deny his shame about his bastard son.

25. Arnold Isenberg, 'Natural Pride and Natural Shame', in *Aesthetics and the Theory of Criticism: Selected Essays of Arnold Isenberg* (Chicago: The University of Chicago Press, 1973) p. 230.

26. See Kaufman, *Shame*, chapter five: 'Restoring the Interpersonal Bridge: From Shame to a Self-Affirming Identity.'

27. Mason and Fossum, *Facing Shame*, p. 174.

28. Isenberg, 'Natural Pride and Natural Shame,' p. 238.

29. Joan Didion, 'On Self-respect', in *Vice and Virtue in Everyday Life*, ed. Christina Hoff Sommers (New York: Harcourt Brace Jovanovich, 1985) pp. 411–12.

30. The same view of how recognizing one's errors is essential to self-respect is at work in McCarthy's fiction. For instance, in 'Ghostly Father, I Confess', the last chapter of *The Company She Keeps* (Harcourt, Brace, and Co., 1942) Meg Sargent realizes in a dream that she cannot acquiesce in her psychoanalyst's 'therapeutic lie', which represents an attempt to stifle the insights of her conscience. 'She could still detect her own frauds. At the end of the dream, her eyes were closed, but the inner eye had remained alert' (p. 304).

CHAPTER 8:   CONCLUSION

1.   T. S. Eliot, 'Religion and Literature', in *Selected Essays*, 3rd edn (London: Faber & Faber, 1951) p. 399.

Index